VIRGINIA PLACE NAMES

DERIVATIONS

HISTORICAL USES

by

Raus McDill Hanson

Emeritus Professor Geography

MADISON COLLEGE

Harrisonburg, Virginia

McClure Press
Verona, Virginia

To

Teachers

Who Persistently

Urged Organization

PREFACE

Individuals probably have different reasons for being interested in the derivation of place names. Those persons, like any other hobbyist or collector, would include the objects or names which fit their interests. A conviction that information should be found and published for nearby areas gives a practical limit to gathering derivations.

A person may ask why a town, a county, a stream, a mountain, or other geographical feature was given its name. In gathering derivations, it becomes evident that the explanations might be grouped under headings: names of persons, some earlier known place, some natural feature, some clever proposal, and in Virginia, the use of some Indian names. The name may tell history, link with an economic interest, or it may link with either tragedy or hilarity.

Persons may have chosen a place's name to honor an outstanding figure in history, a leader in business or community undertakings, an important local land owner, a member of a leading family, or a member of the land development or transportation company prominent in the beginnings of the new community.

This book should be a reference for information as well as entertainment. In addition, it is hoped that in many Virginia localities, persons will gather derivations for many places which could not be included in this book. County and city newspapers will generally be glad to publish items about additional derivations. Local organizations like historical societies are interested in increasing reports about their nearby derivations.

CONTENTS

EXPLANATIONS

A plan or guidance check was needed for the list of derivations which would be gathered to be included. The National Zip Code Directory in 1965 listed nearly 1,300 active postoffices in Virginia; this list made an important beginning. Their present use shows that they serve patrons so they have continued when many other offices have been discontinued. The ninety-six county names were included. The state has about seventy-five mountain peaks with an altitude of 4,000 feet and higher.

The above total of nearly 1,500 names with about 500 other names of streams, land features, and other significant names made a list of 2,000. That list helped to keep the publication from being too bulky.

Research located the information for more than seven-eighths of the original list of 2,000 names. At first, published books, pamphlets, and bound periodicals were searched. The unusual collections of Virginiana in the Madison College Library and the State Library at Richmond were searched. The Geological Survey in Washington, D. C. was visited. This search in publications was the first plan used. All the references in these investigations supplied information for about 500 names.

Efforts were made to get information for the remaining 1,500 of the 2,000 names. As a second plan, Division Superintendents of Schools throughout the state were addressed with a request for the names of persons who might have information for an enclosed list of specific places in his county. Some helpful replies were received.

As a third plan for finding derivations, after an interval of weeks in waiting for replies from Division Superintendents, a request with a list of names for which derivations in his county was still needed was mailed to county university extension agents. Because of their contacts throughout the county, this request asked for the names of persons to be addressed.

Another interval of waiting, and as a fourth plan for getting the explanation, a request with an enclosed list was mailed to local secretaries of Chambers of Commerce. As in the two earlier requests, the inquiry asked for the names of persons who might be addressed.

After another interval, the fifth plan used was a request mailed to a librarian in the area. An enclosed list of derivations still needed in the specific county and a request for persons' names to address were in each letter. Gradually, from these five plans, the information had been gathered for more than 1,000 place names.

A final plan was used for getting these derivations as nearly complete as possible. This sixth plan was to address individual postmasters and ask for long-time residents of the community to address for an explanation of the local post-office name. These persons rated high in their replies.

After using printed information and contacting individuals, the gathered information was organized. This has required more than two and one-half years.

With more than 350 years of history, explanations of the choice of place names in Virginia becomes more problematic than in states organized since 1850 or 1875. There are publications giving information regarding land grants, the settlement of estates, and some diaries include place names used before 1800. If the varied contacts for finding the derivation of such early use of a place name was not found, that information regarding the long-time use of the place name has been accepted for this publication.

Our present-day maps are beginning to include railroads, highways, educational institutions, permanently established places for large group gatherings, as well as other mapped features. The list includes sanitariums, mental hospitals, widely known resorts in addition to those mentioned in the paragraph's first sentence. For the present time, they may be called quasi-place names. These places may have greater influence on numbers of persons than many of the generally accepted list of long-established place names. Derivations were found for several quasi-place names.

As a way of somewhat distinguishing a community and giving it an individuality, some concise information regarding population and transportation is useful. Likewise, for counties, leading employment groups and products give information about the county's present-day interests. These kinds of information give a community a kind of individuality which derivation alone lacks.

The rank of "first" in either Virginia or in the United States belongs to a long list of the place names included. In addition to the "firsts" for the usually accepted place names, different organizations and institutions among the quasi-place names have a record of distinguishing firsts.

Some names like rivers, mountains, divisions of the state, and railroads belong to more than one city or county. These names were placed in the first section of the book under the title, "Larger Areas". All other names of places were grouped in their counties and cities. The index pages (237-253) should help in locating any place in either the Larger Areas or in its city or county.

For persons living in other states, it needs to be explained that in Virginia, a city having a population of 5,000 may become an independent city. Then, it is generally surrounded by a county, but it is not legally included in the county. The location of several sub-station postoffices in the larger cities is indexed by giving the city name. In the book, those larger cities follow the publication's ninety-six counties.

The compiler of this book's information has avoided any suppositions or guesses of his own in writing the book. The derivation of 7.5 percent of the active postoffice names could not be found by using the different inquiries; each of those names is labelled "DU" (derivation unavailable). For all derivations, in which "seemingly", "evidently", "probably", and similar words are included, either a publication or the written statement of an informant used the uncertain words. If the compiler had been willing to use these uncertain words without finding them in published information or from an informant's statement, the label might have been omitted from a number of places.

ACKNOWLEDGMENTS

A very long list of books, pamphlets, and other publications has been used as references. The writers of all this published material should be thanked for getting all that information published rather than hoping that it might be learned by some person at a later time. The hundreds of persons who answered inquiries which supplied information or suggested other persons to address have been helpful although they have never met the compiler. If an unabbreviated list of all these publications and persons had been made, it would claim many more pages in the book. Abbreviations for titles of references used are given on pages 232 to 235.

Many persons who supplied information encouraged the undertaking of the publication of the proposed book. Other persons who learned about the undertaking have commended. The words of a great man of the first century must be used in stating: "I am a debtor".

Raus McDill Hanson

ABBREVIATIONS used in PARAGRAPHS
GIVING INFORMATION regarding PLACES:

DU .... derivation unavailable
elev. .... elevation
ft. .... feet
Mt. .... mount
Pop. .... population
Rt. .... Route
Ry. .... Railway
sq. mi. .... square miles

Railroad Names:

    A&D .... Atlantic and Danville
    ACL .... Atlantic Coast Line
    B&O .... Baltimore & Ohio
    C&NW .... Carolina & Northwestern
    C&O .... Chesapeake & Ohio
    CLIN .... Clinchfield
    CW .... Chesapeake Western
    INT .... Interstate
    L&N .... Louisville & Nashville
    N&PB .... Norfolk & Portsmouth Belt Line
    N&W .... Norfolk & Western
    NF&D .... Norfolk, Franklin & Danville
    NS .... Norfolk Southern
    PA .... Pennsylvania
    RF&P .... Richmond, Fredericksburg & Potomac
    SAL .... Seaboard Air Line
    SOU .... Southern
    VBR .... Virginia Blue Ridge
    VC .... Virginia Central
    VIR .... Virginian
    W&OD .... Washington & Old Dominion
    W&W .... Winchester & Western

Abbreviations used in paragraphs regarding places are explained on this page.

Abbreviations for titles of references used are given on page 232 to 235.

LARGER AREAS

Aarons Creek, boundary between Mecklenberg and Halifax counties, is a tributary of Banister River. It was named for Aaron Pinson by Colonel William Byrd in 1733.   Mathis 13.

Allegheny Mountains have an Indian name meaning "Endless". They are the ridges west of the Great Valley along the western part of the state.
                                                                                                                        Walker 7.

Appalachian Region includes the Blue Ridge and all ridges and valleys west of that ridge. Spanish explorers found a poor Indian village, *Apalchen,* which became the present name Appalachian.   Stewart 18.

Appalachian Trail is considered the longest footpath in the world. Of its 2,049 miles from Mt. Katadin in Maine to Mt. Oglethorpe in Georgia, 355 miles are in Virginia along a maintained trail very close to the crest of the Blue Ridge. It is maintained by the Appalachian Trail Club.   Stewart 18.

Apple Orchard Mountain, elev. 4,224 ft., is on the Botetourt-Bedford line. Oaks growing on the mountain were stunted; they resembled apple trees in shape and formation; named from appearance of the trees. It is site of U. S. Radar Station, established in 1954.   LRI

Appomattox-Buckingham State Forest is named for the two counties in which it is located. Its 19,071 acreage is planned for demonstrating commendable forest practices and outdoor recreation together with including a co-operative wildlife management area.   LRI; EcD counties

Appomattox River for John Smith was "Apamatuck" River, which became Appomattox. It rises in Appomattox County and is bordered by eight counties before it becomes a tributary of the James.   Stewart

Atlantic and Danville Railway serves eight counties and the cities of Norfolk and Danville. It was built in the 1880's and previous to August 1949, it was leased and operated by the Southern Railway. It has inaugurated fast overnight freight service.   Corp I; Com Va 12-1949.

Back Creek drains the valley between ridges of northwestern Bath and Highland counties; it becomes a tributary of the Jackson River. Early settlers coming from the east to the west considered the western section back or remote; hence the name Back Creek.   EcD county; LRI

Back Creek Mountain was used for giving a fort location in 1755-1789. The mountain is parallel, along the southeast side of the stream Back Creek; hence it became Back Creek Mountain.   2 V 106; LRI

Banister River rises in west central Pittsylvania and flows into Halifax County, where it becomes a tributary of the Dan. The old English name was transplanted to Virginia by Richard B. Bannister; the local spelling became Banister.   G-B: GSV 210; GSW: CF.

Big Bend Mountain, elev. 4,000 ft., is on the Bland-Wythe line, seven miles southeast of Burkes Garden. Big Bend refers to a big bend in Big Walkers Mountain north of the fork of Stony Fork.   LRI

Big Reed Island Creek flows across eastern Carroll and into southwestern Pulaski where it empties into New River. Tradition states it was named for an early explorer and hunter, Reed, who early visited the area 1740-1750.   LRI

Big Walker Creek crosses two-thirds of the southern area of Bland County and crosses Giles County, becoming a tributary of New River. It is named for Mr. Walker, who walked into the area, and for whom Big Walker Mountain is named.   LRI

Birsch Creek or Birch Creek rises in southwestern Pittsylvania and flows into Halifax County; it is tributary of Dan River. Land grant (Pittsylvania) 1762 mentions upper fork of Little Creek of Bircher's Creek. Land grant 1765 in Halifax on Birches Creek.   20 V 299; 36 V 26.

Blackwater River crosses Surry and Isle of Wight into Southampton and then flows between Nansemond and Southampton into the Nottoway River. Earlier name Indian River; Act of Assembly 1646 refers to "the black water". Juniper trees in swampy area cause black coloring of the water.   Bohannon 59+.

Blue Ridge extends from the Potomac River to the southern boundary of the state, the first range along the eastern area of Appalachian Region. Early name was The Ledge or the Blue Ledge. (Ledge then meant ridge.) When the atmosphere is clear, the mountains have a veil of violet tint or vapor; the name becomes the Blue Ridge.   Schuright 57+; Percy 2.

Blue Ridge Parkway, total length 477 miles, has 217 miles of winding motor way within Virginia, following the crest of the Blue Ridge, at an average of 3,000 feet above sea level. It includes scenes of mountain ranges, deep valleys, picturesque pioneer dwellings, tranquil farmlands, and rare views of forests with trees and shrubs. It links the Shenandoah National Park with the Great Smokies National Park.   VGb 49; VaVCo 9-1950.

George F. Brasfield Dam, in Chesterfield and Dinwiddie counties, was named for George F. Brasfield, chairman of Appomattox River Water Authority, leader in movement to establish the water supply system. He is a retired industrialist and a former president of the Petersburg Chamber of Commerce.

                                                 T-D 3-2-1967, B-1.

Brushy Mountain, on Smyth-Tazewell line, 4,100+ ft., received its name from the brushy growth on its south side. It extends in the same direction as the Clinch Mountain.   Summers 1439.

Bullpasture River rises in north central Highland and flows through the county to empty into the Cowpasture River in the northern edge of Bath County. In early years, when herds were driven to summer pasture, the bulls could travel over a third ridge to the next stream valley, so it became the Bullpasture.
Wayland SV 331.

Bull Run is a small tributary of Occuquan Creek which rises in Loudoun and drains areas in Fairfax and Prince William counties. In 1730, Robert Carter papers refer to a plantation on Bull Run. It was the location of an early battle in War of 1861-65.   7 V 68.

Byrd Creek is in northeast portion of Fluvanna and crosses the southwest portion of Goochland County; it is tributary of the James. William Byrd owned much land in this section and did surveying.   Weeks

Calfpasture River rises in Augusta County and flows across Rockbridge to become a tributary of Maury River which empties into the James. Herds driven by early residents of Shenandoah Valley to summer pasture in the mountains found that calves tired first. These young animals were left to graze along the first stream; this became the Calfpasture River.   Wayland SV 331.

Camp Pickett, large military installation, covers 46,000 acres in southeastern Nottoway and parts of adjoining counties. In World War II, the government condemned land and moved 300 families from the farms. At times, 70,000 men were in this camp. It is named for the Confederate general, George Edward Pickett (1825-1875). Water supply from Nottoway River; filtered, chlorinated.
Allen 25; VR 11-1952.

Camp Rock, on Scott-Wise boundary, is five miles north of Norton. Pioneers camped on the shelving cliff; name naturally grew from this usage.   LRI

Carolina, Clinchfield, and Ohio Railroad has mileage in Dickenson, Russell, and Scott counties and is known as Clinchfield Railroad, receiving its name from the Clinch River which it parallels for forty miles. It is the shortest connecting line between Ohio River and the Carolinas. Seventy percent of its grading is in bedrock which caused a greater cost in construction but reduced cost in maintenance. It has few bridges.   Corp I; Com Va 6-1950.

Catawba Creek in Roanoke and Botetourt counties. Name is probably from Choctaw *katapa*, meaning *cut off* or *separated*.   Gannett 72

Cedar Creek rises in Frederick and forms part of the boundary between Shenandoah and Frederick counties; it is tributary of North Fork of the Shenandoah. Grant of land in 1731 refers to Cedar Creek. At lower end of stream, the area is covered with cedars, which led to its name.   36 V 63; LRI

Cedar Run in southeastern Fauquier becomes tributary of Occuquan Creek in Prince William County. The name was given in 1731.   Fauquier 48.

Chesapeake and Ohio Railway Company became the incorporation name in 1878. It is the inheritor of the James River Company, the first commercial canal in America, which was chartered in 1785. It is also the line which includes the Louisa Railroad Company which is the basis or original *railroad* predecessor of the present organization; this railroad started in 1836. The name links with the early plan to provide a transportation line from the Atlantic to the Ohio River. The Chesapeake and Ohio operates 751 miles of railway in Virginia.   Corp I.

Chesapeake Bay has an Indian name meaning "Mother of Waters", or "Great Salt Bay". Chesapeake is corrupted from Tschiswapeki or K'tschischwapeki, compounded of *Kitschi,* significantly, highly salted, and *peek,* a body of standing water, a pond, a bay. The southern part of the bay from the Maryland-Virginia line to the Atlantic Ocean is within the area of Virginia.   VaVCo 2-1953;
Com Va 8-1953; 3 V 86.

Chesapeake Bay Bridge-Tunnel is a 17.6 mile complex of three bridges and two tunnels from the Bayside area of the city, Virginia Beach, to Wise Point on the southern tip of Northampton County in the Eastern Shore. The three bridges have a combined length of approximately 12 miles. Each tunnel is nearly a mile long and rests between islands made by dredging from the bottom of the bay. It was opened to traffic in 1964.   VaR 9-1963; DNR 11-4-1966.

Chesapeake Western Railway had Chesapeake and Western Railroad as an earlier name. Originally planned as Washington, Shendun and St. Louis, it was proposed as a coal-hauling railroad from West Virginia to Gloucester Point. Its construction was in the mid-1890's. The former Baltimore & Ohio line between Harrisonburg and Lexington was acquired in 1943; the mileage between Staunton and Lexington was retired. A trackage of 54 miles in Rockingham and Augusta counties is operated; an important part of its traffic links to poultry supplies. The railroad was purchased by the Norfolk & Western in 1954.   Corp I.

Lake Chesdin, reservoir on the Appomattox River which floods an acreage of 3,500 acres between Chesterfield, Amelia and Dinwiddie counties, receives its name from the first syllables of Chesterfield and Dinwiddie. It is planned to contribute to the water supply of cities of Petersburg and Colonial Heights and to Chesterfield County. Recreational use is another contribution.
TD 8-28-1966, 3-2-1967.

Chestnut Ridge, elev. 4,117 ft., on the Bland-Tazewell County line, is named for the chestnut trees once abundant there.   Steeles 1162.

Chickahominy River drains land in Hanover, Henrico, Charles City, and New Kent counties. The Indian word, *checahaminend,* means "land of much grain," so-called because it flows through productive lowlands. Another explanation of the name is "coarse pounded corn people."
Gannett PN 79; Com Va 3-1935.

Clinch Mountains undoubtedly takes the name from the river.

Clinch River flows through Russell and Scott counties to become a tributary of the Tennessee. It takes its name from the hunter who first found it. Another report regarding the river name is that an Irishman fell from a raft and called "Clinch me! Clinch me!"   Addington 11.

Colonial National Historical Park. (See page 236.)

George P. Coleman Memorial Bridge is the largest double swing span bridge in the world; its two 500-foot swinging spans permit passage of the nation's largest war vessels. It extends from Yorktown in York County to Gloucester Point in Gloucester County. It is named for Virginia's second highway commissioner.   VaVCo 6-1950; Historyland.

Conway River is the boundary between Greene and Madison counties. It was named for an early patentee of land.   Yowell 28.

Cowpasture River rises in northeastern Highland, and then crosses Bath into northern Alleghany County to empty into Jackson River. Its earlier Indian name was Wallawhatoola, but settlers changed to Cowpasture River because in the herds of cattle brought to summer pasture, the cows could travel over the second ridge to the second stream, so it was the Cowpasture.

Wayland SV 331; 2 V 103

Craig Creek crosses the southern area of Craig County and flows through the west central part of Botetourt County, becoming a tributary of the James. In March 1754, a road was ordered on Craig's Creek.   30 V 197.

Crooked Run rises in Madison County, flows along the southwestern boundary of Culpeper County, becoming a tributary of the Rapidan River. It is named for its course. March 3, 1729, there is a record of a constable appointed above Crooked Run.   13 V 366; LRI.

Cumberland Mountains along two-thirds of the Virginia-Kentucky boundary have their name derived from the Duke of Cumberland, son of George II; they were named by Dr. Thomas Walker in 1750.   CVHM 21

Currituck Sound extends from North Carolina into Virginia and is within the cities of Chesapeake and Virginia Beach. The area is famous for duck and goose shooting. May 27, 1728, correspondence regarding boundary with North Carolina "to run a due West line from the North shoar of Carotreck Inlet."

32 V 33

Dan River rises in Patrick County and, after flowing in North Carolina, reenters the state in Pittsylvania County and crosses Halifax County to become a tributary of the Roanoke (Staunton) River. In 1728, Colonel Byrd of Westover, a member of the surveying commission of the dividing line between Virginia and North Carolina, named the river Dan.   Clement 23.

Deep Creek flows across northwest Nottoway County and across southeastern Amelia County into Appomattox River. The stream is deeper than nearby Flat Creek; this helps to explain its name.   LRI

Deep Water: Burks Fork drains an area in the southwest portion of Floyd County. Tradition says a party of hunters came to the Indian Valley section. Two of these were Mr. Williamson and Mr. Burke from Richmond. Mr. Burke left the party and went into the area of Burks Fork and the Indian Valley section. Greasy Creek drains an area in the northwestern portion of the county. Tradition that it was custom of Indians in skinning deer under water; then droplets of grease appeared on the water; this gave the name to the stream. The stream flows through Indian Valley District into Carroll County; in Carroll is known as Deep Water.   LRI

Delmarva is the name of the peninsula between Chesapeake Bay on the west and Delaware Bay and the Atlantic Ocean on the east. From the names of parts of three states (Delaware, Maryland, Virginia) having land within the peninsula, some one coined Delmarva.   Stewart 364.

Dismal Swamp is in both Virginia and North Carolina; in Virginia, it is in Nansemond County and the city of Chesapeake. It received its name from the appearance of a wilderness, having a dense forest of juniper, cypress, and other trees, and flowering plants. It remains a paradise of hunters.   Steeles 1163.

Douthat State Park, containing nearly 5,000 acres, has one of the very few remaining stands of virgin timber and embraces mountain scenery. It has been developed for recreation. About 93 percent of the park is in Bath County; the remainder is in Alleghany County. The Douthat Land Company contributed about two-fifths of the land in the park.   Com Va 4-1949.

Dragon Run is between King and Queen and Middlesex counties; the stream is shaped like a dragon.   LRI

Dry Creek is in north central portion of Lunenburg, flows into Brunswick County, and is a tributary of Nottoway River. June 14, 1739, a land petition on Dry Creek was granted.   14 V 343

Lake Drummond, in Nansemond County and the city of Chesapeake, is the largest natural lake in Virginia. It is surrounded by Dismal Swamp. Vegetation makes the water amber-colored. One explanation is that it was named for William Drummond, one time governor of North Carolina.

Steeles 1168; Gannett 109.

Dulles International Airport: Pop. ———. Named as memorial to late Secretary of State, John Foster Dulles (1888-1959), Secretary of State (1953-1959). Largest jet airport in the world, dedicated November, 1962, operated by Bureau of National Capital Airports. It covers 10,000 acres in Fairfax and Loudoun counties. The water supply is from two deep wells.

EcD counties; Com Va 5-1963, 9-1963; Bodie 108.

Eastern Shore is the peninsula on the east shore of Chesapeake Bay which includes the counties of Accomack and Northampton. Persons on the west shore of the bay spoke of the area east of them as the Eastern Shore.

EcD (Northampton County)

Elizabeth River flows northwest between the city of Norfolk on the east and the cities of Portsmouth and Chesapeake on the west; the stream empties into Hampton Roads. Captain John Smith named the river for Princess Elizabeth. Since 1620, shipbuilding has been an important activity on the stream.

Va Highways 9.

Elizabeth River Tunnel, two-lane, 3,400 feet from portal to portal, carries traffic beneath the South Branch of Elizabeth River, between Portsmouth and Berkley, subdivision of Norfolk. VaVCo 4-1952

Fairfax Line, surveyed 1736-37, located the boundary of the grant to Lord Fairfax. It begins at the southwest corner of Maryland and continues along the boundary between Shenandoah and Rockingham counties to and just over the crest of the Blue Ridge, from which point the line follows the Conway, Rapidan and Rappahannock rivers to the starting point on Chesapeake Bay.

Couper 186+, 402.

Fairy Stone State Park in Henry and Patrick counties takes its name from the lucky or fairy stones found in the area; many crosses are of the Saint Andrew's variety, others Roman, and the rarer are Maltese. They are twinned crystals of opaque, reddish-brown iron and aluminum silicate known as staurolite. On September 20, 1933, J. B. Fishburn gave a 5,000-acre tract to the state. It includes a remnant of virgin forest. Attractions include boating, camping, and observing a variety of native plants and animals. VGb 5; Va Cav Spring 1955.

Fall Belt extends from states northeast into states farther south. Its width varies from three to ten miles along a zone or strip made by the harder crystalline rocks of Piedmont Upland meeting the weaker rocks of the Coastal Plain. Streams crossing this area have rapids or falls which influenced its name. On a map, it is shown as a line; although it has width in a zone, belt, or area, and not a line, it has often been called the Fall Line. Va HSSSA 60.

Flat Creek rises in western Nottoway, flows across Amelia into the Appomattox River in northeastern Amelia. The stream is not deep and is spread out; seemingly, this explains the name, because in Amelia County, Deep Creek is deeper. 14 V 229; LRI.

Fredericksburg and Spotsylvania National Military Park includes the battlefields of four major engagements: Fredericksburg, Chancellorsville, the Wilderness, and Spotsylvania Court House in the War of the 1860's. The park preserves the remains of earthworks, roads, and other sites of importance on these battlefields in the city of Fredericksburg and Spotsylvania County.

EcD (county); Willis-Walker 111.

Garden Mountain is along the Tazewell-Bland boundary and reaches 4,000 feet in elevation. It takes its name from Burke's Garden. LRI

George Washington National Forest was established in 1917 as the Shenandoah National Forest. In 1932, the name was changed to George Washington

National Forest in order to avoid confusion with the nearby Shenandoah National Park whose boundaries in places were quite close to the forest boundaries. The boundaries extend from Frederick County through Alleghany and along the James River, together with an area on the Blue Ridge from the James to Rockfish Gap, and Massanutten Mountain. The total area administered by the Forest Service is 918,242 acres; other lands within the boundaries total 718,184 acres. The boundaries include 6 percent of the state's area. The forest provides conservation of water, timber, soil, and wildlife, with an emphasis on fire control and provisions for recreation.   DAI: Va. 54+; Forest Statistics 1967.

Great North Mountain is a ridge of the Alleghenies along the western side of the three counties: Rockingham, Shenandoah, and Frederick. Its name tells that there are lower ridges near the open floor of Shenandoah Valley; compared to the lower ridges, it was Great. Early settlers moving in the valley looked south and saw a mountain ridge; they called it South Mountain; we say Blue Ridge. They looked north and saw the long, high ridge; they said North Mountain. Much of the Great North Mountain is now included in the George Washington National Forest.   Wayland SV 323; Valley Week 10-29-1966.

Hampton Roads is the harbor area or basin which receives water from the James, Nansemond, Elizabeth, and Lafayette Rivers and connects to the Chesapeake Bay. In 1610, the stream near Hampton was named South Hampton River; from this the harbor became South Hampton Roads. A road or roadstead is an open water area in which ships may ride at anchor. The name became shortened to Hampton Roads; this port is the leading North Atlantic port in export tonnage. Seventy-five percent of coal exports bound for Europe leave Hampton Roads.

Allen 8

Hampton Roads Bridge Tunnel connects Willoughby Spit in the city of Norfolk to Hampton. It includes 7,479-foot under water crossing (1 2/5 miles) with the south trestle 6,110 feet long, and the north trestle 3,250 feet long. It was opened August 30, 1957. It is included in US Route 60.   Com Va 8-1957.

Hardware River drains the southern part of Albemarle County, flows into Fluvanna, and is tributary of the James. A land grant, October 24, 1728, mentions Hardware River.   33 V 386.

Benjamin Harrison Memorial Bridge spans the James from Jordan Point in Prince George County to Harrison's Point in Charles City County. It is named for Benjamin Harrison, member of the First Continental Congress, signer of Declaration of Independence, member of Constitutional Convention, and three times governor of Virginia. He was father of William Henry Harrison who became president.   TD 4-16-1967

Hawksbill, altitude 4,049 feet, is the highest point in the Shenandoah National Park. It has an attractive trail, superb wide views, and a few rare Blue Ridge fir trees. It is on the boundary of Page and Madison counties. When viewed from the east side of New Market Gap, in Massanutten Mountain, its outline has the evident shape of a hawk's head and bill.   Wayland SV 10.

Hayter Knob, elev. 4,200+ feet, on Russell-Washington county line, 3 miles south of Elk Garden, was named for a family who were among early settlers in its community.   LRI

Jackson River rises at Hightown and flows from Highland across Bath and Alleghany to join Cowpasture about four miles southeast of Clifton Forge after which the stream is known as the James. It was named for the first settler on its banks.   Gannett 167

James River, named for the English King, is the largest stream which is entirely within Virginia. After crossing Botetourt and Rockbridge counties, it forms either the northern or southern boundary of eighteen counties and five cities. The part of its course above the Fall Belt is important in water power and water supply; below the Fall Belt, it continues to be important for water transportation. It has a drainage area of 9,700 square miles.

James River Bridge is a span 4.6 miles long crossing the James from Bartlett, Isle of Wight County, to Hilton, in Newport News. Both US Routes 17 and 258 cross the bridge.   Historyland.

James River Oyster Seed Area is a multi-million-dollar private oyster growing industry. This "Hatchery" supplies stock to be transplanted in areas where it grows to maturity.   VaVCo 2-1953

Jefferson National Forest, named for the third president, was officially established in 1936 and has a gross area of 2,411,305 acres, three-fifths of which is in Virginia. Roanoke is the location of the unit headquarters. About one-third of the acreage within Virginia has been acquired by the national government. The forest areas extend from the southern boundary of the George Washington National Forest to the Virginia-Tennessee boundary. Areas in twenty counties are within the Jefferson National Forest.   DAI: Va., 55.

John H. Kerr Reservoir (Buggs Island Lake) is in Mecklenburg and Halifax counties and was named for Congressman Kerr (1873-1958), representative from North Carolina 1923-1949. He was father of the Roanoke River Flood Control and Power Project. In the Roanoke River basin, this was the first one of eleven dams constructed; the reservoir has 83,000 acres in area at full flood control pool level; 48,900 acres at average pool level; about three-fourths of the unindated area is within Virginia. There are 7,800 square miles in the watershed above the dam. The lake has a shore line 800 miles in length. Numerous valuable artifacts of Occoneechee tribe of Indians were excavated prior to unindation by the impounded reservoir. The construction had the purposes of: flood control, generation of hydroelectric power, recreation, and preservation of fish and wildlife in and around the lake and in the river downstream. Wild life conservation includes upland game management as well as migratory water fowl refuge area. The reservoir was dedicated June 13-14, 1953.   VaVCo 6-1951, 9-1952.

Lancaster Creek is along the boundary of Lancaster and Richmond counties.

Laurel Fork rises in Floyd and flows into Carroll County. It is named for the many laurels which grew along the stream.   LRI

Lawnes Creek, along the boundary of Surry and Isle of Wight counties, is a tributary of the James and was named for Sir Christopher Lawne, who settled on the Isle of Wight side of the stream.   Bohannon 63.

Lick Creek Natural Area, an 863-acre mountain tract on the slopes of Carter Mountain and Brushy Mountain, is in Smyth and Bland counties. There was a deer lick near the head of the stream and an early resident gave it the name Lick Creek. Cove forests will re-grow on the slopes.   Com Va 11-1964.

Little River flows eastward through the middle of the eastern third of Louisa County and into the northwestern portion of Hanover, there it is a tributary of North Anna. Its name was given because it is a small fork of North Anna. A land transfer, dated April 27, 1758, mentions location on the stream.
                    LRI; 36 V 347+.

Little Walker Creek flows eastward near the northern boundary of Pulaski and into Giles County; it is a tributary of Walker River. It was named for Dr. Thomas Walker.   LRI

Louisville & Nashville Railroad Company was chartered 1850 and began operating between namesake cities in 1859. It entered Virginia in 1891; at present it operates 67 miles in Lee and Wise counties. It serves the coal-producing area within Powell Valley which is an important part of the railroad's overall operation.   Corp I.

Manassas Gap (originally Manassa's Gap), elev. 950 feet, is the lowest wind gap of the Blue Ridge bordering the Shenandoah Valley. It is so low at Linden, on the crest of the divide, that the Southern Railway crosses right over the Blue Ridge without a tunnel.   Wayland SV 669.

Marine Corps Reservation, U.S., has a total area of 57,511.72 acres, with 24,845.72 in Prince William County, 29,266 in Stafford, and 3,400 acres in Fauquier.   EcD county; WP: Va, 346.

Massanutten Mountain is a range fifty miles in length from Strasburg vicinity to Harrisonburg vicinity. As an outlier from the Alleghenies, it splits the valley in two. The meaning of the Indian name, which is more generally accepted, is "potato ground." Another meaning is "Indian basket" from the northern portion or Fort Valley which is shaped like an Indian basket. The early name was Peaked Mountain (pronounced "peak-ed") from its many peaks when seen from the southeast. When Massanutten displaced the earlier name, The Peak became the name of the southeastern bold headland. Sandstone capping resisted erosion so the mountain area remained while its surrounding area was worn away.
                    Wayland SV 8, 322; Couper 433, 697; Strickler 13.

Mattaponi River flows across the central portion of Caroline and between King William and Queen counties; it is tributary of York River. It has an

Indian name. It has a drainage area of 931 square miles. It is one of the finest fresh-water fishing streams. 14 V 289

Meherrin River flows between Mecklenburg and Lunenburg, across Brunswick and Greensville, and between Greensville and Southampton counties into the Chowan River in North Carolina. Meherrin is an Indian word, meaning "island", the name of a tribe in its drainage area. Gannett 204

Middle Peninsula in Tidewater is between the Rappahannock on the north and the York and Pamunkey Rivers on the south. It includes five counties. Its name was given because it is in the middle of the three peninsulas north of the James.

Mobjack Bay is between Gloucester and Mathews counties. It is probably a corruption of an Indian word. In July 1657, a will mentions Mock Jack Bay.
Steeles 1172; 39 V 31

Morris Knob, elev. 4,050 feet, is a peak on Garden Mountain along the Bland-Tazewell county line. May 1777, an Act of Assembly in locating the line between Washington and Montgomery counties included "from the aforesaid to the westerly end of Morris' Knob." Pendleton 364

Namozine Creek, tributary of the Appomattox River, makes the boundary between Amelia and Dinwiddie and Nottoway counties. It was named for an Indian tribe, Nummisseem, which gradually was changed to present-day spelling. Land transfer on Namozine Creek, Aug. 11, 1724. 29 V 101.

New Market Gap, formerly known as Massanutten Pass, had a toll road as early as 1812. It receives its present name from the nearby town, New Market. This wind gap has the boundary of Page and Shenandoah counties. US Route 211 crosses through this gap. WP: Va 617.

New River flows through Grayson, Carroll, Wythe, Pulaski, and along Montgomery, and through Giles counties. A man named New kept an early ferry. Its earlier name, Wood's River, was for Abram Wood, discoverer, who explored the stream in 1654. Dr. Thomas Walker in 1750 named New River.
Roads 25; Allen 23.

Norfolk and Portsmouth Belt Line Railroad Company was incorporated as Southwestern and Atlantic Railroad in 1896; a change in 1898 gave it the present name. It is a connecting railroad providing an interchange service from near Berkley through the environs of Portsmouth and Norfolk to Sewell's Point by the eight standard railroads which in 1898 entered the territory. In addition, it provides switching service for more than 150 local industries. It operates a total of 87.99 miles using tracks owned, leased, and operated under trackage rights.
Corp I.

Norfolk and Western Railway traces to its original predecessor, City Point Railroad, which had completed nine miles from City Point to Petersburg in 1838. This with other lines combined in 1870 as Atlantic, Mississippi and Ohio

Railroad; this was reorganized in 1881 as Norfolk and Western *Railroad*. Continued building and purchasing followed and the road was reorganized as Norfolk and Western Rail*way* in 1896. It has grown by mergers, purchases and much pioneer building to a total of 7,758.8 miles serving fourteen states and the Canadian province of Ontario. One fifth of all this mileage is within Virginia, the largest total mileage of any one railroad within the state. The name links with the construction to the seaport, Norfolk, in 1858, and the determined extension into coal-producing areas in the western edge of the state in the 1880's.   Corp I.

Norfolk-Portsmouth Bridge Tunnel is 3,350 feet long; 2,100 feet under the Southern Branch of Elizabeth River; it was dedicated May 23, 1952. US Route 460 uses this bridge tunnel.   Com Va 6-1952

Robert O. Norris, Jr. Bridge, 9,985 feet in length, crosses the Rappahannock River connecting White Post (in Lancaster County) with Grey's Point (in Middlesex County) on State Route 3. It is sometimes called the Rappahannock Bridge. Robert O. Norris, Jr., of Lancaster County, former State Senator, was a patron of the Revenue Act of 1940, a factor in financing the construction of the bridge.   Historyland; Com Va 10-1957

North Anna River flows through Orange, Louisa, Spotsylvania, and Hanover counties into the Pamunkey River. It was named in honor of Queen Anne; in 1720, the General Assembly passed an act referring to the river North Anna.
                        VaVCo 5-1952; Norris 18.

North Fork Holston River drains areas in Smyth, Washington, and Scott counties. This is one of the streams with a name from Stephen Holstein who settled in the area before 1748.   Roads 25

North Fork of Shenandoah River drains 1,042 square miles in Rockingham, Shenandoah, Frederick, and Warren counties. At Riverton, it unites with South Fork to form Shenandoah River.   Norris 19.

Northern Neck is the peninsula between the Rappahannock and the Potomac and includes the five Tidewater counties: King George, Westmoreland, Richmond, Northumberland, and Lancaster. Its name was given because it is the farthest north of the peninsulas in the state.

Nottoway River rises in Nottoway County, flows along the boundaries of Dinwiddie, Brunswick, Sussex, and Greensville, and through Sussex and Southampton counties. The exploration of the stream is reported in September 1663; a will regarding lands on the river was dated February 4, 1719. Its Indian name, Nottoway, meant "rattlesnake" or "adder", that is enemy.
                        5V 47; 10 V 374; 7 V 341+.

Occohannock Creek empties into Chesapeake Bay; it is the boundary between Accomack and Northampton counties. It has an Indian name. It is listed as a navigable stream, July 1702. A residence was on Occohannock Creek, 1703.
                        1 V 364; 3 W (2) 119.

Occoquan Creek has an Indian name meaning "at the end of the water". It flows north in central Prince William, and along the boundary of Fairfax-Prince William; it is a tributary of the Potomac.   Fauquier 48

Opequon Creek is in southeastern Frederick County and flows along the boundary of Frederick and Clarke to become a tributary of the Potomac. Old pronunciation of the name was O' pe quon. Report that several Indian tribes held their big conference in southern portion of present Frederick County. The Opequon camped on one portion of the stream which has since been known by its long-time name. Survey May 12, 1732, includes "northward to the Operkon river and following its flow."   Wayland SV 62, 89; Couper, I, 188; LRI.

Otter River rises in Bedford and crosses Campbell County; it is a tributary of Roanoke River. Otter names were brought by Scotch colonists who settled in the area; Otter names are frequent in Great Britain.   Bedford 3.

Pamunkey River flows between King William and Hanover and New Kent counties; it is named for the Pamunkey Indians. Drainage area near the mouth at West Point includes 1,419 square miles. Wild rice grows on the stream's marshes which is a favorite food for migratory birds. The beautiful winding stream encourages fishing, duck and goose hunting.
                          Pendleton 377; Gottmann 601.

Panorama, well-known station on Skyline Drive, atl. 2,300; US Rt 211, received name from open view, impressive at each higher level, as US Rt 211 climbs steadily in a series of curves and hairpin turns. Views include forest-covered mountain sides, deep valleys and sparkling runs, and a twisting stream far below.   Wayland SV 5; Va Guide OD 615

The Peninsula has the York on its north side and the James on its south side. It has the colony's first capital and its college, William and Mary, was chartered by the rulers of England. With such centers of group interest, as compared with the other peninsulas, it became *The* Peninsula. In recent years, some have wanted to name it Lower York-James Peninsula or the Williamsburg Peninsula, but those names have only limited use.
                          Va DAI, 57; Roberts: Lower York-James Peninsula, 1.

Peters Mountain, Craig-Giles boundary, received its name from Peter Wright, early settler, hunter and pioneer, who lived near present Covington. In crossing the mountain, he was overtaken by a snow-storm and took shelter under a large projecting rock. It was a very deep snow so he was compelled to remain in shelter several days without food; he was compelled to chew on his moccasins. Eventually, he killed a deer. The mountain's elevation is 4,035 feet.   10 V 185.

Philpott Reservoir, formed by Philpott Dam across Smith River, was completed in 1954. It includes areas in Franklin, Henry and Patrick counties. The dam is located four miles upstream from the village Philpott, from which it was given its name. The lake is 20 miles long and has a shore line of 110 miles. The purposes of the reservoir include: hydro-electric power, increase industrial water supplies, recreation, add to preservation of fish and wild life, and flood control on lower reaches of Roanoke River. The Philpotts, early settlers, were highly respected as community leaders.   VaVCo 9-1950

Piankatank River is the boundary of Middlesex, Mathews, and Gloucester counties. The name was given from the Indians living along the stream. The stream was in the list of navigable rivers, July 8, 1702.   1 V 363.

Piedmont Upland extends from the foot of the Blue Ridge to the Fall Zone, and includes about two-fifths of the state's area. The name means at the foot of the mountains.

Pigg River drains the central and much of the southern portions of Franklin County; it flows into Pittsylvania, and is tributary of Roanoke (Staunton) River. John Pigg patented land about 1742.   Clement 41.

Piney River flows along Amherst-Nelson boundary. Its name is from the unusual growth of pines in its valley.   LRI.

Pollock Knob, on the Page-Madison boundary in the Shenandoah National Park, was named for George Freeman Pollock, long associated with the Skyland area and one of the founders of the Shenandoah National Park. It has an eleva-tion of 3,580 feet, and is about 0.8 mile south of Skyland.   USBdGN 59.

Potomac River is in Maryland and the southern edge of the stream becomes the northern boundary of Virginia. Captain John Smith in 1608 found an Indian "King's House" called "Potomek" and from this the river has its name. One meaning given is "River of Swans". In Algonquin language, the name means "where something is brought". This meaning links with the pre-colonial route which followed the Fall Zone and crossed the east-west route near the Potomac; this made a crossing of trade routes before any Europeans came to the area.
                    Roads 17; Sprouse 23.

Pound River has its sources in northern Wise County; it flows through the northern portion of Dickenson County and is a tributary of Russell Fork. A deep bend in the river almost surrounds a large higher area of ground. Indians and old settlers are reported to have driven animals onto the peninsula because a fence across the narrow neck of land impounded the animals. It was called a pound. Both the town (Pound) which is on and near the peninsula and the stream re-ceived their names from this use.   Addington 196

Powell River rises in north central portion of Wise County and flows through the entire length of Lee County. Ambrose Powell with Dr. Walker carved his name on a tree; this explains the stream name.   Stewart 147; Summers 50.

Propotank River flows along the boundary of King and Queen and Glouces-ter counties; in 1650, a land grant mentions the river.   9 V 107.

Rapidan River is formed by the junction of Laurel Prong and Mill Prong in Madison County; it crosses Orange and flows between Culpeper and Spotsylvania into the Rappahannock. Its name comes from the Rapid Anne.

Gannett 258

Rappahannock River is a tidal stream; the ebb and flow made it an alternative stream; another explanation of its Indian name was the tide moving in was "quick rising waters". Its source is near Manassas Gap of the Blue Ridge and flows across Piedmont and Tidewater so its channel is between fifteen different counties. It has a drainage area of 1,597 square miles.

Steeles 1175; EcD (Westmoreland)

Redrock Mountain, on the Russell-Smyth boundary, 3½ miles northwest of Saltville, has an elevation of 4,434 feet. The red colored rocks jutting from the top gave the mountain its name.   LRI

Richmond, Fredericksburg & Potomac Railroad was incorporated in 1834 and is the only American railroad which has operated through more than a century under its original name and without reorganization. Its charter used the names of the major communities it would serve as its corporate name. Six railroads agreed in 1901 to operate traffic over this one line between Richmond and the Potomac. It operates 110 miles of track in seven counties. It is the last remaining company in which the Commonwealth of Virginia holds stock from earlier investments for encouraging transportation enterprises. It has a remarkable earning capacity and an enviable record for safety.   Corp I.

Rivanna rises in central Albemarle and flows through Fluvanna; it is a tributary of the James. The name is a shortened form of River Anna, named for Queen Anne.

Gannett 264

Roanoke River begins in Roanoke County and becomes the boundary of seven other counties as it crosses the Piedmont into North Carolina. Its basin includes 6,160 square miles in Virginia. The section of the stream which is within the Piedmont is locally known as the Staunton River. As an Indian word, Roanoke means "white shells" or "money".

Rockfish Gap, on the Albemarle-Augusta line, elevation 1,910, is crossed by US Route 250. The Shenandoah National Park and Blue Ridge Parkway meet here. Unsurpassed scenery is viewed from the gap. Rockfish Gap is mentioned in preparations to defend Staunton in 1781 and in mention of transportation in a letter in 1793.   8 V 296.

Rowanty Creek is in Dinwiddie and Sussex counties and was named for a local Indian tribe.   Steeles 1176

Russell Fork enters Dickenson County about the middle of Dickenson-Russell line and flows north into the Breaks of the Cumberland. It receives its name because its sources are within Russell County.   Sutherland 13.

Sandy River flows through central eastern Pittsylvania into Halifax County; it is a tributary of Banister River. Land grant mentioned on Sandy River in 1745. Sandy River Church in October 1773.   25 V 299

Saylor's Creek Battlefield Park, 220 acres, in Amelia and Prince Edward counties, was the scene of the last major engagement between Lee's and Grant's armies, with a mass surrender of 6,000 men and six generals of the Confederate army taken prisoner on April 6, 1865. Hillman House, built 1770, used by the Unionist forces as hospital, has been restored.

VaVCo 12-1950; EcD (county).

Seaboard Coast Line Railroad formed July 1, 1967, by the merger of Seaboard Air Line and Atlantic Coast Line railroads. The name chosen emphasizes the prestige and good will in both names of highly respected companies. The merged railroad operates 341 route miles in Virginia, located in six cities and ten counties. The predecessors of both companies were chartered in Virginia. The Seaboard traces to the Portsmouth and Roanoke Railroad chartered in 1832, opened as far as Suffolk in 1834 and completed to Weldon on the Roanoke River in 1836. The Coast Line traces to the Petersburg Railroad, chartered in 1830 and completed to Weldon on the Roanoke in 1833.   Corp I.

Seminole Trail became the name of U. S. Rt. 29 as it crosses Virginia from Washington, D. C. through Danville to the Virginia-North Carolina boundary; this naming was voted by the 1928 General Assembly. Other states farther south through which U. S. Rt. 29 passes do not use the name.   LRI

Shenandoah Mountains is a name applied locally to the ridge of the Alleghenies forming the western boundary of Augusta and Rockingham counties.

Wayland SV 319

Shenandoah National Park includes 193,645 acres (302 square miles) and extends along the crest of the Blue Ridge from Front Royal to the vicinity of Waynesboro. It is 77 miles long and has an average width of four miles with its greatest width of 13 miles. It has over 200 miles of hiking and horseback trails, trout streams stocked annually, shelters and campsites, together with unparalleled scenery. Congress approved its establishment in May 1926; its two-fold purpose includes preserving the area in its natural condition and providing the accessible and available area for the enjoyment of people. The unparalleled scenery offers graceful, curving mountains, blanketed with thick forests, rocky crags, canyons, and panorama views of valley and nearby uplands.

VaVCo 10-1947, 4-1952; Lambert 7, 50, 67.

Shenandoah River begins at Riverton with the uniting of the North Fork and South Fork and flows through Warren and Clarke counties into Maryland. The stream name developed through Gerando, Sherando, Shenadore, to become Shenandoah. The name in Algonquin Indian is for "Daughter of the Stars".

Va HSSA 10; Norris 19.

Shenandoah Valley, produced by erosion of the plateau between the area of the present Blue Ridge and the Alleghenies, has a much-used name. The area drained by the Shenandoah River and its tributaries begins near the Augusta-Rockbridge counties boundary and includes drainage from seven counties. Geologists have generally spoken of the Shenandoah Valley as it includes the area beginning near Buchanan in Botetourt County because ridges from the Blue Ridge and the Alleghenies almost meet and divide the open area of lowered land. In more recent years, the state has been divided into regional areas of commerce. Roanoke is the headquarters of the Shenandoah Valley Chamber of Commerce; this influences many persons to consider that the Shenandoah Valley includes all of the area between the Blue Ridge and the Alleghenies north of Roanoke in Virginia. VaVCo 10-1940, 8.

Sinking Creek, in Craig and Giles counties, goes underground near Hoges Chapel and this disappearance gives it the name. The record of a settler on the stream dates from 1757. 30 V 191; LRI.

Skyline Drive is the mountain top surfaced highway along the crest of the Blue Ridge for one hundred miles through the Shenandoah National Park. It follows the old Indian Trail along which runners carried messages between tribes. It provides an ideally engineered road for visitors to relax and view the unusual scenery. The first section of the park was opened in 1934 and the completed roadway became available in 1939. VGb 39, 42.

Smith Creek flows through the center of Rockingham County to the north into Shenandoah County where it becomes a tributary of the North Fork of Shenandoah. Its earlier name was Elk Run. A land patent, November 12, 1735, was for a tract on Smith's Creek. Couper I, 224.

Smith River rises in Patrick County, flows across Henry from the northwest corner to the southeast corner to become a tributary of the Dan in North Carolina. Was formerly Irwin River. It is believed that early land owners were named Smith. LRI

South Anna River rises in Louisa and crosses Hanover to unite with North Anna forming the Pamunkey River. The streams were named for Queen Anne. VaVCo May 1952, 5.

South Branch of Shenandoah River is formed by South River and Middle River joining at Port Republic. The stream drains areas of Augusta, Rockingham, Page, and Warren counties, having a total drainage area of 1,570 square miles. When Spotswood saw this stream, he named it Euphrates. Its headwaters drain the southern part of the Shenandoah drainage area. Stevens 245.

South Fork Holston River is in Smyth and Washington counties. The north portion of South Holston Lake, formed in the TVA developments, is in Washington County. Stephen Holstein was an early settler in the area. Roads 25; Preston 154.

South Holston Lake, formed by damming South Fork Holston River in Sullivan County, Tennessee, provides all types of outdoor recreation.

South Mountain, in Augusta and Rockingham counties, (see North Mountain), is an old name of the Blue Ridge.   Wayland SV 42.

Southside Virginia is largely south of the James River and east of the Blue Ridge. Until recent years, it emphasized tobacco growing more than its livestock and its use of land for tree production. This with long-time residence of much of the population has contributed to a consciousness of being a distinct area of the state.

Southwest Mountains were given that name because they extend toward the southwest from the Rappahannock to the James River; they are the first range of hills when a person comes from areas farther east. The earlier name was Chestnut Ridge. A deed in 1733 refers to Southwest Mountains.
Mead 111; 39 V 137.

Southwest Virginia is the part of the state west of the crest of the Blue Ridge and drained by streams which are tributaries of the Ohio River. It has been called the Mountain Empire. Fifteen counties are included.
Com Va 3-1954.

Staunton River had Hocomawanach as its earliest name; other names have been Rorenock and Ocoaneechi. The commissioner of the North Carolina-Virginia boundary in 1728 named it for Lady Rebecca Staunton Gooch. The stream drains seven Virginia counties. The stream begins as Roanoke River in Roanoke County and is Roanoke River after entering North Carolina; the Virginia portion of the stream east of the Blue Ridge continues to be known as the Staunton River by many residents of its area.   Crouch 3.

Swift Run Gap, on the boundary of Rockingham and Greene counties, with an elevation of 2,370 feet, is at the intersection of US Route 33 and the Skyline Drive. A monument with its information tells Governor Spotswood with his troop passed through the gap September 5, 1716.   Lambert 22.

Thornton Gap, on the boundary of Page and Rappahannock counties, has an elevation of 2,304 feet, and is at the intersection of US Route 211 and Skyline Drive. The name is from Colonel Francis Thornton who settled here in mid-18th century.   WP: Va 614.

Tinker Creek flows through the southern part of Botetourt County; then south through Roanoke County to become a tributary of Roanoke River. Its name comes from the legend that a number of deserters in the Revolutionary War hid in nearby Tinker Mountain; they made pots and pans; therefore they were called "tinkers".   Va HSSA 19

TVA is the much-used name for Tennessee Valley Authority, inaugurated in 1933, which includes the tributary areas in Southwest Virginia drained by the

Powell, Clinch, and Holston rivers which are in the drainage of the Tennessee River.   Lit.Dig.,11-18-33, p.15.

John Andrew Twigg Bridge, 2,090-feet in length, connects Middlesex and Mathews counties across Piankatank River and was dedicated September 23, 1953. In 1911, John Andrew Twigg founded Twigg's Ferry across the river.
                                                              Com Va 10-1953

Upper Chippoak Creek, boundary of Surry and Prince George counties, is a tributary of the James. In 1610, Chepoke, brother of Pipisco, chief of Quiough-cohannicks, lived near the mouth of the creek. A grant of land on Chippoaks Creek was recorded November 16, 1635.   4 V 87; 5 V 98.

Valley Turnpike Company was chartered in 1838 to construct a macadamized road from Winchester to Staunton. Later, it was extended to the Potomac River and to the southwest to Roanoke. Before white explorers were in the area, buffaloes and Indians followed the course of the trail, which Major de L'Enfant surveyed for the historic Great Valley Pike. It was a toll road until midnight August 31, 1918. It became the route of the Lee Highway, and is now US Route 11.   Wayland SV 30, 344.

Vaughans Creek is a boundary of Appomattox and Prince Edward counties. April 5, 1737, there is the record of a petition for a grant of land on Vaughans Creek.   22 V 193

Walker Mountain, in Washington, Smyth, Bland, and Pulaski counties, was named for Dr. Thomas Walker, who led an exploring party in the region about 1750.

Warm Springs Mountain got its name from the famous Warm Springs, a very early gay and fashionable resort. Its elevation is 4,000+ feet and is on the boundary between Alleghany and Bath counties.   LRI

Warwick Swamp crosses the southern portion of Prince George and flows into northern Sussex County; it is a tributary of Blackwater River. A deed dated March 13, 1787, gives the location on the north side of Warwick Swamp.
                                                              7 W (2) 184.

Whiterock Mountain is within Russell, Tazewell, and Smyth counties, and has an elevation of 4,550 feet. White colored rocks seen jutting from the mountain top give it its name.   LRI

Willis River flows east in southeastern Buckingham and into Cumberland County. A land grant on Willis River was recorded in 1730.   36 V 144

York River was first called Pamunkey River; then became Charles River. In 1642, it was named York River at the same time that Charles River shire became York shire. It is a tidal estuary formed by the uniting of Pamunkey and Mattaponi River at West Point. Four counties border on the estuary.
                                                              Kibler 77.

ACCOMACK COUNTY

An Indian tribe, Accomacs, inhabited the Eastern Shore, so the name Accomac was given to all of the Eastern Shore when it was made one of the original shires in 1634. In 1663, the present county was formed. Area: 470 sq. mi.; Pop. 30,635; Pop. per sq. m., 65.2. General Assembly in 1940 decided that the name of the county should have this spelling: Accomack. More than one-third of county is wooded. It is the state's leading county in acreage harvested and bushels produced of soybeans, in hundredweight of Irish potatoes produced and bushels of sweet potatoes produced, and in the quarts of strawberries produced.

Long 165; GSW:CF.

Accomac, county seat, means "Other Side of Water Place" or "The Other Side Place". Earlier names have been Freeman's Plantation, Metompkin, Courthouse; then Drummondtown, after Henry Drummond, landowner, 1793-1818; was Accomac Court House 1832-1893; then Accomac. Pop. 414; US Rt. 13.

Wood 16; Turman 135+.

Assateague Island has a record of land patent before 1687. Assateague means "Stony River". Lighthouse on the island has been in service since 1833. Wild horses from Assateague Island are offered for sale in Chincoteague Pony Penning. Legend is that Spanish ship wrecked early in 16th century; ponies from wreck came to island for food and shelter. In 1945, the United States government bought the Virginia part of the island and established the Chincoteague National Wildlife Refuge, covering 8,809 acres. The National Seashore Park was formed September 1966. VaVCo 2-1953; EcD county; Turman 247.

Assowoman means "Rock Cave". Pop. 200. Wood 17.

Assowoman Inlet is a natural waterway 7½ miles long, along the northwest side of Assateague Island. In 1938, the U. S. Coast and Geodetic Survey decided the name should be Assateague Channel, but local usage continues with Assowoman Inlet. Wood 17

Atlantic derives its name from the Atlantic Ocean, which has its name from Greek for the sea beyond Mount Atlas. Village population 350.

Steeles 1159

Belle Haven, residential community, traces to early 18th century; a Mr. Bell baked in a large outdoor oven so place was Bell's Oven. In 1762, plantation was called Belle Haven. Town took the name of plantation; incorporated 1898; Pop. 371. ESS (county) 12; Whitelaw I, 570.

Bloxom has the name of an early postmaster, William E. Bloxom. Ry PA; elev. 20; incorporated 1953; Pop. 349. PO Dept Archives

Chincoteague gets its name from Cingo-Teague tribe, meaning "Beautiful Land across the Water". The town's Volunteer Fire Department has annual round-up of Assoteague ponies, parade, and auction as fund-raising undertaking. Pop. 2,131. VaVCo 2-1953.

Chincoteague Island is the largest inhabited island in Virginia. Chincoteague Wildlife Refuge makes possible birds living and migrating along great Atlantic flyway which has dense human population. Wildlife Refuge has beautiful marshes, ponds, and thick woods. Bridge connects island to mainland since 1923.
VaVCO 2-1953; Gottmann 165.

Craddockville had a popular name of Farmer's Interest in 1820. "Craddock" was the name of the estate of the first rector of St. George's of Pungoteague, which links to the present village name. Lieut. Craddock probably made an early settlement in June 1614. Pop. 150. Wood 37; VaVCO 8-1949.

Daugherty, earlier Bull Run, had postmasters by the name of Daugherty for more than 40 years. Pop. 150. PO Dept Archives

Davis Wharf: Miss Maggie E. Davis was postmistress in early 1890's. Pop. 50. PO Dept Archives

Eastern Shore Branch of University of Virginia is two-year community college located in vicinity of Wallops Island. Ann.Bul.

Eastern Shore Truck Experiment Station is near Painter; has been maintained since 1912. It serves commercial vegetable interests of Accomack and Northampton counties. Va Govt 53.

Fox Island, in Chesapeake Bay at northern edge of county, received the name from the tradition that foxes were raised there in colonial days. Another explanation is that presumably this island is mentioned in court records in 1874 and that a man named Fox could have been granted an early land patent.
GSW: CF; Turman

Greenbackville: Pop. 300. The name was from the paper money issued by the U. S. Government in 1862; it was called greenback. One explanation of the name is that one acre of land was sold in 1866 for $100 and the local comment was that the buyer covered it with greenbacks. Another explanation has been that an acre of marsh with oyster beds nearby brought $100 and the same remark was made. Turman et als

Greenbush: Ry PA; Pop. 200. The earlier name was Eliza's Flat until Stewart Mathias bought the local store. Tradition says he named the place from an evergreen bush. In an election in 1885, it failed to get the courthouse moved from its present location. Turman et als

Guilford Creek enters Pocomoke Bay from the southeast. A record, dated May 21, 1727, is regarding land on Guilford Creek in Accomack. 33 V 175.

Hacksneck receives its name from Dr. George Hack who patented 900 acres in 1665; at the place, there is a large neck of land on the eastern side of Chesapeake Bay. Pop. 175.   Turman 69; GSW: CF.

Hallwood has its name from the Hall family; Henry Hall married Mary Shae, whose early ancestors acquired land in the 18th century. Ry PA; elev. 15; incorporated 1958; Pop. 269.   Whitelaw II, 1258.

Harborton was Hoffman's Wharf before 1893; it was an important landing for steamers before the county had a railroad.   EcD (county).

Hopeton received its name from the Hope family, prominent in the area for years. Ry PA; Pop. 200.   Turman et als.

Hopkins: first postmaster's name, John H. Hopkins, 1886.
PO Dept Archives

Horntown: two explanations of the name are given; two branches of Savage Creek there resembled a pair of horns; or, peddlers blew horns to advertise wares in early days. Pop. 250.   Whitelaw I, 261; VaVCo 2-1953

Horsey: in 1890's, two postmasters' names were Horsey. Pop. 50.
PO Dept Archives

Jenkins Bridge: earlier name of causeway, Jenkinson's Bridge; name from landowner in 1699. Name became Jenkins Bridge. Pop. 100.
Whitelaw II, 1288.

Keller was formerly Pungoteague Station; but was named for contractor who built the railroad through the neighborhood. Ry PA; elev. 40; Pop. 263.
ESS county 12

Lee Mont: Pop. 125. Named for General R. E. Lee. This was Woodstock until Postoffice application was made in 1878. Since there was already Woodstock in Shenandoah County, the proposed name was rejected. Confederate feeling was strong on the Eastern Shore, and a rejection from Washington raised it. The first children on the Shore to have transporation to school at public expense were from Lee Mont and Bayside to Hunting Creek in 1902.   Turman et als

Locustville has been a postoffice since 1835; it was probably named from the locust trees in the area.   Turman et als

Mappsville has its name from Samuel Mapp, store and land owner; US Rt 13; Pop. 150.   Whitelaw II, 1225.

Mears has its name from postmistress, Kittie Mears; the Mears were landowners in 1717; Ry PA; Pop. 40.   PO Dept Archives; Whitelaw I, 602.

Melfa: Ry PA; Pop. 400. It was named for an official of the Pennsylvania Railroad when the station was opened; it is uncertain whether his name was Melfer or Melfa. The village replaced Fair Oaks, one mile east.   Turman et als

Metomkin Inlet has a name of Indian origin; it is between Metomkin Island and Cedar Island.   GSW: CF.

Metomkin Island is midway of the county on the Atlantic coast. Its Indian name means "To enter into a house".   VaVCO 2-1953

Modest Town was Sunderland Hall in the late 18th century: Pop. 75. Two prim ladies kept a boarding house here when it was a stage coach stop and post office. Tradition says the name was for them. Court records mention Helltown, one mile to west, so naming seems logical.   Turman et als

Nelsonia: US Rt 13; Pop. 100. Named for a local family.   Steele 1172

New Church: Ry PA; Pop. 250. The name was given because locality had the last Anglican Church built in the county during colonial years.   Turman 145

Oak Hall is in the center of plantation Oak Hall dating from 1671; post-office name is Horsey; Ry PA; elev. 20; Pop. 240.   Whitelaw II, 1319.

Onancock, meaning "Foggy Place", was an Indian village in 1670; was Port of Entry in 1680 and county seat until 1786; name is corruption of "auwannaku". Incorporated 1880. Pop. 1,759; increase Pop. 1950-60, 30.0%.
                                        Wood 17; Whitelaw II, 1408.

Onley, named for home of Henry A. Wise, governor of Virginia, incorporated 1950; Ry PA; Pop. 415. Headquarters of Eastern Shore Produce Exchange, organized 1899, considered earliest example of cooperative marketing in Virginia. It has the chief strawberry auction.
                            VaVCo 2-1953; Wood 34; Com Va 4-1953.

Painter: Ry PA; Pop. 349; incorporated 1950. The village was named for an official of Pennsylvania Railroad when the station was opened.
                                                        Turman et als

Parkers Marsh Natural Area, a 760-acre tract on the Chesapeake Bay side, is about four miles northwest of Onancock.   LRI

Parksley: Ry PA; elev. 45; Pop. 850. On land part of which owned by Edmund Bailey Parkes in 1742. First station name Matomkin, but conflict with nearby postoffice, so changed to Parksley.
                                    PO Dept Archives; Whitelaw II, 1110.

Parramore Island, one time called Teach's or Feche's, presuming that pirate buried treasure there. Then Cedar Island until 1857 when a storm destroyed the cedars. Became Parramore Island because Parramore family owned the land. It was largely undisturbed; never settled; commercial fishing and clamming are permitted.   ESS county, 13.

Pungoteague, from "pungotekw", meaning "sand fly river", dates from 1660. Was first county seat and had first dramatic performance in New World, August 27, 1665. Pop. 50.   Whitelaw II, 1408; Gannett 255.

Quinby: Pop. 200. Name from prominent attorney who inherited land from Upshur family through his mother who was a descendant of the original patentee. The area is still called Upshur's Neck.   Turman et als

Sanford is on part of the "Free School Land" bequeathed by Samuel Sandford in a will written and probated in London, April 1710. Pop. 180.
                                                                                                    Turman 196+.

Saxis (or Saxis Island), a corruption of names, traces to Sikes Island patented by Robert Sikes in 1666. Sykes became Saxis April 1896 in Postoffice records; incorporated 1959; Pop. 577.   Whitelaw II, 1276.

Saxis Marsh Wildlife Refuge, of Virginia Department of Conservation and Development, started in 1957, contains 5,000 acres and is a waterfowl feeding and nesting area. It had been a muskrat farm from 1873 to 1957; that land use became unprofitable.   Turman 248

Tangier, with an area of five square miles of land and swamp, has a name derived from Tanja, because Indians made small clay vessels which reminded John Smith of similar clay bowls which he had to fashion as a Turkish slave. It was first settled by a fishing family from Cornwall, England, in 1680. Located in Chesapeake Bay, twelve miles west of Onancock. The men are employed in fishing, oystering, and crabbing. Pop. 876.   VaVCo 8-1949; Wood 32-34.

Tasley: Ry PA; elev. 40; Pop. 200. Its name is from the Tazewell family which owned the land on which the town of Cape Charles was built until the railroad was planned. Governor Littleton Waller Tazewell of the 1830's was buried there and his body was moved to Norfolk after the land went out of the Tazewell family's ownership.   **Turman et als**

Temperanceville was Crossroads until 1824; then, four land-owners sold land with the provisions that whiskey should not be sold and the name was changed to Temperanceville. US Rt 13; Pop. 400.   ESS county 6.

Wachapreague, meaning "Little City by the Sea", on the east coast, was originally called Powellton because Powell Brothers owned the land. There was confusion with Powellton in Brunswick County, so the name was changed to Wachapreague. Incorporated 1902; Pop. 570.   Wood 17; ESS county 13.

Wallops Island was patented by John Wallop in 1672. On July 1, 1959, the National Aeronautics and Space Administration began maintaining a launching area on the island. In 1960, a bridge and causeway connected with the mainland at Assowoman.   Whitelaw 1241+.

Wattsville is named for Nancy Watts, land owner; Pop. 100.
                                                                                                    Whitelaw 1335.

Withams: Pop. 50. Charles W. and M. E. Withams built a mill in the area in the second decade of the 1900's and the village grew up around it and took the name.   Turman et als.

ALBEMARLE COUNTY

The county was formed in 1744, formally organized February 4, 1745, and named for William Anne Keppel, second Earl of Albemarle, nominal governor-in-chief of the colony seventeen years. Area: 739 sq.mi.; Pop. 30,969; increase in Pop. 1950-60, 16.2%. Over one-half of county forested. Shenandoah National Park and Blue Ridge Parkway, land owned by federal government, include 2.9% of county area. Occupational group rank: manufacturing, trade, agriculture. Farm products rank: livestock, dairy, fruits.   VGb 24.

Barracks Road received the name from quarters in 1779 to house 4,000 British and Hessian prisoners. Huts and barracks of the camp were in a wooded area of a high hill known as "The Barracks". Camp broken up November, 1780. It is now a shopping center and has a branch postoffice of Charlottesville.
                                                                                       St. Claire 33+.

Batesville, formerly Oliver's Store, in the southeastern part of the county, was named for Mr. Bates who had a blacksmith shop here. Pop. 150; elev. 605 ft.   LRI

Boonesville: Pop. 25, elev. 749, is in the extreme northern part of the county.
                                                                                       DU

Boyd Tavern: Pop. 10. On Three Chopt Road was early travelers' stopping place. In stage coach route between Richmond and Charlottesville was Shepherd's Inn. Proprietor of Tavern, Mr. Boyd.   St. Claire 17.

Charlottesville: Rys C&O, SOU; elev. 480; area 6 sq.mi.; Pop. 36,000; increase in Pop. 1950-60, 13.3%; US Rts 29, 250. Site patented in 1737 by William Taylor. It was established as a town in 1762, named for Princess Charlotte of Mecklenberg-Sterlitz, young bride of George III. It became the county seat in 1761; courthouse built 1830. In May and June, 1781, it was the temporary seat of Virginia government. It is an independent city; its municipal water supply is from watershed on Moorman's River, treated.   St. Claire 38+.

Cismont: Pop. 200; elev. 491; in eastern section of the county. The name in Latin for "on this side of the mountain". About 1836, Nicholas Meriwether built his home upon top of a hill and gave the name Cismont. In 1890's, the village which had been Bowlesville from blacksmith named Bowles; then Brown's Store; took the name of the nearby manor. Each year, Thanksgiving Day, there is the traditional outdoor ceremony, "Blessing of the Hounds".   WPA: JA 87.

Cobham, in northeastern part of county, was named for village Cobham, in Surrey County, England. Pop. 40; elev. 401.   Mead 244

Covesville: Ry SOU; elev. 805; Pop. 150; US Rt 29; in southwestern part of county. Nearby Cove Presbyterian Church dates to 1769; supposition there is connection in village name.   LRI

Crozet was named for Col. Claude Crozet, president VMI, construction engineer of C&O tunnel under Blue Ridge. Name had been Waylands for early owner of large acreages. Ry C&O; elev. 720; Pop. 900. Drainage area of 436 acres and two springs furnish municipal supply of water; treated.

St. Claire 92.

Earlysville received its name from John Richard Early, early resident of community; in north central part of county. Pop. 40; elev. 646.

WPA: JA 141.

Esmont, settlement started about 1905-06, named for nearby house, built before 1850. Elev. 450; Pop. 100. Branch of C&O connects with Nelson and Albemarle Railroad to Schuyler in Nelson County.   WPA: JA 87.

Free Union: Pop. 60; elev. 589. It is in the northwestern part of the county; was Nicksville for a Negro blacksmith. A free union church was established there, which gave the present name.   Steeles 1165.

Greenwood was named by Issac Hardin, 18th century settler; earliest name Greendwood; later became Greenwood. Was Greenwood Depot when applied for postoffice in December 1853. In 1913, became Greenwood. Ry C&O; Pop. 250; elev. 1,080.   PO Dept Archives.

Hatton, on the James River in the southeastern corner of county, was Hatton Grange before 1850; it is often known as Mountain View, because of unusual view of Blue Ridge on the west. Ry C&O; Pop. 25; elev. 291.   WPA: JA 82, 84.

Heards: Pop. 60; elev. 1,061; in southwest portion of county.   DU

Howardsville was laid out on land patented by Allen Howard in 1730; it is in southwestern corner of county on James. Ry C&O; Pop. 50; elev. 400.

WPA: JA 86.

Institute of Textile Technology was chartered by textile executives in 1944. It is supported as a co-operative venture by textile mills from Canada to Texas. It is planned for post-graduate only, offering degrees Master of Science and Doctor of Philosophy, with a two-fold purpose: research and training for the textile industry.   Ann.Bul.

Ivy derives its name from Ivy Creek, which is referred to in deeds as early as 1750. Along the creek, much *kalmia,* an evergreen frequently mistaken for ivy, is found. Its early name was Woodville; then Ivy Depot; became Ivy. Ry C&O; elev. 545; Pop. 250.   WPA: JA 129.

Keene, in south central part of county, was named for man who married into Randolph family. Pop. 25; elev. 552.   WPA: JA 77.

Keswick, in north central part of county, was doubtless named for the home of poet Southey in Cumberland County, England. Keswick Farm had been called Turkey Hill, probably from number of wild turkeys there. Railway station was Keswick Station until shortened to Keswick. Ry C&O; elev. 434; Pop. 300.

Mead 217.

Mechum River, tributary of Moorman's River, is in southwestern part of county. Land purchase record on Mechum's River, 1772. 19 V 325

Miller School, in western part of county, was provided with funds by Samuel Miller and opened in 1878. It was planned to provide occupational training. Pop. 20; elev. 700. WPA: JA 22, 132.

Monticello, in Italian meaning "Little Mountain", was designed and built by Thomas Jefferson, now owned and maintained as a national shrine by Thomas Jefferson Memorial Foundation. The restoration began in the early 1920's. Elev. 867. VGb 26; St. Claire 67, 70.

Moorman's River: Charles Moorman, Quaker, acquired land 1735. Later in land patent gave the stream its name. It is a tributary of the Rivanna.

WPA: JA 137.

Newcomb Hall (branch postoffice of Charlottesville) on University of Virginia campus, named for John Lloyd Newcomb (1881-1954), president University of Virginia, 1933-1947. LRI

North Garden, in south central part of county, has its name from luxuriant nearby area. Ry SOU; elev. 645; Pop. 200. WPA: JA 93.

Piedmont Fruit Research Laboratory investigates plant diseases and insects attacking fruits. Com Va 9-1953

Sanitarium (State Tuberculosis Hospital); Blue Ridge Sanitarium; has accommodations for 270 patients. Elev. 336.

Scottsville: John Scott was owner of Scott's Ferry and founder of Scottsville. David Scott was owner of land on which first Albemarle courthouse was built; was county seat 1744-1761. Wide view of nearby lowland gave protection from Indian attacks and undesirable persons in earliest days. In 18th century, it was shipping center and manufacturer of flat-bottom boats. Ry C&O; elev. 275; Pop. of portion in Albemarle County 292. Municipal water from treated supply from James River. Rawlings 1, 27, 32.

University of Virginia: Pop. 5,300. Thomas Jefferson fought for more than thirty-six years to establish the University of Virginia. With the help of Joseph Cabell, a bill was passed in the General Assembly in 1816 which provided the necessary funds. January 25, 1819, the charter of Central College was converted into that of the University of Virginia; all of the original buildings are classical in design. First session opened March 7, 1825. Honor system was established in 1842. Graduate studies and professional departments are widely recognized.

Ann. Bul.

Whitehall, in the northwestern portion of the county, was an election precinct known as Glenn's Store, William Maupin's Store, Maupin's Tavern, Miller's Store, Shumate's Tavern, until 1835. Then, it was named Whitehall for a White family living in the community. Pop. 55; elev. 722.

Woods: HA 22; WPA: JA 136.

ALLEGHANY COUNTY

Formed in 1822, named for Allegheny Mountains; the name means "endless" as natives saw the range from the valley floor. Settlement began before 1750. Area: 446 sq.mi.; Pop. 12,128; Pop. per sq.mi., 27.2; 70.9% county area forested; 46.8% county area in George Washington National Forest. Rank occupational groups: manufacturing, public facilities, trade. Rank agricultural income: livestock, dairy, poultry. (The legal spelling of the county name is "Alleghany".) Long 168

Alleghany: Ry C&O; elev. 2,056; Pop. 150. The name is from a pre-historic race of mound builders, the Alleghi. Steeles 1158.

Boys Home, Covington, maintained by the Episcopal Church; a non-sectarian home for boys.

Cliftondale: Pop. 100. Clifton was the name of the early home of an iron master in Rockbridge County; he was owner of present Clifton Forge. Cliftondale is a subdivision of Clifton Forge. Arritt

Clifton Forge: Ry C&O; elev. 1,086; Pop. 5,600; US Rts 60, 220; Interstate 64. Named for James Clifton's iron furnace in Iron Gate Gorge. Century-old forge has been restored. Prior to incorporation in 1884, town was Williamson. Became independent city in 1906. Location of C&O large repair yards, offices, and is a junction point. Chesapeake and Ohio General Hospital 205-bed is here. Water from Smith Creek; filtered, chlorinated. VaVCo 2-1951.

Covington: Ry C&O; elev. 1,242; Pop. 11,062; increase Pop. 1950-60, 88.8%; US Rts 60, 220. Interstate 64. Earlier name Merry's Store; townsite surveyed and platted by Dr. James Merry. Incorporated as Covington in 1833. Dr. Merry was probably a relative of Prince Edward Covingtons and named the town for a relative. It became an independent city in 1952. West Virginia Pulp and Paper Company established in 1899. Water from mountain stream and Jackson River; chlorinated, filtered. Arritt

Dunlap Creek flows from the southern boundary as a tributary of Jackson River. It was named for Captain James Dunlap, killed at Fort Upper Tract in 1758; he had received early land grant in 1753. Arritt

Falling Spring, nine miles northeast of Covington, has a flow of 7,000 gallons per minute; it rates as the second largest in flow among Virginia springs. Falls over a rock 200 feet into the valley. VaVCo 2-1951; Bodie 151.

Falling Spring Creek in the northwest portion of the county is a tributary of Jackson River.

Gathright Dam on Jackson River near Covington is named for Thomas Morton Gathright, owner of game preserve, or gentlemen's hunting and fishing preserve.   Arritt.

Gathright Wildlife Management Preserve, named for Thomas Morton Gathright, who acquired picturesque mountain land.   Arritt.

Iron Gate: Ry C&O; elev. 1,020; Pop. 716. Jackson River cuts water gap, Iron Gate, through White Mountain. Town down stream takes name from gap. Water supply, mountain spring, three wells.   Morton 96.

Jordan Mines: Pop. 30. It was named for an early iron man. Elev. 1,450.
                                                                              Steeles 1168.

Dabney S. Lancaster College, two-year community institution, established in 1964; has 167-acre campus. It is named for former State Superintendent of Public Instruction and later President of Longwood College.   Ann.Bul.

Lowmoor: elev. 1,155; Pop. 900; US Rts 60, 220. Correct name should be Low Moor. Low-Moor Iron Company is source of community name. Augustus Low, of New York, was in the company owning iron orelands. Moor reported as name of Cincinnati engineer. Water from spring, chlorinated.   Arritt.

Ogle Creek is in western area of northwest portion of county; unites with Dunlap Creek. It received name from an early family.   Arritt.

Potts Creek flows northeast from southeast portion of county; tributary of Jackson River. Earlier name Carpenter Creek. It was named for John Potts who settled along the stream before 1770.   Arritt.

Selma: Pop. 850; near to and southwest of Clifton Forge.   DU

South Covington is part of Covington; it has a postoffice.

Sweet Chalybeate: elev. 2,000; Pop. 75. Named for a local spring. Chalybeate means water well-supplied with salts of iron. Red Springs Company was incorporated 1836. Spring flows nearly 1,500,000 gallons each day.   Morton 91.

Wilson Creek flows from Douthat State Park south; it is tributary of Jackson River. It was named for the first family to settle in the neighborhood.   LRI

AMELIA COUNTY

Amelia County, organized 1734, was named for Princess Amelia Sophia, youngest daughter of George II of England. Area: 366 sq.mi.; Pop. 7,815; Pop. per sq.mi., 21.4. Nearly three-fourths entire area wooded. Rank occupational groups: agriculture, manufacturing, trade. Rank agricultural income: dairy, crops, livestock. Roads 67; EcD county

Amelia C. H. (RR name Amelia): Ry SOU; elev. 630; Pop. 630; US Rt 360. April 4-5, 1865, Lee's army disappointed because supplies had gone on to Richmond; lost time here while foraging.

Ammon: Pop. 10. Biblical name, Gen. 19:38. Steeles 1158.

Bush River: Land grant mentions 337 acres on stream to Richard Jones, Jr., Sept. 28, 1728. Land grant, June 10, 1741. 62 V 449; 15 V 234

Chula is Choctaw for Red Fox. Ry SOU; Pop. 125. In east central portion of county. Steeles 1162

Jetersville: Ry SOU; elev. 430; Pop. 175; US Rt 360. Named for first postmaster, Thomas E. Jeter. In southwestern portion of county. Sheridan entrenched here April 4, 1865. Grant and Meade arrived April 5; these positions were across Lee's line of retreat to Danville. Armstrong 49.

Mannboro: Pop. 25. In southeastern portion of county. Named for an early settler. Steeles 1171

AMHERST COUNTY

Founded 1761, the county was named for Lord Amherst, successful British commander in French-Indian War. Area: 467 sq.mi.; Pop. 22,953; increase Pop. 1950-60, 12.9%; Pop. sq.mi., 49.1. Nearly three-fourths of county area wooded. 18.2% county area in federally-owned areas. Rank occupational groups: manufacturing, trade, agriculture. Agricultural income rank: livestock, field crops, fruit and nuts.   Long 71+.

Amherst: Pop. 1,200; increase Pop. 1950-60, 15.6%; elev. 629; US Rts 29, 60. Incorporated 1910. Two buildings at crossroads were known as "The Oaks", some say "Seven Oaks". This was a community center before location became county seat. County seat in 1807 when county reduced by formation of Nelson County. Water supply from Buffalo River; filtered, chlorinated.
Percy ACS 121+.

Bald Knob, 4,000 feet elev., in northwest portion of county, had a bald area.
EcD county

Clifford: Pop. 135; elev. 770. Incorporated as Cabellsburg in 1795; later New Glasgow, short time county seat of Amherst County. Colonel Nicholas Cabell, son of Dr. William Cabell, physician, surveyor, and very early settler in area, was interested in raising fine horses; links to early race track in community. Academy at New Glasgow, now Clifford, is claimed as influence to founding Sweet Briar College.   Percy ACS 7, 30, 60, 71.

Colony (Lynchburg Training School and Hospital): Pop. 2,000. Colony for epilepsy and mental deficiency was chartered 1906; opened May, 1911. In the grounds are earthworks erected in June 1864, to defend Lynchburg against Sheridan's advance from the east.   CVHM 22.

Lowesville: Pop. 50; elev. 740. First postmaster Lowe Fulcher; this explains name Lowesville.   LRI

Madison Heights: Pop. 700; US Rt 29. Probably received name from a tobacco warehouse known as Madison warehouse; was an early river town. When river transportation used, hogsheads of tobacco were lowered to double-dugout canoes or bateaux on the river. Water supply from Graham Creek; filtered, chlorinated.   VA HSSA 22.

Monroe: Ry SOU; Pop. 800; elev. 650; US Rt 29. In southeast portion of county. In 1960, Father Judge Mission Seminary opened for students wishing to complete four years of high school and two years of college required for the order. Postoffice Potts was established Aug. 1, 1897. Name changed to Monroe February 24, 1905. James Monroe Watts was postmaster; hence Monroe adopted. Water supply from Harris Creek; filtered, chlorinated.   LRI

Mt. Pleasant, 4,098 feet elev., is in the northwest portion of county. Panorama from this peak presents contrasts — from the sharp-nosed mountains and deep-seated valleys of the Blue Ridge to the wide-spreading expanse of the Piedmont Upland.

Naola: Pop. 50; elev. 850. In southwest portion of county. One tradition that Italians working digging canal named for town in Italy.   LRI

Pedlar River rises in the northwest portion of the county and flows south as a tributary of the James. Land grant, 1762 on Pedlar River.   7 V 76.

Riverville: Ry C&O; elev. 500; Pop. 50. In eastern portion of county; its location on the James River is one explanation of the place name.   LRI

Snowden: Ry C&O; elev. 671; Pop. 25; US Rt 501. Is in the western portion of county. Hope Ferry or Waugh's Ferry, now Snowden, was an important crossing of the James for early migrants. In the 1880's, Davis, a Welshman, renamed the village for Mount Snowdon in Wales, but with limited education, he spelled it Snowden.   LRI

Sweet Briar: Ry SOU; elev. 702; Pop. 950; US Rt 29. Elijah Fletcher, teacher in Clifford Academy, married one of the students he tutored. During the years he lived in Lynchburg, as capable manager of the Plantation, he improved it and prospered. Their daughter, Indiana Fletcher-Williams, in memory of her own daughter, provided for Sweet Briar College which opened in 1906. The estate was Sweet Briar plantation. It is in the east central part of the county. Water supply: impounded lake, springs, well; filtered, chlorinated.

Percy ACS, 71, 73+, 76.

Sweet Briar College, name chosen by Mrs. Fletcher because of great number of sweet briar roses on the plantation. Boxwood gardens of the campus are among the most extensive of English box in this country. College founded on plantation of 8,000 acres in 1900; opened 1906; granted first Bachelor of Arts degrees in 1910.   Chr-Mas 503.

APPOMATTOX COUNTY

Appomattox County, formed in 1845, was probably named for a tribe which once lived along the James River. The river name "Apamutiky" in the Algonquin language meant "a sinuous tidal estuary". Another meaning of the word is "tobacco plant country". Area: 343 sq.mi.; Pop. 9,148; Pop. per sq.mi., 26.7. Three-fourths of county wooded. Leading occupational groups: manufacturing, agriculture, trade. Rank agricultural income: field crops, dairy, livestock.

Long 166; VaVCo 1-1951

Appomattox became county seat in 1892. Ry N&W; elev. 825; Pop. 1,184; increase Pop. 1950-60, 8.2%; US Rt 460. Wells provide municipal water.

Appomattox Court House National Historical Park has an area of 970 acres; it was formed April 10, 1940. It commemorates the surrender of General Lee's army on April 10, 1865. The McLean House and many other buildings have been restored; in addition, many points of interest are identified by markers. Clover Hill Tavern was built in 1819; around this the village, Clover Hill, developed. This became the county seat when the county was formed in 1845.

EcD county; VGb 47.

Bent Creek: Pop. 30; US Rt 60. In northwest corner of county.   DU

Evergreen: Ry N&W; Pop. 150. Its name was given because in earlier years, the location was surrounded by evergreens.   Steeles 1164.

Pamplin was named by a local resident. Ry N&W; elev. 680; Pop. 312; US Rt 460. The village is on the county line of Appomattox and Prince Edward counties. The Pamplin Clay Pipe Factory, said to be the largest clay pipe factory in the world, has a capacity of 20,000 pipes daily.   Steeles 1174

Spout Spring was given its name because a large spring spouts out from the side of a hill. Pop. 100; US Rt 460.   Steeles 1177

ARLINGTON COUNTY

Formerly Alexandria County, earlier name Bellehaven, formed in 1847 from part of District of Columbia retroceded to Virginia. Renamed Arlington in 1920 for Arlington estate. The county has no incorporated community. It is the third smallest county in size in the United States. Area: 24 sq.mi.; Pop. 163,401; Pop. per sq.mi., 6,808.4; increase Pop. 1950-60, 20.6%; US Rts 1, 29, 50, 211. New courthouse built 1898 at Fort Myers Heights, now called Claredon. County contains National Cemetery and National Airport. County controls its own secondary road system. Compared to Virginia counties, county ranks first in the persons 25 years old and older in their years of high school or more completed, 71.6%. Rank occupational groups: public administration, on duty with US armed forces, trade.   Roads 83; Va R 9-1955.

Arlington Hall was once a girl's school, now home of Signal Corps.
                                                                        Va R 9-1955.

Arlington National Cemetery: Arlington House was built in 1802. Federal Government confiscated Arlington May 24, 1861. March 3, 1883, Congress appropriated the necessary $150,000 to pay son of General and Mrs. Robert E. Lee for Arlington Heights, 480 acres. First burials in 1864. Arlington Cemetery, largest, most beautiful, most famous of all national cemeteries under the control of United States government. Thousands of nation's brave dead are buried in the cemetery. On highest point, Tomb of Unknown Soldier, guarded day and night; the tomb is cut from a single block of marble. Body brought from France in 1921 and decorated with Congressional Medal of Honor. In grounds, historic Lee Mansion with exquisite furnishings, gardens, and architecture.
                                                                  Bodine 67; Va HSSA 6

Eads (sub-postoffice): In early 1930's, with a new alphabetical street naming pattern, Eads replaced "E" as a street name. It was named for the prominent engineer, James Buchanan Eads, who bridged the Mississippi at St. Louis and improved South Pass of the Mississippi delta. The sub-station took the name of the street location.   LRI

Fort Myer: established as Fort Whipple in 1863, was named in honor of Major General Whipple who died in 1863. General Albert J. Myer, post commander 1870-1880, was honored by the present fort name. It has had different military units at different times.   Lee AC 31, 116.

Francis Scott Key Bridge across the Potomac, built in 1923, was named in honor of the composer of "The Star Spangled Banner".   Arl St

George Mason Bridge, opened in 1962, was named for the writer who in 1776 drafted the Virginia Bill of Rights and the first Constitution of Virginia.
                                                                  Arl St; Detweiler 4.

Marymount College, two-year institution, established 1950 is one of Marymount schools, fostered by the Congregation of the Religious of the Sacred Heart of Mary.   Ann Bul.

Memorial Bridge constructed in 1932 connects vicinity of Lincoln Memorial in Washington to entrance of Arlington National Cemetery. It has six lanes and is 2,163 feet in length.   Rev. of Reviews, 9-1933; Pop. Sci., 7-1931.

National Airport is a civilian airport owned by the United States Government. In 1940, Summer Hill Plantation (150 acres) and dredged land added became National Airport; area 750 acres. It is three and one-half miles from the heart of downtown Washington; one of the world's most modern commercial flying fields.   Va R 9-1955

Pentagon is the largest office building in the world — five floors, five sides, five rings; sprawls over 42 acres, on grounds of approximately 300 acres; has 17½ miles of corridors; employs 45,000. A pentagon is a five-sided figure having five angles; *penta* means five in Greek.   VGb 36; Lee AC 55.

Preston King (sub-station postoffice) was named for the first casualty in line of duty during World War II from the local area, June 19, 1943.   LRI

Rochambeau Memorial Bridge was built in 1950; named after French General Jean Baptiste Rochambeau, who was commander of French troops during Revolutionary War. He fought with General Washington at Yorktown. The bridge was named by Congress.   Arl St 21; LRI.

Rosslyn belonged to property deeded to Caroline Lambden and her husband, William Henry Ross. From their names, they called it "Rosslyn Farm". In 1869, the farm was sold to Rosslyn Development Corporation. The name was spelled with two N's in 1900.   Lee AC 78, 166.

Shirlington was named for the shopping center, "Shirlington Shopping Center", which name was given because of nearness to Shirley Highway. The highway was named after the former Commissioner of Highways of the State of Virginia.   LRI

South is in the southern part of Arlington County; all mail carriers delivering in the southern part of the county worked out of this station.   LRI

AUGUSTA COUNTY

Formed in 1738, named for Augusta of Saxe-Gotha, wife of Frederick, Prince of Wales, mother of George III. The county's earliest area extended to the Mississippi on the west and the Great Lakes on the north. Some of the oldest records of colonial days are in Augusta County Courthouse, invaluable documents of those times are on file. Area: 986 sq.mi.; Pop. 37,363; Pop. per sq.mi., 37.9; increase Pop. 1950-60, 9.4%. Over half total area forested. 32.5% of county area is federally-owned areas. Compared to other counties in the state, it leads in the number of sheep on the farms and in the tons of all hay produced. Rank occupational groups: manufacturing, agriculture, trade. Rank agricultural income: livestock, poultry, dairy.   Roads 80; VaVCo 10-1949

Augusta Military Academy, at Fort Defiance, was founded in 1865. Began as Augusta Academy; became Augusta Military Academy in 1890.
                                                                    TD 5-9-1965.

Augusta Springs: Ry C&O; elev. 1,680; Pop. 300. Is located near base of Elliott Knob. Water had reputation of valuable medicinal qualities in early 19th century.   EcD county

Baker Spring southeast of Waynesboro flows 5,300 gallons per minute; hardness of 50; is an advantage to Waynesboro.   Bul Spg V 53.

Bald Knob in Blue Ridge east of Steeles Tavern has a lookout tower in George Washington National Forest. The name is influenced by earlier times when Indians kept places having scant vegetation barren by burning in favor of use as a signal station.   LRI

Basic City began east of South River in 1889; it was chartered in 1890, and consolidated with Waynesboro in 1923. It was named after Jacob Reese's basic process for making steel.   Com Va 5-1941

Betsy Bell and Mary Gray, twin hills near Staunton, are named from the ballad of the 17th century. Two girls died of a plague in 1645. From the romantic legend of the two hills near Perth, Scottish Covenanters named two hills in County Tyrone near Omaugh. Scotch-Irish descendants gave the names to two hills near Staunton.   Gordon 101++.

Blue Ridge College near Weyers Cave on US Rt 11 is a two-year state community institution which opened in 1967.   LRI

Buffalo Gap is in the west central portion of the county. Buffaloes used the gap in moving from one side of the range to the other; a remnant of the buffalo trail is visible on a Cowpasture bluff; their use gave the name. A hard surface highway and the C&O Railway go through the gap.
                                            Gordon 189+; Wayland SV 58.

Churchville: Ry C&O; elev. 1475; Pop. 400; US Rt 250. It is located in the lovely valley of Jennings Branch. An early log church was used by several denominations; later several denominations built their own churches; this led to naming for many churches in a small place.   LRI

Craigsville: Ry C&O; elev. 1,515; Pop. 978. Early settlement was called Marbledale because marble was mined. Craigsville was named for an early set-ler. It has been incorporated since 1950.   ESS county 26.

Crimora: Ry N&W; Pop. 500; US Rt 340; elev. 1,260. A land owner gave the site for the railroad station in 1881 if he might name the place for his sweet-heart. The community ranked as chief producer of manganese in 1885-1891. Water supply from mountain stream and spring.   Steeles 1163.

Cyclopean Towers (been called Natural Chimneys), were carved by erosion; they are near Mt. Solon. It is the location of an annual jousting tournament, a test of horsemanship and skill, since 1821.   VaVCo 5-1963.

Deaf and Blind, Virginia School for: (Staunton). It was established in 1839 and is state supported. The applicants are from those between 6 and 20 years of age.   Va Govt 52.

Deerfield: Pop. 200; elev. 1,737. Is in Calfpasture valley; deer were plenti-ful; the name memorializes those native animals.   Wayland SV 325

DeJarnette State Sanitarium, founded 1928, is an institution for mental and nervous afflictions and alcohol and drug addictions. Friends and relatives of the patient must pay the approximate cost for maintenance and operation of the sani-tarium. Named for Dr. Joseph Spencer DeJarnette (1866-1957), superintendent Western State Hospital, 1906-1947.   Va Govt 67; LRI

Elliott Knob is in North Mountain; elev. 4,473; it has lookout tower in George Washington National Forest. Andrew Elliott was an early surveyor; the knob was probably named for him.   LRI

Fairfax Hall, four-year private college-preparatory girls school in Waynes-boro. It was Brandon Institute 1920-1932. In 1932, it was named Fairfax Hall in honor of Thomas, sixth Lord of Fairfax, of Greenway Court.
Couper II, 1240; LRI.

Fishburne Military Academy in Waynesboro was founded in 1879. James A. Fishburne established a day school which became a boarding school. At present, has the advantages of military training plus the goal of high citizenship.
EcD county; Couper 1231.

Fishersville: Ry C&O; Pop. 700; elev. 1,320; US Rt 250. An early settler by the name of Fisher explains the name.   ESS county 20.

Fordwick: Ry C&O; Pop. 150; elev. 1,485. Formerly The Ford. Wick is an old English word for village. The name was suggested by F. H. Lewis, mean-ing "the village at the ford". Since 1899, Portland Cement has been manufac-tured.   Steele 1165.

Fort Defiance: Ry CW; Pop. 100; elev. 1,247; US Rt 11. The village was named Fort Defiance when the railroad built through the community in 1874-75; named in honor of fort built surrounding the Old Stone Church in 1755.

ESS county 81.

Grand Caverns were discovered in 1806; long known as Weyer's Cave. Rock layers shoved up in vertical position favored a great number of shield-like formations.

Com Va 5-1949; DNR 11-5-1966.

Greenville: Ry N&W; elev. 1,545; Pop. 400; US Rt 340. It was named for Nathaniel Greene. Near the village, Washington and Lee University had its beginning.

Steeles 1166.

Kables (part of Staunton): named for Captain William E. Kable, founder of Staunton Military Academy.

Steeles 1168.

Lewis Creek flows through Staunton; it is a tributary of Middle River. John Lewis settled at the location of Staunton in 1732.

Va HSSA 15.

Lyndhurst: Ry N&W; elev. 1,394; Pop. 150. It was named by George C. Milne, an Englishman, for Lord Lyndhurst.

Steeles 1170.

Mary Baldwin College, in Staunton, was Augusta Female Academy 1842-1895. It is the oldest senior college for women of the Presbyterian Church of the United States. It was named to honor Mary Julia Baldwin, woman educator and principal, 1863-1897. It became a junior college in 1916 and a four-year institution in 1923. It is a liberal arts college.

Ann.Bul.

Middlebrook: elev. 1,840; Pop. 140. It is named from the clear stream which crosses Main Street near the center of the village. It had a postoffice as early as 1840. Its water supply is from a spring.

Catlett 23.

Middle River flows from the northeast area of the county to the southeast area in the eastern portion of the county. It is the middle stream of the three largest streams flowing from the west side of the Valley to empty into the South Branch of the Shenandoah.

LRI

Mint Spring: elev. 1,562; Pop. 75; US Rt 11. It was named for a local spring which was surrounded by mint.

Steeles 1172

Mount Sidney: Ry CW; elev. 1,260; Pop. 500; US Rt 11. It was named by Samuel Curry for Sir Philip Sidney. Its water supply, four wells; chlorinated.

Steeles 1172.

Mount Solon: elev. 1,322; Pop. 140. It was named by Samuel Curry for the Greek philosopher.

Steeles 1172

Naked Creek, in the central portion of the northeastern part of the county, is a tributary of Middle River. The bare banks along the stream gave it the name.

Wayland SV 325

New Hope: Pop. 125. John Kerr, home near village, made a land entry for 400 acres in 1772. The wife of the early settler wanted to abandon the clearing. The husband was confident that they could take on new hope. This led to the community's name.   Couper I, 349.

Park: postoffice station in Waynesboro. It was named because it is near the southern terminus of the parkland included in Shenandoah National Park.   LRI

Shen Valley Airport, near Weyers Cave, serves three cities: Staunton, Waynesboro, and Harrisonburg; and two counties, Augusta and Rockingham. In time schedules, it is often designated as Staunton.   LRI

South River has its headwaters in the south central part of the county; it flows to the northeast as the third of the three largest streams belonging to the drainage area of the South Branch of the Shenandoah.   LRI

Spottswood: elev. 1,844; Pop. 100. It was named for Governor Spotswood.
                                                   Steeles 1177.

Staunton: (independent city); Area 9 sq.mi.; Rys C&O, CW; elev. 1,385; Pop. 23,000; increase Pop. 1950-60, 11.6%; US Rts 11, 250. Its earlier name was "Mill Place". William Beverly donated twenty-five acres "at his mill-site" near the center of his "Manor of Beverly" for the location and erection of a court house and jail in 1738. The town was laid off in 1748; it was named in honor of Lady Staunton, wife of colonial Governor Gooch. It was chartered in 1749; incorporated 1871; established by the General Assembly 1761. The first vestry meeting of Trinity Episcopal Church 1736. Virginia Assembly met in town June 7-23, 1781; they avoided capture by the British Colonel Tarleton. City manager plan began January 16, 1908. Water supply, mountain reservoir, auxiliary spring: filtered, chlorinated. (The city name is pronounced *stan' t'n*).
                                          EcD county; Catlett 13.

Staunton Military Academy founded 1860 as Staunton Male Academy by William H. Kable; in 1863, it became Staunton Military Academy. Senior school: four years college preparatory plus one year post graduate. Plans for culture, education, and self-reliance linked to Truth, Duty, and Honor.
                                          VaVCo May 1951; Va R Dec 1955.

Steeles Tavern: elev. 1,671; Pop. 160; US Rt 11. Named for David Steele, Revolutionary soldier. It is also known as Midway.   Morton: Rbr Co 137

Stuart Hall, founded 1843 as Virginia Female Institute, renamed to commemorate the widow of the Confederate leader J. E. B. Stuart; Mrs. Stuart became principal in 1880. Offers college preparatory; property of three Episcopal dioceses of Virginia.   VaVCO 5-1951.

Stuarts Draft: Ry N&W; elev. 1,385; Pop. 600. Stuarts, early settlers, owned a little valley called a draft; this gave name Stuarts Draft for the town. Nearby Shenandoah Acres, resort and vacation spot.   Catlett 25.

Swoope: Ry C&O; elev. 1,650; Pop. 40. Early settler A. Jacob Swoope lived near the village location; he became Staunton's second mayor; likelihood station named for him.   LRI

Verona: Ry CW; elev. 1,280; Pop. 500; US Rt 11. The name is probably from Venezia — Veronese. Early postoffice in Bowling's Mill; when roller mill installed, named Rolla. Postoffice was Rolla; railroad station Verona. Postoffice name became Verona when another postoffice in Virginia having that name was discontinued.   LRI

Waynesboro (independent city): Ry C&O; N&W; elev. 1,405; Pop. 17,000; increase Pop. 1950-60, 27.0%; Area: 7 sq.mi.; US Rts 250, 340. Earlier name Teesville from Tees Brothers. In 1801, town named for General Anthony Wayne. Incorporated 1834. Became independent city in 1948. Rank occupational groups: manufacturing, trade, professional services.

Willis-Walker 18, 83.

West Augusta: Pop. 10; elev. 2,012 ft.; US Rt 250.

Western State Hospital, in Staunton, founded 1828, institution for mentally ill.   Va Govt 67

Weyers Cave: Ry CW; elev. 1,150; Pop. 300. Bernard Weier, Wyer, or Weyer discovered caverns in 1806; named station Weyer's Cave to attract tourists to cavern. The charter of the first chapter of Future Farmers of Virginia, which had been organized in the Weyers Cave High School, was received in 1927. The idea spread and became the Future Farmers of America which was organized in Baltimore in November 1928 and is now chartered by the United States Congress; the organization now has 450,000 members in some 9,000 chapters.

Couper 755++, 1179+; DNR 5-29-1962

Woodrow Wilson Birthplace, manse at Staunton in 1846, now a national shrine, was dedicated May 4, 1941. Woodrow Wilson Birthplace Foundation, Inc., has been refurnished with treasured family possessions, furniture, and maintains the lovely Victorian garden.   VaVCo 10-1949; Com Va 10-1959.

Woodrow Wilson Rehabilitation Center at Fishersville was dedicated November 1947 and provides service to the maimed, crippled, and afflicted in vocational training, active group recreation, and self-care. Enrollees come from 40 states and foreign countries.   Com Va 8-1963

BATH COUNTY

Bath County has several remarkable springs and baths, which is one explanation of its name; another is that it is named for the English town Bath. It is a resort county extensively known for golf courses, thermal springs, horseback riding, mountain hiking, and scenic highways. Over 50 hunt clubs have headquarters in the county. Area: 540 sq.mi.; Pop. 5,335; Pop. per sq.mi., 9.9. Almost nine-tenths area in forests. Land owned by federal and state governments, 52.1%. First settlers in 1745; county formed 1790. Rank of occupational groups: agriculture, manufacturing, trade. Rank agricultural income: live stock, field crops, poultry.　　　　　　　　　　　　　　　　　　　Long 175; Roads 73.

Bacova: Pop. 175. Name was from first letters of *Bath*; first letters of *Co*unty; and abbreviation for Virginia; compose Bacova. Elev. 1,841 ft.　　LRI

Bald Knob: elev. 4,228 ft.; 3 miles south of Healing Springs. At its high elevation, only scrub oaks grow, so led to name Bald Knob.　　　　　　LRI

Bolar: elev. 2,240; Pop. 45. Named for Colonel John Bolar of Bath. Has mineral springs; one, largest in county, flows 52 gallons per minute. Temperature of springs 66 degrees, highest in state for volume of flow.
　　　　　　　　　　　　　　　　　　　　　　　　　　Morton High 161.

Burnsville: elev. 2,390; Pop. 50; in north central part of county. Earlier name, Red Hole Valley. Many disliked name; changed to more acceptable name for large number of Burns family located in area.　　　　　　　　LRI

Healing Spring: elev. 2,200; Pop. 200; US Rt 220; in south central part of county. It was named for the thermal mineral spring, temperature 77.2.
　　　　　　　　　　　　　　　　　　　　　　Steeles 1167; Gannett 153

Hot Springs: Ry C&O; elev. 2,195; Pop. 200; US Rt 220. It was named for springs having a temperature of 103.8 to 90. Earliest hotel erected 1766. Homestead Hotel is largest business in the county, employing several hundred. Homestead owns 17,000 acres, famous as pleasant-weather resort with variety of sports including months of ice-skating and skiing; 3,000-foot ski run can be covered by artificial snow, has a 500-foot drop.　　　　　Bodie 122

Mad Sheep Mountain: elev. 4,256 ft.; 16½ miles north of Hot Springs. Sheep grazed area before acquisition by George Washington National Forest. Many times sheep would eat "loco weed" from tops of mountain; the results led to the name.　　　　　　　　　　　　　　　　　　　　　　LRI

Mad Tom Mountain: elev. 4,050+ ft.; 16 miles north of Hot Springs. Mad Tom, poor colored slave who first became lost about 1800, went crazy here.
　　　　　　　　　　　　Kenny: West Virginia Place Names, p. 396.

Millboro: Ry C&O; elev. 2,195; Pop. 300. In approximately 1829, Lowman family built Millboro Roller Mills for grinding wheat and corn. Postoffice took name from mill.   LRI

Millboro Spring: elev. 1,344; Pop. 50.

Mill Creek in southeastern area is tributary of Cowpasture River.   DU

Nimrod Hall: elev. 1,307; Pop. 25. Windy Cove Presbyterian Church near village was organized 1753.   DU

Paddy Knob: elev. 4,494 ft.; 8 miles southwest of Monterey. Bear Hollow begins at Paddy Knob; Paddy was Negro term for a bear.   LRI

Warm Springs: elev. 2,371; Pop. 300; US Rt 220. County seat, first court May 10, 1791. Springs have temperature 95.2 and 94. Gentleman's Pool Spring flows 1,200 gallons per minute.   VaVCo 2-1951

Williamsville: elev. 1,661; Pop. 40; on Va. Rt. 678. It receives name from one of first postmasters, William Lockridge.   Morton High, 16.

BEDFORD COUNTY

County was formed in 1753 and named for the fourth Duke of Bedford, English statesman. Area: 770 sq.mi.; Pop. 31,028; Pop. per sq.mi., 40.3; increase Pop. 1950-60, 4.7%. About 60 per cent of county is wooded. Jefferson National Forest and Blue Ridge Parkway include 4.9% of county area. Rank occupational groups: manufacturing, agriculture, trade. Rank agricultural income: dairy, livestock, field crops.   VaVCo 11-1950.

Bedford: Ry N&W; elev. 1,017; Pop. 5,921; increase Pop. 1950-60, 45.8%; US Rt 340. Was Liberty in 1782; became Bedford City in 1890; word "city" dropped in 1912; county seat. City municipal water supply from Stony Creek reservoir; filtered, chlorinated.   Parker 16, 18, 20+; Bedford HG 16.

Big Island: Ry C&O; elev. 595; Pop. 500; US Rt 501. Named for island in James River, 1½ miles long and ¼ mile wide; said to be the river's largest.
                                                                    Parker 27.

Big Otter Creek. Otter names brought from Scotland by colonists who settled in area. Scores of "Otter" place names in Scotland and England.
                                                              Com Va 5-1952

Boonesboro: pop. 100; US Rt 501. Named for Daniel Boone's visit to friend here before their trip to Kentucky.   Parker 27.

Buffalo Creek named for presence of animal in the area. Early records of buffalo in Pittsylvania and Franklin which adjoin Bedford.   LRI

Coleman Falls (RR name Coleman): Ry C&O; elev. 595; Pop. 100. Named for local family.   Steeles 1162

Difficult Creek was probably named from early settlers having difficulty with Indians.   Crouch, second page.

Eagle Eyrie: elev. 1,280; US Rt 501. Nicholas Davies named his hunting lodge Eagle Eyrie. The estate was purchased by the Baptist General Association of Virginia in 1950. Summer assemblies gather for programs.
                                                              Crouch, fifth page.

Elk Creek was named for presence of elk in the area.   LRI

Elks, National Home of the, is located within Bedford (city) and is maintained for elderly and retired members of the organization; it was dedicated May 21, 1903. Its grounds are a show garden.   Com Va 5-1952

Forest: Ry N&W; elev. 873; Pop. 250; US Rt 460. It was established in 1850's; name from "Poplar Forest", nearby home of Thomas Jefferson.
                                                                    Parker 17

Goode: Ry N&W; elev. 720; Pop. 250. Named for family of Hon. John Goode.   Parker 28

Goodview: Ry N&W; Pop. 50. It is believed that the unusual view in-fluenced the name.   LRI

Hardy: Ry N&W; Pop. 100. Robert Hardy owned land in the big bend of the Staunton River where the station and village are located.   Parker 31.

Huddleston: Ry N&W; Pop. 85. The name is from Henry Huddleston Rogers, financier of the railroad.   Parker 32.

Lowry: Ry N&W; elev. 760; Pop. 120. The land for the railroad station was donated by Nelson Lowry.   Parker 28.

Moneta: Ry N&W; elev. 860; Pop. 170. Postoffice was named for the first postmaster in 1882.   ESS county, 28.

Montvale: Ry N&W; elev. 1,012; Pop. 500; US Rt 460. Was Buford's Gap, because Capt. Paschal Buford, War 1812, owned large area; became Bu-fordville because owner gave land for railroad. It is in large basin surrounded on three sides by spurs of Blue Ridge, so name became Montvale in 1890.
                                             Parker 29; Bedford HG 15.

Norwood: Pop. ———. Woods north or in northern part of county; North Woods became Norwood.   LRI

Peaks of Otter in northwestern part of county on spur of Blue Ridge which juts into county; Sharp Top elev. 3,875 and Flat Top elev. 4,001. The name is from a ridge in Scotland having similar appearance; another theory is that the name is from Cherokee "Otteri", meaning mountain or high hill.
                                             Com Va 5-1952

Smith Mountain Reservoir is along the southwestern border. The mountain was named for two brothers living in Pittsylvania County; they owned a large area on the mountain. They hunted and trapped in the area as early as 1750's. One was named Gideon Smith; other brother is reported to have gone farther west into Tennessee and to have been killed. The reservoir and dam are named for the mountain.   LRI

Stewartsville: Ry N&W; Pop. 150. Its earlier name was Crossroads; the name is from Stewart Brothers, principal property owners.   LRI

Thaxton: Ry N&W; Pop. 150. Named for local family.   Steeles 1178

Villamont: Pop. 200; US Rt 460. It was named Peel Brook for an early settler, Dr. Peel. Because of the discovery of iron, it was given the name Iron-ville; the iron boom collapsed. About 1893, the promoters gave the name Villa-mont, which means "Village in the Mountain".   Parker 30; LRI

BLAND COUNTY

Formed in 1861; named for Richard Bland, Revolutionary leader. Area: 369 sq.mi.; Pop. 5,982; Pop. per sq.mi., 16.2. Nearly three-fourths county area forested. 8.9% county area in Jefferson National Forest. Rank occupational groups: manufacturing, agriculture, trade. Rank agricultural income: livestock, dairy.   Roads 93.

Bastian: elev. 2,826; Pop. 700; US Rts 21, 52. Earlier name was Parkersburg from Parker Hornbarger. It was changed to Bastian for F. E. Bastian, railroad manager. Camp Roland on Wolf Creek near Bastian is owned by Boy Scout Council.   Bland 241.

Bland: county seat: elev. 2,470; Pop. 500; US Rts 21, 52. Was called Crab Orchard Creek. Name changed to Selden for James Alexander Selden. In March 1891, name became Bland.   Bland 237.

Bland Correctional Farm, institution of state penal system, near Mechanicsburg in eastern part of county.   EcD county.

Ceres: elev. 2,608; Pop. 75; is oldest settlement in the county. Was named Ceres in 1879 for Goddess of Agriculture, a farming community.   Bland 236

Clear Fork in north central area of county was named because the stream is always clear.   LRI

Laurel Creek in north central area of county was named for the abundance of laurel shrub in this area.   LRI

Lick Creek, near Ceres, in the northwestern area of the county. A deer lick near the head of the stream caused an early settler to give it the name.   LRI

Rocky Gap: Pop. 250; US Rts 21, 52. In north central portion of county. Name from abundant rock and in mountain gap.   Bland 242

BOTETOURT COUNTY

Formed in 1769, named for Lord Botetourt, Governor, 1768-1770. At its formation, the western county boundary was the Mississippi River. Area: 548 sq.mi.; Pop. 16,715; Pop. per sq.mi., 30.5; Pop. increase 1950-60, 6.0%. Nearly three-fourths county area wooded. 20.1% county area in federally-owned area. Ranks as state's leading county in clay production. Rank occupational groups: manufacturing, agriculture, trade. Rank agricultural income: livestock, dairy, poultry.   Roads 83

Amsterdam: elev. 1,339; Pop. 100; US Rt 220. Named by German settlers after Amsterdam, Netherlands.   LRI

Blue Ridge: Ry N&W; elev. 1,240; Pop. 900. Named for Blue Ridge which surrounds village.   LRI

Buchanan: Ry C&O, N&W; elev. 862; Pop. 1,349; increase Pop. 1950-60, 4.9%; US Rt 11; Interstate 81 nearby. Town first known as Pattonsburg, named for Col. James Patton, early explorer. Later named for John Buchanan, son-in-law of Col. Patton, deputy surveyor of Augusta County. Old James River and Kanawha Canal terminated at Buchanan. Water supply from two wells and spring; chlorinated.   Pendleton 167.

Cloverdale: Ry N&W; elev. 1,146; Pop. 500; US Rts 11, 220. John Breckenridge's plantation "Cloverdale" was included in Furnace Plantation; furnace supplying iron developed 1808. Town which grew up was called Cloverdale.
                                                                             Kegley 511

Daleville: Pop. 125; US Rt 11; Interstate 81 nearby. Early settlers named Dale are source of name. Colony Brethren located at New Amsterdam, near Daleville. Daleville College merged with Bridgewater College in 1924.   LRI

Eagle Rock: Ry C&O; elev. 935; Pop. 450; US Rt 220. Earlier name, Eagle Mountain, named for eagle-shaped rock on mountain overlooking town. Later, changed name to Eagle Rock.   LRI

Fincastle: elev. 1,257; Pop. 403; US Rt 220. County seat was Botetourt Courthouse two years. In 1772, legislature established town of Fincastle on 40 acres planned by Israel Christian in 1770. Town named for George, Lord Fincastle.   Long 139; Kegley 405.

Glen Wilton: Ry C&O; elev. 1,000; Pop. 30. Named by out-of-state iron workers where a furnace was established. Water supply from mountain spring and stream; chlorinated.   LRI

W. C. Karnes Spring, 6½ miles north of Buchanan, near Purgatory Creek, ranks third among Virginia springs in its flow per minute, 6,000 gallons. Named for land owner.   LRI

Lithia: Ry N&W; elev. 1,060; Pop. 101.   DU

Looney Mill Creek flows in the southeastern area of county; empties into the northern part of Back Creek. Named for pioneer family by name of Looney who settled at stream's mouth.   LRI

Nace: Ry N&W; Pop. 65. Named about 1892 for George Nace, original owner of land.   Steele 1172

Oriskany: elev. 1127; Pop. 110. Over long period of years, iron ores from Oriskany deposits were mined in northwestern section of county. Iron ore from mines of vicinity smelted in Richmond made armor for iron-clad Merrimac.

EcD county

Springwood: Ry C&O; Pop. 125. Originally Jackson; present name from Spreading Springs close by.   LRI

Troutville: Ry N&W; elev. 1,603; Pop. 524; US Rt 11; Interstate 81 nearby. It was named for Trout family.   LRI

BRUNSWICK COUNTY

Formed in 1720, the county was named for the House of Brunswick, which came to the English throne, when George I was crowned. Area: 579 sq.mi.; Pop. 17,779; Pop. per sq.mi., 30.7. The region was explored in 1650. In 1714, Fort Christanna was the first school for Indians. Christanna is a combination name of Christ and Anna, the queen. The county is the location of Brunswick stew: the name has changed from squirrel stew to Matthews stew (disgruntled cook) to Haskins stew (family preserved recipe) to Brunswick stew (county of origin). Nearly three-fourths land in forests. Rank occupational grouping: agriculture, manufacturing, trade. Rank agricultural income: field crops, livestock, dairy.

Roads 66; VaVCo 11-1952

Adsit: Ry N&W; Pop. 20. Chosen as the community name in 1906 or 1907, it was named for one of the vice presidents of the Virginia Railway.   LRI

Alberta: Rys N&W, SAL; Pop. 430; US Rt 1. Alberta was first Walthall's Store. One explanation of the present name is that it is for the Canadian province. The other explanation is that it is for an official of the Seaboard Railroad. Water supply is from a well; filtered, chlorinated.

Bell-Heartwell 72; Witten 11.

Ante: Pop. 20. In southeastern portion of county.   DU

Brodnax: Ry NF&D; Pop. 561; increase Pop. 1950-60, 12.4%; US Rt 58. Named for prominent family whose home was near community. Incorporated 1915. Largest cotton market in state.   VaVCo 11-1952.

Danieltown: Ry N&W; Pop. 40. Settlement of Daniels; settlement explains postoffice Danieltown.   LRI

Dolphin: Ry N&W; Pop. 35. Land-owner gave right-of-way to Virginia Railway in early 1900's if he might choose the name of the small town. He chose Dolphin.   LRI

Ebenezer Academy, first Methodist School in Virginia, opened 1767; building burned 1795; passed out of Methodist hands about 1800. At dedication, Bishop Asbury reported to have said: "Here I raise my Ebenezer." It is considered the forerunner of Randolph-Macon College.

Sweet 306; Bell-Heartwell 33.

Ebony: Pop. 100. In southwestern corner of county.   DU

Freeman: Pop. 100. In east mid-central portion of county.   DU

Gasburg: Pop. 100. In south central portion of county.   DU

Great Creek flows southeast in central portion of county, through Lawrenceville, is tributary of Meherrin River. Will, dated Jan. 19, 1721, mentions Great Creek.   4 V 285.

Lawrenceville: Ry NF&D; Pop. 1,941; US Rt 58. Courthouse in 1732 near Cochran; in 1746, moved near Thomasburg; in 1783, moved to Lawrenceville. James Rice gave land for townsite in 1814 so was granted privilege of naming the settlement; one report is named for Lawrence, a favorite horse. Another explanation is was named for Captain James Lawrence whose well-known words were, "Don't give up the ship." Water supply from Great Creek; auxiliary from Meherrin River; filtered, chlorinated.   WP: Va 474; VaVCO 11-1952.

Meredithville: Pop. 60. Name Meredith given to postoffice in stage coach days when David Meredith petitioned Post Office Department to have postoffice established because stage changed for fresh horses nearby. Location has been changed several times.   LRI

Rawlings: Ry SAL; Pop. 50. A Mr. Rawlings arranged for railroad siding to load saw mill products for shipment; called Rawlings Siding. When postoffice established, it was given name Rawlings.   LRI

St. Paul College, third oldest Negro vocational and industrial school in United States, founded by Rev. James Solomon Russell, born a slave, educated at Hampton Institute. At Lawrenceville, sponsored by Protestant Episcopal Church, founded 1888. It now confers B.A. and B.S. degrees; emphasizes teacher and business education.   Ann.Bul.

Seward Demonstration Forest began when Dr. Walter Merritt Seward gave 3,600 acres to the University of Virginia. It provides an area for studying the science of foresty and the art of cutting, sawing, manufacturing and marketing forest products.   Bell-Heartwell 67.

Sturgeon Creek, so called from the dexterity an Occa-wee-chy Indian showed in catching one of these royal fish. Stream flows east in northern third of county and is tributary of Nottoway River.   36 V 205

Triplett: Pop. 250. Triplets were born about the time the postoffice was named. The tradition is that the postoffice name was proposed from the community event.   LRI

Valentines: Pop. 40; in southeast portion of county. Named for the first postmaster.   LRI

Waqua Creek flows near Danieltown and Warfield. A deed gives land location on Waqua Creek, Feb. 1, 1748.   29 V 508

Warfield: Ry SAL; elev. 318; Pop. 80. It was named for Warfield, the first president of Seaboard Air Line Railroad.   LRI

White Plains: Pop. 50. Earlier names, Richardsons; then Harrisons Store; these names were for postmasters. Became White Plains in 1825; some jokingly say named when snow on ground because soil of that area is extremely red. LRI

BUCHANAN COUNTY

Formed in 1858; named after James Buchanan, President 1857-1861. Exploration of county dates from 1750. Area: 508 sq.mi.; Pop. 36,724; Pop. per sq.mi., 72.3; increase Pop. 1950-60, 2.7%. About 85.3% area forested. Among state's coal-mining counties, Buchanan mines greatest amount. Ranks as state's leading county in value and receipts from minerals. Rank occupational groups: trade, educational services, manufacturing. Rank agricultural income: field crops, livestock, fruit.   Roads 76

Big Rock was named for a large local rock. Ry N&W; elev. 895; Pop. 300. In northwest portion of county.   Steeles 1159

Conaway (RR Conoway): Ry N&W; Pop. 200. In mid-western portion of county. Received name from Conaway Creek.   LRI

Council: Pop. 35. In southwestern portion of county.   DU

Davenport: Pop. 40; elev. 1,541. In extreme south portion of county. Named for William Davenport, first postmaster, about 1885.   Steeles 1163

Grundy: Ry N&W; elev. 1,050; Pop. 2,287; increase Pop. 1950-60, 17.4%; US Rt 460. First postoffice, Jan. 1857, Mouth of Slate. Name changed to Grundy, Aug. 1858; was made county seat in 1858. Named for U. S. senator from Texas at time Buchanan County was formed. Municipal water supply from drilled wells; chlorinated.   LRI

Harman: Ry N&W; Pop. 700. In northwestern portion of county. Name from H. E. Harman family and coal company located on Hull Creek about 1935.
                                                                      LRI

Hurley: Ry N&W; Pop. 400. In north central portion of county. Probably named for family of S. B. Hurley, founder Mountain Mission Home for under-privileged and orphan children.   LRI

Jewell Valley: Ry N&W; Pop. 300. In southeast corner. Many persons having Jewell as family name lived there.   LRI

Keen Mountain: Ry N&W; elev. 1,408; Pop. 150. Many families in community have Keen as family name. In mid-southern portion of county.   LRI

Leemaster: Pop. 100. Name of log cutter for lumber firm about 1908; community given his name. In mid-western portion of county.   LRI

Levisa Creek. Early land grants refer to stream as "Levisa or Louisa Fork" of the Sandy River. It flows from the central to the northwest boundary of the county.   LRI

Mavisdale: Pop. 400. In south central portion of county.   DU

Maxie: Pop. 370. When postoffice was established, a long list of names was sent as proposals; the P. O. Dept. chose Maxie. In northwest portion of county.   LRI

Murphy: Pop. 35. Named for Richard Murphy, first postmaster; he was also Justice of the Peace in community for some time. On western boundary of county.   LRI

Oakwood: Ry N&W; Pop. 250. In southwest portion of county.   DU

Patterson: Ry N&W; elev. 1,130; Pop. 400. In east central portion of county. Patterson brothers established coal company and postoffice named for them.   LRI

Pilgrim Knob: Pop. 100. In mid-eastern part of county. Name explanation is that community store kept Pilgrim Knob coffee; the name is from the coffee marketed.   LRI

Prater: Pop. 75. In northwest portion of county.   DU

Roseann: Pop. 250. W. S. Leckie, founder of Panther Coal Company, at Roseann, named the postoffice for his daughter. In north central portion of county.   LRI

Rowe: Pop. 125. Named for a local family. In south portion of county.   LRI

Royal City (part of Grundy, but has separate postoffice). There was a contest for suggestions for naming the postoffice. Walter Jackson, storekeeper, sold Royal brand shirts; he suggested Royal City.   LRI

Slate: Pop. 60. It received its name from nearby Slate Creek. In northeast portion of county.   LRI

Stacy: Pop. 100. Several county officers have had that family name. In mid-eastern portion of county.   LRI

Vansant: Ry N&W; elev. 1,114; Pop. 850. In mid-western portion of county. Lumber company dealing in yellow poplar had name Vansant Kitchen Company. It was named for a partner of the company.   LRI

Venia: Pop. 30. Venia Buchanan has been the only postmaster. In southern portion of county.   LRI

Whitewood: Ry N&W; elev. 1,675; Pop. 40. In southeast portion of county.   DU

Wolford: Pop. 250. John Wolford was an early settler there. In northeast portion of county.   LRI

BUCKINGHAM COUNTY

Formed in 1761; named for Duke of Buckingham or Buckinghamshire in England. Area: 576 sq.mi.; Pop. 10,877; Pop. per sq.mi., 18.9. Area settled shortly after 1700. Buckingham Church, built in early 1700's, still in use. First chartered women's college in Virginia, Buckingham Female Collegiate Institute, operated New Canton, 1837-1863. More than three-fourths county area forested. Rank occupational groups: manufacturing, agriculture, trade. Rank agricultural income: livestock, field crops. VaVCo 9-1949

Alcoma: Pop. 25. In central portion of county. DU

Andersonville: Pop. 65. In southern portion of county. Was Gary's Store. When first free delivery from this postoffice, R. M. Anderson was the postmaster. About 1902, the office became Andersonville. LRI

Arvonia: Ry C&O; Pop. 700. In northeastern portion of county. Quarrying slate began commercially 1780. VaVCo 9-1949

Buckingham: elev. 500; Pop. 218; US Rt 60. Earlier name Mayville; also called Buckingham Courthouse. VaVCo 9-1949

Dillwyn: Ry C&O; elev. 649; Pop. 515; US Rt 15. In mid-eastern portion of county. Gold mining 1830-1860. Sayres Spring supplies municipal water; treated for carbon dioxide removal; chlorinated. EcD county

Geographical Center of Virginia is close to Mt. Rush, which is at the junction of US Rt 60 and State Route 24. Latitude 37" 30.6' N., Longitude 78" 37.5' W. Bodie 138.

Lee Experimental Forest is planned for a Piedmont experimental area. Named for General Robert E. Lee. A detailed soil survey was made so the soil type of each unit is known. Trees are suited to each working unit; there will be systematic cutting, and records will be kept for each unit. An area of about one-seventh of the total area was not included in the systematic forestry plan in order to compare the growth and returns from that one-seventh with the records from the planned units. Com Va 12-1946

New Canton: Ry C&O; elev. 290; US Rt 16. On James River near northeast corner of county. Postoffice established January 1, 1802, on lands of William Cannon — name "New Cannon"; became New Canton. 10 V 100

Slate River flows northeast across county; tributary of James. Will dated May 25, 1747, bequeaths lands on Slate River. 22 V 318

Sprouse's Corner: Pop. 40; US Rts 15, 60. DU

Walton Fork: Land granted to Thomas Patterson, dated August 20, 1747, from George II, signed by Sir Wm. Gooch, about 700 acres on the branches of Walton's Fork of Slate River. LRI

Willis Mountain, elev. 1,159 ft., in southeast corner of county. Willis was colonial name in county. Kyanite mined and processed here. Will dated Sept. 4, 1749, bequeathed plantation near Willis's Mountain. 22 V 216

CAMPBELL COUNTY

Formed in 1781; named for General William Campbell, hero of King's Mountain, 1780. Area: 524 sq.mi.; Pop. 32,958; Pop. per sq.mi., 62.9; increase Pop. 1950-60, 14.1%. About 65% county area wooded. Rank occupational groups: manufacturing, trade, agriculture. Rank agricultural income: field crops, livestock, dairy.   Roads 69

Altavista: Ry N&W, SOU; Pop. 3,299; US Rt 29. Named for a farm owned by Henry Lane. Staunton River furnishes water power favoring development; largest cedar chest industry in United States. Water supply from two wells; chlorinated.   LRI

Brookneal: Ry N&W; elev. 599; Pop. 1,070; increase Pop. 1950-60, 21.1%; US Rt 501. Earliest settlements near town 1736. Town name from intermarriage of Brooks and Neal families. Water supply from Falling River; wells auxiliary; filtered, chlorinated.   Early 91-94.

Central Virginia Community College, in Lynchburg, formerly part of University of Virginia system, became separate institution 1967.   Ann.Bul.

Concord: Ry N&W; elev. 835; Pop. 400; US Rt 460. Old Concord Furnace near Concord supplied military materials from nearby iron deposits during Revolutionary War. Community name from three Presbyterian churches of that section: Old Concord, New Concord, and Little Concord.   Early 104

Evington: Ry SOU; Pop. 200. Station on Southern Railroad built on land owned by Miss Evie Smith; station name from hers.   Early 107.

Falling River rises in northeast portion, flows through eastern portion; tributary Staunton(Roanoke) River. Febr. 7, 1732, court appointed commissioner for receiving taxes at Ross Hook's store in Falling River.   8 W (2) 120.

Fort Hill (sub-station postoffice); at edge of city limits, Confederate army threw up breastworks to defend city of Lynchburg; the area later became known as Fort Hill, one of the city's seven hills.   LRI

Gladys: Ry N&W; elev. 770; Pop. 180; US Rt 501. Earliest name, Connelly's Tavern; later Pigeon Run because huge flocks wild pigeons came annually to feed on nuts and acorns in forests. Railroad station in 1890 called Woodlawn; later name changed to Gladys, after name of railroad stockholder's daughter. In southeastern portion.   Early 120+

Hat Creek Presbyterian Church, established 1742, county's oldest church; fifth building on same site. Near Brookneal. John Ervine was leader of earliest settlers. Hat Creek in southeast portion.   EcD county

Leesville: Ry N&W; Pop. 50. In southwestern corner of county.   DU

Long Island: Ry N&W; Pop. 75. In southeast, near county boundary. Named for island in Roanoke (Staunton) River.   LRI

Lynchburg (independent city); Ry C&O, N&W, SOU; elev. 631; Pop. 57,000; increase Pop. 1950-60, 14.8%; US Rts 29, 360, 501. John Lynch built ferry here in 1756; settlement grew, built tobacco warehouse, and in 1786 applied for charter for town Lynch's Warehouse, later Lynchburg. Incorporated 1805; became independent city 1852. Water supply from reservoir on Pedlar River; auxiliary station on James; filtered, chlorinated, fluorinated. Rank occupational groups: manufacturing, trade, services.   VGb 48; EcD (Campbell County)

Lynchburg College began in 1903 as Virginia Christian College; name changed to Lynchburg College in 1919. Liberal arts; co-educational institution affiliated with Disciples of Christ.   Ann.Bul.

Lynch Station (RR Clarion): elev. 735; Ry SOU; Pop. 400. Near southwest corner of county. Named for a Lynch family.   LRI

Miller Park (sub-station postoffice). Across street from city park named "Miller Park". Name from that park.   LRI

Naruna: Ry N&W; elev. 645; Pop. 250; US Rt 501. In southeast corner of county. Name said to have Indian origin.   Early 122

Randolph-Macon Women's College, founded 1891, liberal arts with high standards of scholarship; in 1916 was first independent college for women to receive charter to Phi Beta Kappa. Has scenic campus of 100 acres. Methodist-related institution.   Ann.Bul.

Rivermont (sub-station postoffice): Ry SOU. Name originated before founding of city; section on high bluff overlooking James. From River Mountain, shortened to River Mont, to one word, Rivermont.   LRI

Rustburg: Ry N&W; elev. 897; Pop. 350; US Rt 501. County seat. Rustburg was made the county seat when Jeremiah Rust donated land for a courthouse.   EcD county

Timberlake: Pop. 750. Large lake at intersection of three streams which form Buffalo Creek; village named "Timber Lake". In northwestern portion of county. Water supply, springs and wells.   Early 43

Virginia Theological Seminary and College organized 1886; Negro college of "self-help" and "spiritual independence". In Lynchburg.   Ann.Bul.

CAROLINE COUNTY

Formed 1727; named for Queen Caroline, wife of King George II. Area: 544 sq.mi.; Ry RF&P; Pop. 12,725; Pop. per sq.mi., 23.4; increase Pop. 1950-60, 2.0%. 23 percent county area in A. P. Hill Military Reservation. 78.6 percent county forested. County is Virginia's leading producer sun-cured tobacco. Rank occupational groups: manufacturing, trade, agriculture. Rank agricultural income: field crops, livestock, dairy.

Alps: Pop. 15. In eastern portion of county. About 1912, P. O. Dept. chose name from ones proposed. Hilly section so name appropriate. Reported as only postoffice having that name in the United States.   LRI

Balty: Pop. 20. In western portion of county.   DU

Bowling Green: County seat. Pop. 528; US Rt 301. Name from Hoomes family estate in England; oldest house in vicinity was built by Major Thomas Hoomes after receiving land grant in 1670; when county seat was located, he donated land for the public buildings.   EcD county

Chilesburg: Pop. 85. In northwest corner of county. Named for Chiles family.   Wingfield 36.

Corbin: Pop. 25. In north central portion. Named for colonial family.   Wingfield 36

Gether: Pop. 20. In southeast portion near North Anna River.   DU

Guinea (or Guiney's): Ry RF&P; Pop. 75; without postoffice. In north central portion. Town named for local Guinea family. House is near Guinea where General Stonewall Jackson died after being wounded on Chancellorsville battlefield.   Wingfield 37.

A. P. Hill Military Reservation includes 70,000 acre wild life management area of Camp Hill. Reservation area, 76,981 acres. The post is named in honor of Lieut. Gen. Ambrose Powell Hill, C.S.A., who was killed while defending Petersburg.   Bodie 59.

Ladysmith: Pop. 50; US Rt 1. In northeast portion of county.   DU

Lorne: Pop. 100; in south portion of county.   DU

Milford: Ry RF&P; elev. 100; Pop. 250. In central area of county. Until November 2, 1792, it was head of navigation on the Mattaponi; at present, railway station for Bowling Green. Tradition that ford crossed Mattaponi at location of present village; mill may have been there; this may have influenced the present name. It may have been named for Milford, England.   Wingfield 287.

Mount Creek flows northeast in the northwestern portion of the county; tributary of Rappahannock. Stream name used in land grant in 1705.

Wingfield 300.

Polecat Creek flows east in the southwest portion of the county; tributary of Mattaponi River. Probably named from many polecats or skunks in the area. Name used in land grants in 1691.   24 V 369, 371; 38 V 76.

Port Royal: Pop. 128; US Rt 301, 17. In mid-eastern area of county. Town was established 1744; was one of principal shipping points on Rappahannock. Thomas Roy founded Port Royal; called Port Roy for several years. Possesses oldest charter of any Masonic lodge in the United States, given by Grand Lodge of Scotland, in Edinburgh, dated Dec. 1, 1755.   Wingfield 283; Gwathmey 181.

Rappahannock Academy: Pop. 5; US Rt 17. In northeast portion of county. Postoffice named for academy; legislative petition, Dec. 5, 1808, to establish academy.   Wingfield 37.

Ruther Glen (Caramel Church): Ry RF&P; Pop. 200. In mid-western portion of county. Was Chesterfield Station; name changed to Ruther Glen to avoid confusion. Scottish Ruther Glen was associated with Wallace and Bruce. Near this village, Ruther Glen is old home of the Moncures, "Ellerslie", named for home of Wallace in Scotland. Superintendent of railroad chose Ruther Glen as name of the station.   Wingfield 291+.

Shumansville: Pop. 30. In south central portion of county. Named for Shuman family.   Wingfield 37

Sparta: Pop. 30. In south central portion of county. Postoffice was established within last 100 years. Name Sparta for the community dates to Revolutionary period; local documents used the name. Probably, early settlers knew Greeks had trouble with warlike tribes, Spartans, so gave their community its name. The name Sparta was accepted for the postoffice.   LRI

Woodford: Ry RF&P; Pop. 25. In north central portion. During many years, railroad station was Woodslane. Woodford named for General William Woodford who was born in community.   Wingfield 291.

CARROLL COUNTY

Formed in 1842; named for Charles Carroll of Carrollton, Signer of Declaration of Independence. Area: 494 sq.mi.; Pop. 23,178; Pop. per sq.mi., 46.9. County borders on North Carolina and is largely on the west slope of the Blue Ridge. Land in federally-owned areas, 1.9%. About 40 percent in forests. Leading occupational groups: manufacturing, agriculture, trade. Rank agricultural products: dairy, livestock, field crops.   Roads 96.

Beamers Knob: elev. 3,400 ft., is in the southwestern portion. Beamer family, early settlers, lived near and owned part of hill. Descendants are residents of the area.   Alderman

Big Reed Island River and Little Reed Island Creek, according to tradition, were named for an early explorer and hunter named Reed, who often visited this area in the 1740-50 years.   Alderman

Cana: Pop. 65. In the southwestern corner of the county. Given Bible name by early settlers in selecting postoffice name.   Alderman

Dugspur: Pop. 40; elev. 2,700. In northeastern portion of county. Early roads of county largely north and south. An east-west road from the north-south roads crossed hills, streams, and hollows and was built by hand labor. It was a spur dug leading from the main road, so the community name, Dugspur.

Alderman

Fancy Gap: Pop. 50; elev. 3,100; US Rt 52. Col. Ira Coltrane in his boyhood drove a team with others crossing the mountains. He saw a possible route with more advantage than the "Good Spur Road" then in use. He named the impressive and beautiful gap in the Blue Ridge, "The Fancy Gap". It is on the Blue Ridge Parkway. The village and postoffice took the name Fancy Gap from Coltrane's description. An impressive piece of engineering work is shown in the construction of US Rt 52 through the community.   Alderman

Galax takes its name from the decorative mountain evergreen. Town originally called Bonaparte. Independent city. Area: 3 sq. mi.; elev. 2,382; Pop. 5,254; Ry N&W; US Rt 58. City owns 900 acres at headwaters of Chestnut Creek on Blue Ridge as source of municipal water supply. (Part of Galax in Grayson County).   Alderman

Hillsville was named for the Hills family, early Quaker settlers. Pop. 905; elev. 2,570; US Rts 52 and 58. The town is the county seat.   Alderman

Lambsburg, in the south central area of the county, near North Carolina line, was named for Wilmot Lamb, first settler. Pop. 250; elev. 1,400.

Alderman

Laurel Fork: Pop. 25; US Rt 58. In southeastern corner of county; it was named for the creek along which many laurels are still growing.   Alderman

Sylvatus: Pop. 100; elev. 2,213. In middle northeastern part of county. Sylvatus Smith was prominent resident when mines were opened there, and post-office was named for him.   Alderman.

Woodlawn: Pop. 30; elev. 2,520; US Rts 28, 221. In west part of county, was named for Colonel James Wood who received grant of 2,800 acres by King George II.   Alderman

CHARLES CITY COUNTY

Formed 1634, one of the original eight shires; named for the King's son, later Charles I. Settlement began 1613. Old courthouse built of hand-made bricks with oyster-shell mortar. Area 184 sq.mi.; Pop. 5,492; Pop. per sq.mi., 29.8; increase in Pop. 1950-60, 17.5%. Seventy-five percent area forested. Rank occupational groups: manufacturing, agriculture, trade. Rank agricultural income: field crops, livestock, poultry.   EcD county

Barnetts: Pop. 75. Named for family of Barnetts who lived in area many years ago.   LRI

Berkley Plantation dates to 1619; five cousins settled; location first official English thanksgiving within nation. It became known as Harrison's Landing, present mansion built in 1726, birthplace of Benjamin Harrison, signer of Declaration of Independence, and President William Henry Harrison. During July and August, 1862, it was headquarters of General McClelland. The bugle call "Taps" was composed here by General Butterfield. 7.2 miles west of Charles City.
                                                                CVHM 9.

Charles City Courthouse: Pop. 20. Courthouse of original county built about 1730.

Harrison's Lake, U.S. Fish and Wildlife Service has Fish Hatchery in southwestern portion of county; 254.31 acres. Named for President Harrison.   LRI

Ruthville: Pop. 150. Named for Mrs. Ruth Brown-Huckles. Village is seat of Negro community life. Elam Baptist Church, known as Old Elam, considered third regularly organized Negro Church in Virginia.   LRI

Walkers Dam, on Chicakahominy River, north central boundary, Newport News water supply. Named for H. B. Walker family.   LRI

CHARLOTTE COUNTY

Formed 1764, named for Queen Charlotte, wife of King George III. Area: 467 sq.mi.; Pop. 13,368; Pop. per sq.mi., 28.6. The county is Virginia's leading producer of fire-cured tobacco. Rank occupational groups: agriculture, manufacturing, trade. Rank agricultural income: field crops, dairy, livestock.

Roads 70

Aspen: Ry N&W; Pop. 40. In mid-central portion of county. **DU**

Barnesville: Pop. 50; US Rts 15, 360. About 1920, R. P. Barnes built store and called place Barnes Junction; added business; secured postoffice. Greyhound Bus changed name to Barnesville. In southern portion of county. **LRI**

Charlotte Court House (Charlotte Courthouse): Pop. 555; increase Pop. 1950-60, 39.7%. In 1756, "The Magazine", storage depot. In 1759, Daltonsburgh, believed in honor of Catherine Dalton, wife of Lieutenant Governor, Francis Fauquier. In 1836, Maryville, in honor of Colonel Clement Read. In 1874, Smithville in honor of Smith family, residents of the town. In 1901, Charlotte Court House, authorized three words. Water supply from spring and two wells; chlorinated. **VaVCO 7-1952**

Cub Creek flows south from central western portion, tributary of Staunton (Roanoke) River. Land grant on Cub Creek, Jan. 14, 1739. **14 V 343**

Cub Creek Church. Settlement on Cub Creek before 1734; once called Caldwell Settlement. Earliest Presbyterian Church in South Virginia; church built 1735. **18 V 40**

Cullen: Ry N&W; Pop. 150. In northeastern portion of county. **DU**

Drakes Branch: Stream Drakes Branch flows through town. Uncertain which was named first. Nickname: Duck's Puddle. Ry SOU; Pop. 759; increase Pop. 1950-60, 85.1%. **Prid-Pr 19**

Patrick Henry Boys Plantation is the official title of the 1,000-acre farm which had been Patrick Henry's home bought in 1794; he lived there 1796-1799. Patrick Henry Memorial Foundation purchased Red Hill in 1944; it is in northwest portion of the county. Boys 10 to 18 years old will be housed in units of six to ten boys and provided guidance for overcoming mistakes. They will be employed on the farm and will be paid wages. **VaVCO 7-1952; Com Va 9-1950**

Horsepen Creek is in southern portion of county; tributary of Roanoke Creek. Will dated April 30, 1770, mentions Horsepen Creek. **2 V 321**

Keysville: named for John Keys, early landowner and tavern keeper in the vicinity. Ry SOU; elev. 625; Pop. 753; increase Pop. 1950-60, 6.2%; US Rts 15, 360. In northeastern portion of county. **Prid-Pr 20**

Madisonville: named for Henry Madison, legislator from the county. Pop. 40. In northern portion of county. Prid-Pr 22

Ontario: Ry SOU; Pop. 100. Canadian in area at time postoffice established in 1888 suggested Ontario as its name. Tourists from Canada frequently post mail to have it sent from Ontario. Near east boundary in northeast portion. LRI

Phenix: Ry N&W; Pop. 259. In northcentral portion of county. Name advised for selection when railroad was being built in 1906; from legend, name has meaning "rise from its own ashes". Since beginning, town has had several fires. Office of Home Development Co.; LRI

Randolph: Ry SOU; Pop. 60. Near mid-southwestern boundary. Named for Richard Randolph, pioneer estate owner. Prid-Pr 21

Red House: Pop. 50. In northeastern corner of county. DU

Red Oak: Pop. 50; US Rts 15, 360. In southern portion of county. Named for twelve large red oak trees; all twelve have died, but until the last one, it was the largest and oldest on US Rt 15 from New York to Florida. LRI

Roanoke Creek with tributaries drains nearly all of eastern half of Charlotte County; tributary of Staunton (Roanoke) River.

Saxe: Ry SOU; Pop. 125. In central southwest portion. Was Carrington's Mill for Judge Carrington, the younger; name changed to Saxe by Vermonter in honor poet of his state. Prid-Pr 21

Southside Virginia Research Station, 22 acres, investigations relating to production of field crops and dark tobacco. Com Va 9-1953

Turnip Creek drains western side of county, tributary of Staunton (Roanoke) River. Land grant, August 5, 1737, mentions Turnip Creek. 14 V 7

Wards Creek flows south through central part of county, tributary of Roanoke Creek. Land patent issued October 6, 1637, on Captain Ward's Creek. Grant, July 13, 1635, gives location on Ward's Creek. 3 V 186

Wyliesburg: Pop. 150; US Rts 15, 360. In southeastern portion of county. Wylie family lived in community years ago; village derived name from them. LRI

CHESTERFIELD COUNTY

Formed in 1748; named for Philip Stanhope, Fourth Earl of Chesterfield whose name is a synonym of courtly grace and polished dignity. Area: 460 sq.mi.; Pop. 71,197; Pop. per sq.mi., 154.8; increase Pop. 1950-60, 19.6%. County was settled in 1611 and 1613. Near Falling Creek, first iron furnace in English America in 1619. First county in state to sell revenue bonds for expansion of centralized water system; Gregory's Pond on Falling Creek, source of water supply for large area heavily populated; filtered, chlorinated. Nearly three-fourths county area wooded. Rank occupational groups: manufacturing, trade, construction. Rank agricultural income: poultry, field crops, livestock.

Roads 68; EcD county; VaVCo 6-1952

Bermuda Hundred: named in remembrance of those wrecked in Bermuda. Town established on James at mouth of Appomattox in 1611.　　Stewart 58.

Bon Air: Ry SOU; Elev. 205; Pop. 3,000. In north central portion. Name is French for "good air". In 1880's, popular family resort. Department of Welfare has training school for delinquent girls in community.

Steeles 1160; EcD county

Broad Rock: near east boundary in northwest portion. Pop. 1,000. In early 19th century, there was a Broad Rock Race Track which attracted famous race horses. Its surrounding area is still known as Broad Rock.　　LRI

Buford (sub-station postoffice): Pop. ———.　　DU

Chester: Ry SAL; elev. 145; Pop. 2,000; increase Pop. 1950-60, 71.2%. In east central portion of county.

Chesterfield: Pop. 135; Court House located 1750.

Colonial Heights (independent city): Area: 7 sq.mi.; Pop. 9,587; increase Pop. 1950-60, 57.8%; US Rt 1. Incorporated 1926; independent city 1948. In southeast corner county.　　EcD county

Ettrick: Pop. 3,200. In southeast corner of county. Legend that Scotch merchants were early settlers and named for town in Scotland. First name, Ettrick Banks; then Ettricks; now Ettrick. Virginia Negro Baptist Children's Home chartered 1947.　　LRI

Falling Creek flows across northern Chesterfield and is tributary of the James. On the creek, the first iron furnace built in America in 1619; destroyed by Indians in the massacre of 1622. A physician's record, March 7, 1623, mentions Falling Creek.　　Roads 40; 19 V 144.

Farrar Island: land deed to Wm. Farrar, June 11, 1637. It was a peninsula until Dutch Gap Canal was cut. During long time, was property of Farrar family.
7 V 69+; 8 V 67.

Matoaca: Pop. 1,200. Near southeast corner of county. Named after Matoax, Indian name for Pocohontas.   VaVCo 6-1952

Midlothian: Ry SOU; elev. 270; Pop. 400; US Rt 60. Coal mined from 1730 to 1865. In northwest portion of county. Named for county in Scotland.
Gannett 207

Pocohontas State Forest, 5,000 acres in central area of county.
EcD county

Pocohontas State Park in central area of county, 2,004 acres. Day-use park, hiking trails, playing fields, picnic facilities, 156-acre lake, youth group camps.
EcD county

Pocoshock: Pop. ————. Named for an Indian name of a creek which meanders across Chesterfield County three to five miles south of Richmond.   LRI

Stratford Hills: Pop. 5,000. Real estate development.   LRI

Swift Creek flows east in eastern two-thirds of southern part of county. Land transfers located on Swift Creek, Oct. 19, 1677.   32 V 389

John Tyler Community College in Chester opened in 1967.   LRI

Veterans Administration Hospital: McGuire Hospital was transferred to the Veterans Administration on March 31, 1946. (See McGuire Hospital, Richmond city).   Lutz: Ch 347

Virginia State College: combination land grant college, college of liberal arts, and college of education. Established 1882; opened 1883, as Virginia Normal and Collegiate Institute. In 1902, became Virginia State College for Negroes; in 1946, Virginia State College. Has 400-acre farm for training agricultural students. Grants bachelors and masters degrees.   Ann.Bul.; Com Va 2-1957

Winterpock: Pop. 130. In southwest portion of county. In 1703, group patented 4,000 acres in vicinity of present village of Winterpock.
Lutz: Ch 66+.

CLARKE COUNTY

Formed 1836; named for George Rogers Clarke, conqueror of the Northwest. Earliest settlement in county about 1740. Area: 174 sq.mi.; Pop. 7,942; Pop. per sq.mi., 45.6; increase Pop. 1950-60, 12.3%. One-third county area forested. Rank occupational groups: agriculture, manufacturing, trade. Rank agricultural income: livestock, dairy, field crops.　　　　　　　　Roads 82

Berryville: Paths on road to Winchester crossed north-south route; became gathering place for young men meeting to drink, play, quarrel, and engage in fisticuffs; was known as "Battletown". Benjamin Berry divided portion of land into lots; Berryville established by General Assembly Jan. 10, 1803. Became county seat. Ry N&W; elev. 602; Pop. 1,645; increase Pop. 1950-60, 17.4%; US Rt 340. Municipal water supply: two wells, a mountain shed supply, and an auxiliary spring; softened, filtered, chlorinated. Near center of west portion.

Gordon 47+; EcD county

Blandy Experimental Farm of the University of Virginia. At Boyce, field laboratory, 722 acres. George F. Blandy, New York broker, willed acres plus a sum of money to be endowment fund; will probated March 30, 1926. The White Arboretum is developed with the farm.　　　　　　　　LRI

Boyce: Ry N&W; elev. 583; Pop. 384; increase Pop. 1950-60, 3.2%; US Rt 340. Near center of west portion of county. Named for Col. U. L. Boyce, owner of nearby estate. Earliest records of town in 1770; incorporated 1910.

EcD county; Norris 482.

Millwood takes its name from upper mill in village. Village had mill prior to 1769; Colonel Nathaniel Burwell built several mills in neighborhood. Near center of west portion of county. Pop. 400; elev. 496; US Rt 50. Blue Ridge Hunt Club at Millwood boasts as oldest hunt club west of Blue Ridge.

ESS (county) 23; VaVCo 12-1949

Old Chapel near center of county between Millwood and Berryville, built in 1783, said to be oldest Episcopal Church west of Blue Ridge. Stone edifice took place of Cunningham's Chapel, log structure, erected before 1751. Elev. 559.

Wayland SV 17, 25; Norris 463.

Wadesville: Ry B&O. In northern portion. Named for Wade family.

ESS (county) 30.

White Post: Ry N&W; elev. 624; Pop. 200; US Rt 340. In extreme west portion. Takes its name from post set and probably white-washed as marker to direct to Greenway Court, seat of Lord Fairfax.　　　Wayland SV 26; Roads 44.

CRAIG COUNTY

Formed 1851; named for Robert Craig, Member of Congress. Area: 336 sq.mi.; Pop. 3,356; Pop. per sq.mi., 10.0. Region first explored 1751; permanent settlers 1774. Four-fifths county area forested. 52.1% of area in Jefferson National Forest. Rank occupational groups: manufacturing, agriculture, trade. Rank agricultural income: livestock, poultry.   Roads 92; EcD county.

Arnold Knob, 3,929 ft. elev.; along Craig-West Virginia line. A man named Arnold owned a farm on north side of mountain, so high peak was named Arnold Knob.   LRI

Craig Springs: named for Congressman. Pop. 50 (summer Pop. 250). Near north central boundary of county.   EcD county

Craig Creek crosses southern area of county. In March 1754, a road ordered on Craig's Creek.   30 V 197

Johns Creek, from western border crosses northern and central sections of county; tributary of Craig Creek. March 1756, mouth of John's Creek, a branch of Craig's Creek, at which place a fort was to be erected.   15 V 248, 250.

C. E. Leffel Spring, Cassie E. Leffel owner, 2.2 miles southwest of Newcastle. Has flow of 5,000 gallons per minute.   LRI

New Castle (census name Newcastle): County seat. Pop. 200; elev. 1,493. Established as fort by Governor Dinwiddie in 1756 was at first New Fincastle. Confusion with Fincastle, so became New Castle.   WP: Va 433

Paint Bank: elev. 1,868; Pop. 100. In northwestern part of county. Paint ore in bank of nearby creek; mined to small extent during World War.   LRI

CULPEPER COUNTY

Formed 1748; named for Lord Culpeper, governor of Virginia, 1680-1683. Settlement began in 1714. Area: 383 sq.mi.; Pop. 15,088; Pop. per sq.mi., 38.8; increase Pop. 1950-60, 13.9%. Local farmers first in state to install artificial hay driers. 46.4% county area forested. Rank occupational groups: agriculture, trade, manufacturing. Rank agricultural income: dairy, livestock, poultry.

Long 136

Boston: Pop. 40; US Rt 522. In west corner of county.　　　　　　　DU

Brandy Station: Ry SOU; Elev. 355; Pop. 300; US Rts 15, 29. In east central portion of county. Early cross-roads, called Crossroads. Tavern sold hard liquor; including brandy having potent quality for which travelers recommended. During War 1812, soldiers expected to patronize; too often insufficient supply. Disgruntled used large letters and wrote BRANDY on inn wall. Became known as Brandy House. Railroad built in 1854 and station named Brandy Station. Nearby many cavalry engagements in 1861-65.　　　　LRI; Waite.

Culpeper: Area 7.5 sq.mi.; Ry SOU; elev. 510; Pop. 5,900; US Rts 15, 29, 522. County seat in colonial days named Fairfax; confusion between Fairfax in Culpeper County and Fairfax Court House in Fairfax County; in 1870, General Assembly changed name to Culpeper. Location Virginia Baptist Home for Aged. Water supply from reservoir on Mountain Run; coagulated, settled, filtered, chlorinated.　　　　VaVCO 7-1949

Elkwood: Ry SOU; Pop. 60. In mid-center of east portion of county. Elkwood was name of Cunningham estate. Postoffice established on or adjacent to this estate. Four miles southeast, battle at Kelly's Ford, March 17, 1863.

LRI; Waite

Hazel River flows through northern portion of county, tributary of Rappahannock. Earlier name Gourdvine River, source on Hazel Mountain. Oct. 28, 1730, grant of land between Hazel River and North River.　　36 V 350; LRI

Jeffersonton: Pop. 300. In northeast portion of county. Town named for Thomas Jefferson; postoffice established in 1779. Suffix *ton* added to distinguish from Powhatan County postoffice.　　　　LRI

Lignum: Pop. 120. Established in wooded area; postoffice given name which in *Latin* is for *woods*, as proposed by the Rev. Frank P. Robertson, father of A. Willis Robertson, in 1880. In southeast portion of county.　　LRI; Waite.

Mitchells (RR Mitchell): Ry SOU; Pop. 100. In south central portion of county. "Uncle Billy Mitchell" opposed railroad going through small part of his land. John Wharton, favorite friend, promised name station Mitchell and engineer salute with loud blowing of engine whistle each trip if could build through property.   LRI; Waite.

Mountain Run flows through central and southeastern portions of county; tributary of Rappahannock. Nov. 1, 1726, deed recorded "in Fork of Rappahannock on the south side of Mountain Run."   36 V 229

Rapidan: Ry SOU; Pop. 220. In southwest corner of county. Village on Rapidan River, named for Queen Anne, "rapid Anne".   Gannett 258.

Reva: Pop. 130. In center of extreme west portion of county. Walter Burgess, instrumental in getting postoffice established, named for his daughter, Reva Burgess.   LRI; Waite

Richardsville: Pop. 40. In southeast portion of county. Named for Richards family. Richard's Ferry on Rappahannock near this town.   LRI; Waite

Rixeyville: Pop. 100. In north central portion of county. Named for Rixey family; came to county in 1804.   LRI; Waite

Stevensburg: Pop. 25. Near mid-center of southeastern portion of county. Was York in colonial times, oldest town in county. Named Stevensburg for General Edward Stevens (1744-1820), Revolutionary hero of Culpeper.

LRI; Waite

CUMBERLAND COUNTY

Formed 1748; named for Duke of Cumberland, second son of George II. Area: 288 sq.mi.; Pop. 6,360; Pop. per sq.mi., 22.1. 8.4% county area in Cumberland State Forest. About three-fourths county area is forested. Rank occupational groups: agriculture, manufacturing, trade. Rank agricultural income: field crops, livestock, poultry.   Roads 68.

Cartersville: Pop. 85. Named after descendant of King Carter. Was overnight stop for boats on James River in late 1700's.   LRI

Cumberland: elev. 475; Pop. 250; US Rt 60. County seat, named for Prince William Augustus, Duke of Cumberland.

Muddy Creek in northeast portion of county. Land records as early as August 17, 1725 gave location of land on Muddy Creek. After each rain, stream very muddy from the runoff.   34 V 353; LRI

Tamworth: Pop. 25. On Muddy Creek. Proposal that be postoffice name. Several postoffices in United States use that name; P. O. Dept. submitted list of names to pick from. Tamworth chosen; only one other postoffice in United States has that name.   LRI

Willis River flows north through the county. Land grant by Council at Capitol, July 7, 1730, gave location near Willis's River.   36 V 144

DICKENSON COUNTY

Formed 1880; named for W. J. Dickenson, prominent public man. Area: 335 sq.mi.; Pop. 20,211; Pop. per sq.mi., 60.3. First permanent settler, "Fighting Dick" Cooley; about 1810, built three-walled cabin. More than nine-tenths county area wooded. 4.1% county area in Jefferson National Forest. Mining is leading occupation, followed by these groups: trade, educational services, manufacturing. Rank agricultural incomes: field crops, livestock, fruit and nuts.

Roads 76; VaVCo 8-1955

Bee: Pop. 50; elev. 1,482. In southwestern portion of county. Named for little girl named Beatrice. LRI

Birchleaf: Pop. 100. In mid-eastern portion of county. DU

Breaks: Pop. 100. In northeastern corner of county. Ravine or gorge through the Cumberland Mountains is called "The Breaks"; named from that feature. LRI

Breaks Interstate Park: Russell Fork has canyon five miles long; river bed with rock formation 1,600 feet above in center of gorge. Russell Fork plunges downhill 400 feet in the five miles of gorge. Stream roars, surges, and tugs at huge boulders. Gorge through Cumberland Mountains forming largest canyon east of Mississippi. Carolina, Clinchfield & Ohio Railway and Highway 80 are constructed through the gorge. Walls have vegetation of spruce, laurel, ivy and other plants. Breaks Interstate Park Commission voted by Virginia and Kentucky legislatures; area 1,250 acres; dedicated September 5, 1955.

VaVCo May 1953; Com Va 10-1957

Clinchco: Ry CLIN; Pop. 975. In central portion of county. Name from railroad name (Clinchfield) and Clinchfield Coal Corporation. Water: well; filtered, chlorinated. Sutherland 45

Clintwood: elev. 1,784; Pop. 1,400. In northwest portion of county. Became county seat 1882; chartered 1894. Increase Pop. 1950-60, 2.4%. Early name, Holly Creek; renamed Clintwood in honor of Senator Henry Clinton Wood of Scott County. Water: four wells; filtered, chlorinated.

Com Va 8-1955

Cranesnest River flows northeast as tributary into Pound River. Named because cranes built nests in small caves honeycombed in towering sandstone cliffs. Sutherland 270

John W. Flanagan, Jr. Dam: 250-feet-high, rockfill dam across Pound River, 1.8 miles upstream from mouth of Pound River, dedicated September 24,

1966, unit in flood-control system for the Big Sandy Basin. Named for John William Flanagan, Jr., member of Congress, 1931-1945.

DNR 9-20-1966; WWA vol. 24.

Haysi: Ry CLIN; Pop. 485; elev. 1,600. Named for Charles M. Hayter and a Mr. Sypher, partners in a small store. In northeast portion of county.

WP: Va 538

Isom: Pop. 50; elev. 1,460. In northwest portion on Pound River. Named for Isom Mullins.

Steeles 1168

Lick Creek, in southwest portion of county, flows into Russell Fork at Sandlick, where a salt spring brought a large number of native animals to lick its brackish waters.

LRI

McClure: Ry CLIN; Pop. 500. In central portion of county. Named for McClure River; Captain McClure was killed there by the Indians.

Sutherland 47

McClure River rises in south central portion of county; flows northward across county; tributary of Russell Fork. In April, 1774, party commanded by McClure pursued Indian Chief Logan; Logan ambushed and defeated McClure on the creek; this gave creek its name.

Summers 145

Nora: Ry CLIN; elev. 1,505; Pop. 200. In southwest portion of county. Nora was Mouth of Open Fork of McClure River, earliest county seat; then Ervinton; now Nora. Named for first postmaster, Nora Dorton.

LRI

Sandy Basin is named for its sandy soil. In the northeastern portion of the county.

Sutherland 150

Trammel: Ry CLIN; Pop. 500. Trammel was named for Trammel Creek; early hunters found name of Trammel cut in beech tree and named stream for him. Report that he was captured by Indians and taken to Kentucky. In south central portion, near county boundary.

Sutherland 48

Vicey: elev. 1,432; Pop. 50. (In both Dickenson and Buchanan Counties). In central east portion of Dickenson.

DU

DINWIDDIE COUNTY

Formed 1752; name from Robert Dinwiddie, Governor 1751-1756. Area: 507 sq.mi.; Pop. 22,183; Pop. per sq.mi., 43.8; increase Pop. 1950-60, 17.8%. Nearly three-fourths area forested. Rank occupational groups: manufacturing, agriculture, trade. Rank agricultural income: field crops, livestock, poultry.

Roads 66

Carson: Ry ACL; elev. 152; Pop. 160. In southeast corner of county. At time railroad wreck, a telegram was sent reading: Cars off and cars on. The last two words of telegram gave name, Carson.

Steeles 1161

Central State Hospital established 1869, first mental hospital for Negroes in America. Recently serves all mental persons of vicinity. Located west of and near Petersburg.

Va Govt 67

Church Road: Ry N&W; Pop. 65. In north central portion. Church Road was name of a country road leading to a church.

Steeles 1162

Dewitt: Ry SAL; elev. 295; Pop. 100. Slightly south of mid-center of county. Named for Dewitt Smith, a local resident.

Steeles 1163

Dinwiddie: Ry SAL; elev. 235; Pop. 200; US Rt 1. County seat. Lieutenant-General Winfield Scott, born here 1786, admitted to bar 1806, had law office here in early life; became commander U.S. Army 1841-1861. Military engagements 1864-65.

Ford: Ry N&W; Pop. 30; US Rt 460. In northwest portion near eastern boundary of west third of county. Name from Fred Ford, first station agent; sometimes known as Ford's Depot.

ESS county 35

Fort Lee: named for General Robert E. Lee, Commander of Confederate Armies; President Washington and Lee University 1865-1870. Camp Lee, 3,500 acres, World War I, one of large cantonments. Was Wild Life Preserve of Virginia Commission of Game and Inland Fisheries from April 1927 until October 1940. After World War II, in April 1950, became Fort Lee. Chief quartermaster center of the United States. East of Petersburg.

Hatcher Run flows east in the northern portion of county; tributary of Rowanty Creek. Named for man Hatcher; possibly Henry Hatcher of expedition of Abram Wood about 1673.

Butterworth

McKenney (corporate name McKenny); Ry SAL; elev. 300; Pop. 519; increase Pop. 1950-60, 9.0%; US Rt 1. In southwest portion near eastern boundary of west third of county. Named for William R. McKenney, Seaboard Air Line Railroad's lawyer and owner large tracts of land in vicinity.

Glick 23

Monk's Neck Creek, tributary of Rowanty, was Moccasin Neck Creek, which developed into its present name.   Butterworth

Petersburg (independent city): Ry ACL, N&W, SAL; elev. 15; Pop. 37,000; increase Pop. 1950-60, 4.8%; US Rts 1, 460. Site of city formerly Indian trading post Appamatuck. In 1645, Fort Henry, colonial fort to resist hostile Indian attacks, established. Peter Jones succeeded Abram Wood as proprietor trading post and place became Peter's Point. In Sept. 1732, Colonel William Byrd, II, proposed naming Petersburg. Village laid out 1748. In 1784, four settlements united as Petersburg. Became city March 16, 1850. Walnut Hill annexed in 1921. Soldiers of War of 1812 earned title "The Cockade City".
                                              Va Doc 25, 22+; VaVCo 7-1963

Petersburg National Military Park borders southern side of city of Petersburg. Established by act of Congress approved July 3, 1926, has gross acreage of more than 1,500 acres. Commemorates military operations in 1864-65. Thirty-two locations included in route of tour to see points of interest.
                                              Lykes: Petersburg Natl. Mil. Park, 46, 56.

Petersburg Training School for Negro mental defectives is near the city.
                                              Va Govt 67.

Richard Bland College (Petersburg), two-year institution, authorized 1960, named for Richard Bland, Virginia statesman. Confers Associate of Arts degree.
                                              Ann.Bul.

Saponey Church, five miles southeast of Dewitt, built 1729, oldest in county, is still in use.

Sappony Creek in south central and southeast portion. Saponi were a warlike Indian tribe who lived in Brunswick County area before 1740. Land grant, Feb. 8, 1727.   32 V 374.

Stony Creek flows from central portion of county to the southeast. Many rocks and bowlders near the source give the stream its name.   Butterworth

Sutherland: Ry N&W; Pop. 65; US Rt 460. In northwestern portion of county. Named for local family.   Steeles 1178

Whiteoak Creek flows in northwest portion of county; tributary of Stony Creek. Named from abundance of white oak trees in its area.   Butterworth

Wilsons (RR name Wilson): Ry N&W; Pop. 150; US Rt 460. In northwest corner of county. Named for local family.   Steeles 1180

ESSEX COUNTY

Formed 1691; named for Essex County, England. Captain John Smith and explorers visited county in 1608; settlement began 1652. Area: 250 sq.mi.; Pop. 6,690; Pop. per sq.mi., 26.8; increase Pop. 1950-60, 2.5%. More than two-thirds land wooded. Rank occupational groups: manufacturing, trade, agriculture. Rank agricultural income: field crops, livestock, poultry.   Roads 86

Bowlers Wharf: Pop. 125. In eastern fourth of county. Named for Thomas Bowler who settled here and built a home in 1663; the house is still standing and occupied. Ferry across Rappahannock at now Bowler's Wharf. Bowler's Ferry in 1730; public warehouse. Salt water fishing guides and boats at Bowlers Wharf.   Garnett TT 28; LRI

Caret: Pop. 5; US Rt 17. At western edge of mid-portion of county. First courthouse near Caret; there 1665-1693. Named by P. O. Department. Vauter's Church near Caret been used continuously since before 1719.

                                                        EcD county; LRI.

Center Cross: Pop. 200; US Rt 17. In eastern fourth of county. Earlier name Hermitage. Two highways cross; about in center of county; probable explanation of name.   Garnett TT 88

Champlain: Pop. 80. Near center of west third of county. Named for early seat of Garnett family. The farm still retains the name.   LRI

Chance: Pop. 20. In northern part of west third of county. Named by P. O. Department.   LRI

Dunnsville: Pop. 50. At western edge of eastern third of county. Named after Mr. Dunn, early storekeeper. US Rt 17. Salt water fishing guides and boats here.   LRI

Hoskins Creek flows east across central portion of county; tributary of Rappahannock. Named for Bartholomew Hoskins who was first person to patent land around the creek.   LRI

Howertons: Pop. 20. Near western edge of eastern third of county. Named for Howerton family who lived in the area.   LRI

Hustle: Pop. 65. In western part of west third of county. Named by P. O. Department.   LRI

Laneview: Pop. 25. In extreme east part of county. Locally stated that named for the long straight lane or road that leads to Rappahannock River.

                                                                     LRI

Loretto: Pop. 34; US Rt 17. In central area of west third of county. Name in use as early as 1861.

11 C 161

Millers Tavern: Pop. 50; US Rt 360. Near western edge of eastern third of county. Was wayside and early tavern and stopover on the road that led from Richmond to Tappahannock.

LRI

Mount Landing: Pop. 10. In northern part of middle third of county. Early landing place on Mt. Landing Creek. The farm located here still bears the name.

LRI

Occupacia Creek flows east across northern portion; tributary of Rappahannock. Indian name.

LRI

Piscataway Creek; seemingly identical with *Kiismaquindi*, which means "place of the old great beaver". Stream flows east across central portion; tributary of Rappahannock.

Hodge II, 262

St. Margaret's School, an Episcopalian school for girls, at Tappahannock. It is named for St. Margaret of Scotland, a queen whose chapel is still in use in Edinburgh, Scotland.

LRI

Supply: Pop. 35. In extreme west portion of county. Oldest resident unable to give reason for choosing postoffice name.

LRI

Tappahannock: First, Hobb's Hold, meaning land holden under a grant; not Hobb's Hole. Indian language guttural, begin word with a "T" instead of "R", name of town Tappahannock. Name means "on the rise and fall of water", or "on the running water". Pop. 1,086; increase Pop. 1950-60, 7.4%; US Rts 17, 360. Became permanent location of courthouse in 1728. Before 1800, overseas ships sailed from Tappahannock. In 1682, port was called New Plymouth. Water supply from wells.   EcD county; Garnett TT, 18+, 52+; WP: Va 452.

Upright: Pop. 100. In south portion of east third of county. Name probably from perpendicular weather-boarding of first store, or description of community's moral character.

Garnett TT, 71.

FAIRFAX COUNTY

Formed 1742; named for Lord Fairfax, proprietor of the Northern Neck. First settlement, Hunting Creek Bay (southern edge Alexandria). Area: 405 sq.mi.; Pop. 275,002; increase Pop. 1950-60, 179.0%. 52.8 percent county area in forests. County is in megalopolis. County seat first at Freedom Hill near present-day Vienna; then at Alexandria 1754-1799; moved to Fairfax 1799. State's leading county in sand and gravel production. Rank occupational groups: public administration, trade, construction. Rank agricultural income: livestock, dairy, poultry. Roads 83; EcD county

Accotink Creek is in central and east portions of the county. Land patent in 1677 gives location on drains of Accotink. 30 V 326

Annandale: Pop. 21,000. In east central portion. Name probably comes from Earl of Annandale, 13th century knight of Scotland. US Rt 236. Carey

Back Lick Run, near Annandale; in 1755, mention of road up Back Lick Run. 35 V 311

Baileys Crossroads: Pop. 2,600. Probably named after Hachaliah Bailey of circus fame who owned land and used it for winter quarters for his shows. Carey

Burke: Ry SOU; Pop. 150. In south central portion of county. Named for prominent family. IHS Fairfax

Cameron Run along boundary Alexandria-Fairfax County. Named for Thomas, 6th Lord Fairfax, Baron of Cameron. 34 V 40, 45.

Centreville: Pop. 600; US Rts 29, 211. In southwest portion of county. Earlier name, New Gate. Name from location about equidistant from Leesburg, Middleburg, Warrenton, Georgetown, and Alexandria. Martin: Gaz 168

Chantilly: Pop. 400; US Rt 50. Earlier name Ox Hill. Chantilly was name of farm in 1816; name came originally from Chateau Chantilly in France. Farm name given to postoffice. In southwest portion. LRI

Clifton: Ry SOU; Pop. 230. In south central portion. Two explanations of name: one, Wyckliffe family from England were large property owners; name from old English "Cliff by the Ye". The other, Otis family, influential, came from Orange-Clifton, New Jersey. Community name given by Harrison Gray Otis. LRI

Community (name for Hybla Valley): Pop. 4,000. In mid-east portion. Named by postmaster. LRI

Difficult Run is in west fourth of county; flows north; tributary of Potomac. Was location of county line in 1732; location of land in will dated Feb. 6, 1755.

4 V 102++; 36 V 180.

Dogue Creek, named after Indian tribe of Dogues (Doeg); creek marked boundary of patent 1675. Tribe had evil reputation; name survives as "dawg" in "mean as a dawg". In mid area of east one third of county; tributary of Potomac. Sprouse 9+

Dunn Loring: Ry W&OD; Pop. 1,500. In mid-third of county. Originated 1885, development plans by Loring Land Improvement Company; name from members of company, General Lanier Dunn and Dr. Loring, a Washington oculist. Souvenir Program, community, 11

Fairfax (independent city in 1961): elev. 365; Pop. 19,500; US Rts 29, 50, 211. Named for sixth Lord Fairfax, grandson of Lord Culpeper. When Alexandria became part of District of Columbia in 1779, county seat moved to present location. Water supply from Goose Creek in Loudoun County.

VaVCo 3-1952; Lee AC 21

Fairfax Station (RR Fairfax): Ry SOU; Pop. 175. Near center of county.

Falls Church (became independent city 1948): Area 2 sq.mi.; Ry W&OD; elev. 365; Pop. 12,500; increase Pop. 1950-60, 35.3%; US Rts 29, 211. Nearness to Falls of Potomac and Episcopal Church built 1734 gave locality its name. Incorporated 1875. Among state's independent cities, has highest rank of 73.4% persons 25 years old and older who have completed high school or more. Rank occupational groups: public administration, trade, duty with armed forces. Water purchased from District of Columbia; filtered. ESS (Fairfax); VGb 36

Fort Belvoir (military reservation): Pop. ———. In southeast portion of county. Expanded during World War II. Former name Fort Humphreys. Present name from Col. Fairfax establishing residence named Belvoir, in honor of his ancestral home in England. Name means "beautiful to see"; earlier pronunciation "Beever". 4 V 102; Sprouse 6; GSW CF; Callahan 115+; 119.

Four Mile Run received its name in 1694 on a land grant because it is located four miles north of Great Hunting Creek. It is a tributary of the Potomac and flows just south of the National Airport. Sprouse 13

Franconia: Ry RF&P; Pop. 3,000. In center of eastern one-third of county. Owner of Franconia Farms granted right-of-way to railroad so named station for his property. LRI

Great Falls: Pop. 400. On Potomac in northwest portion of county. Named from "cataract" 35 feet high as one of the series of rapids where river descends 90 feet; about 15 miles upstream from Washington.

Webster's Geog. Dictionary, 418.

Great Falls Park at point where Potomac River falls 76 feet in short distance of few hundred feet. Carey

Greenway: Boarding School, Madiera School for Girls. Pop. ———. Near Potomac in west one-third of county. Greenway from Greenway Court, home of Lord Fairfax.   LRI

Gunston Hall, a state-owned historical house, once the home of the Revolutionary statesman, George Mason. The mansion and its gardens have been restored and are maintained by the National Society of Colonial Dames of America, and the site is one of the Nation's most notable privately operated historic sites. The house was built in 1758 by the fourth George Mason, author of the Virginia Bill of Rights. Site includes 555 acres from 5,000 of the eighteenth century plantation. The name Gunston is from the Staffordshire residence of the Fowke ancestors of Mason.   Va. Cav., Summer 1951; Roads 18

Herndon: Ry W&OD; elev. 365; Pop. 1,960; increase Pop. 1950-60, 34.1%. On west boundary of county in northwest portion. Named for Captain William Herndon, lost at sea 1857.   ESS county 26

Langley: Central Intelligence Agency on 400-acre tract; near Potomac in mid-section of county. Multi-story building more than one-fifth size of Pentagon. Rolling woodland; modern concrete building blends into the hills and pines.
Com Va 4-1958; DNR 2-18-1967

Little River: Pop. ———. A branch or contract postal station was established in 1963. It received its name from State Route 236 (Little River Turnpike) which goes west from Alexandria. The old toll road and main highway derived its name from its terminus Little River in Loudoun County.   Carey

Lorton: Ry RF&P; Pop. 300. In south portion of east one-third of county. Named for postmaster's home in Cumberland County, England, in 1875. Nearby, District of Columbia's correctional institution, 3,500 acres.   LRI

McLean: Pop. 12,500. In north portion of the central part of the county. Named for Edward McLean, one of the original founders of Great Falls and Old Dominion electric line.   Detweiler 16

George Mason College, opened 1957; part of University of Virginia. In 1960, institution named George Mason. In 1966, offered programs for Bachelor's degrees.   Ann.Bul.

Merrifield: Pop. 1,000. Earlier name, Mills Cross Roads. Then, Slabtown, probably from number of sawmills; slabs sold for firewood. Name Merrifield honors G. A. L. Merrifield of Falls Church, faithful Sunday School worker.
Souvenir Program, Community 9

Mosby: Pop. ———. Is included with Jefferson Village but has a separate postoffice. Named for John Singleton Mosby (1833-1916), lawyer and Confederate soldier, who was scout for Gen. J. E. B. Stuart; in 1863, he recruited an independent body of fighters which became known as Mosby's Rangers.   Carey

Mount Vernon: Pop. ———. Near Potomac in mid-area of eastern part of county. Commander expedition against Cartegena in Spanish colonies, Admiral Edward Vernon; expedition met disaster. Lawrence Washington, captain of colonial troops, named his plantation for his admiral, Mount Vernon. George Washington came into possession of Mount Vernon in 1752. Estate purchased by Mount Vernon Ladies Association in 1858; purpose to preserve and guard the home and tomb of Washington.   Stewart 144

Nebasco Creek crosses U. S. Rt 1 north of Dumfries; the Indian word means "at the point of rocks".   LRI

Newington: Ry RF&P; Pop. 100. It was the Truro Glebe of 1734; later known as "Newington".   Carey

Northern State Mental Health Institute has two-fold purpose of treating acutely ill mental patients and restoring to their normal residence in their communities as soon as possible.

Northern Virginia Community College, comprehensive institution, of University of Virginia, opened 1965 at Bailey's Crossroads. Main campus developing at Annandale.   Ann.Bul.

Oakton: Pop. 350. In mid-area of central portion of county. Formerly Flint Hill. Large oak tree in center of village was chief factor in changing name.   LRI

Pimmitt River in north central portion of county. Land grant on Pommett's Run, Nov. 21, 1715.   17 V 115

Pohick Creek: land patent on Pohick in 1677. Pohick from pohickory, Indian name for American tree.   30 V 326; Com Va 3-1935

Reston: Pop. 100. Developer Robert E. Simon; whose initials form first syllable of town name. Planned development; seven villages, each having "town center" as retail area; villages with woodland in between. Variety of house type; trees, lake, garden spots, recreation sites. Total area: 6,750 acre tract.
                                        New Republic 10-7-64; Fortune 12-64.

Seven Corners (shopping center): Pop. ———. The name is from the number of roads and highways which converge on a single intersection.   Carey

Henry G. Shirley Memorial Highway (State Route 350) crosses county from Woodbridge vicinity through Falls Church and Alexandria to Arlington. The highway was named for the former State Commissioner of Highways.
                                        Official Information

Springfield: Ry SOU; Pop. 15,000. In west portion of eastern third of county. Present development began 1952. Name from large springs in vicinity.   LRI

Sunset Hills: Ry W&OD; Pop. 100. In northwest portion. Wife of owner chose Sunset Hills because of magnificent view from ridge near village as a person looked at setting sun across wide valley at sunset behind Blue Ridge and Bull Run Mountains.   Carey

Vienna: Ry W&OD; elev. 345; Pop. 15,200; increase Pop. 1950-60, 463.8%. In northern area in west part of central section of county. Early county seat at Freedom Hill near present-day Vienna. Vienna named after New York community; requirement of prospective resident. Water supply, drilled wells; plus supplement from Falls Church. **ESS county 24**

Wellington: Pop. 8,000. Probably named for Wellington House a short distance from Wellington Station, a stop on the old Washington, Alexandria and Mt. Vernon Electric Railway. The house may have had its name changed from Walnut Tree Farm to Wellington after the battle of Waterloo. **Carey**

West Falls Church (sub-station postoffice of **Falls Church**).

FAUQUIER COUNTY

Formed in 1759; named for Francis Fauquier, Governor, 1758-1768. Settlers were in vicinity in 1712. "Elk Marsh" settlement in 1714. Area: 660 sq.mi.; Pop. 24,066; Pop. per sq.mi., 36.5. About two-thirds county area forested. Boasts supporting more hunts than any other county in Virginia or in the nation. Rank occupational groups: agriculture, trade, construction. Rank agricultural income: livestock, dairy, field crops.   Roads 81; Cavalcade Sum. 1959

Ashby's Gap in Blue Ridge; pioneer family crossed it. Earliest record Ashby's Bent Gap.   Fauquier 51

Bealeton: Ry SOU; elev. 290; Pop. 75. In south portion of east one-third of county. Right-of-way for Orange and Alexandria Railroad given by Beale family in 1850. John Marshall born in Germantown, now Bealeton. Fauquier 82

Broad Run: Ry SOU; Pop. 20. In the northeast area of county. Stream Broad Run led to name of postoffice when railroad built through community.
LRI

Calverton: Ry SOU; Pop. 220. First called Owl Run; then Warrenton Junction; name Calverton by family who came from Calvert County, Maryland.
Fauquier 82

Carter Run flows southeast in western portion of county; tributary of Rappahannock. Captain Thomas Carter in July 1724 took grant of land at mouth of stream.   Fauquier 48

Cassanova: Ry SOU; Pop. 100. In mid-portion of middle third of county. First called Three Mile Switch after railroad was built, and next named Melrose. Next called Cassanova for a Mr. Cassanova who lived at Rock Hill.
Fauquier 81+

Catlett: Ry SOU; Pop. 200. In north portion of east one-third of county. Named for John Catlett, early patentee. Originally, Catlett's Station.
Fauquier 82

Cedar Run flows east across the northern middle third of the county. Its name was given in 1731.   Fauquier 48

Delaplane: Ry SOU; Pop. 50. In northwest portion of county. It was Piedmont Station until 1874. Washington Delaplane operated a store.
Fauquier 80

Goldvein: Pop. 100. In southeast corner of county. Name reminiscent of gold rush in vicinity.   Fauquier 82

Hume: Pop. 130. In southwest portion of county. Named for local family.
Steeles 1168

Markham: Ry SOU; elev. 550; Pop. 100. In mid-portion near west boundary. Formerly The Hollow, also Farrowsville. Name changed for James Markham Marshall, first president of railroad branch in 1854.   Fauquier 81

Marshall: Ry SOU; Pop. 500. In center of western half of county. Thomas Marshall, Chief Justice's father, bought land in 1773. Early name Salem; changed to Marshall, March 8, 1882. Water supply, well; aerated, filtered, chlorinated.   Roads 21; Fauquier 78.

Midland: Ry SOU; Pop. 100. In western mid-portion of east one-third of county. Named for Virginia Midland Railroad.   Steeles 1171

Morrisville: Pop. 100. In south portion of east one-fourth of county. Named for local family.   Steeles 1172

Orlean: Pop. 75. In south part near boundary of west and middle thirds of county. Reported that named for large estate formerly in area.   LRI

Paris: Pop. 100; US Rt 50. In northwest corner of county. One explanation: village founded by Revolutionary soldier who served under Lafayette, and named village in honor of France's capitol. Other explanation: Lafayette in travel while visiting America was impressed with beauty of village and asked that it might be named Paris. Water supply, springs, well.
                    VaVCo 5-1950; V HSSA 9.

Rectortown: Ry SOU; Pop. 250. On south boundary in east one-third of county. Was Maidstone for Lord Fairfax's estate in England. Became Rectortown; John Rector lived here in 1772.   Fauquier 78

Remington: Ry SOU; elev. 275; Pop. 288; US Rts 15, 29. In southwestern area of county. Until 1850, Millview; then Bowenville. In 1853, railroad Rappahannock Station. In 1890, Remington.   Fauquier 82

Somerville: Pop. 25. Near southeast boundary. Named for Somerville family.   LRI

Sumerduck: Pop. 40. In southeastern portion of county. Stream, Summerduck; many ducks on stream and nested; explains name of stream. Village name (spelled with one 'M') was taken from name of stream.   Fauquier 47, 82.

The Plains: Ry SOU; elev. 565; Pop. 484; increase Pop. 1950-60, 19.4%. Formerly, name was The White Plains; confusion with White Plains, New York, so name shortened. In north portion of middle third of county. Water supply, well; chlorinated.   VaVCo 5-1950

Upperville: Pop. 350; US Rt 50. Near Loudoun County line. Located in upper portion of county. Piedmont Hunt at Upperville dates from 1840; considered oldest in country.   Steeles 1179; VaVCo 5-1950

Warrenton: Ry SOU; Pop. 3,522; elev. 635; increase Pop. 1950-60, 84.8%; US Rts 15, 29, 50, 211. County seat established 1760. Town laid off 1790; incorporated January 5, 1810. Formerly Fauquier Court House; renamed for Dr. Joseph Warren, who started Paul Revere on his ride; fell as General at Bunker Hill. Water supply from Cedar Run; filtered, chlorinated.
                    VGb 30; V HSSA 51

FLOYD COUNTY

Formed 1831; named for John Floyd, governor of Virginia, 1830-34. Area: 383 sq.mi.; Pop. 10,462; Pop. per sq.mi., 27.3. County area nearly one-half forested. 1.1% county area in Blue Ridge Parkway. Rank occupational groups: manufacturing, agriculture, construction. Rank agricultural income: dairy, live stock, field crops.   Roads 74

Alum Ridge: Pop. 40. In north portion of west one-third of county. Name from springs containing alum. Also, name of ridge and magisterial district. LRI

Buffalo Mountain in southwest portion of county. Is chief mountain in height (elev. 3,970) — so named because of its shape.   LRI

Burks Fork. (See page 236.)

Check: Pop. 55; elev. 2,520; US Rt 221. In eastern one-fourth of county. One story is that a store was a favorite meeting place for a group of checker players.   LRI

Copper Hill: elev. 2,720; Pop. 40; US Rt 221. In extreme northeast portion. Mr. Tonycrafty supposedly prospected for copper at Copper Hill.   LRI

Copper Valley: Pop. 30. One mine by name of Tonycrafty did operate in the county. Presence of copper ore.   LRI

Floyd: was Jacksonville, for President Andrew Jackson; became Floyd. Pop. 487; elev. 2,431; US Rt 221. County seat. Town water supply from Dodd Creek; filtered, chlorinated.   WP: Va 434

Indian Valley: Pop. 75. In northwest portion of county. Tradition that this area was summer hunting grounds of Cathaway Indians who lived in what is now West Virginia. A Parkway naturalist some years ago from research seemed to believe Indians came from Cherokee tribe in North Carolina. Still many arrow heads in this area.   LRI

Little River drains much of county; flows northeast and becomes tributary of New River. Begins in eastern part of county as "Head of the River"; one stream in western part of county is called West Fork, meaning west fork of Little River.   LRI

Simpsons: Pop. 100. Near center of eastern one-third area of county. From family name.   LRI

Willis: Pop. 70; US Rt 221. Near center of western one-fourth of county. Earlier name was for a family Hylton. In late 1890's, changed to another family name, Willis.   LRI

FLUVANNA COUNTY

Formed 1777; name honors Queen Anne; Fluvanna or Flueve-Anna; Anna's River was in early years used to designate the upper part of James River. Area: 282 sq.mi.; Pop. 7,227; Pop. per sq.mi., 25.6; increase Pop. 1950-60, 1.5%. 66.8% county area forested. First rural accredited high school in Virginia in Fluvanna. Rank occupational groups: manufacturing, agriculture, educational services. Rank agricultural income: livestock, field crops, poultry.

EcD county; Roads 63

Bremo Bluff: (RR Bremo) Ry. C&O; elev. 222; Pop. 100; US Rt 15. In southeast corner of county on James. In Revolutionary times, Bremo grant to General Carey C. Cooke. Bremo is name which Cooke family brought from England; village of Breamore in County Wilts, England. Bremo Bluff is near Bremo, beautiful home designed by Thomas Jefferson in 1815. Water supply, well.

News Leader 9-5-193-.

Bybee: Pop. 20. In northeast portion. Named for local church which was named for its leader.

Steeles 1161

Carysbrook: Ry C&O; Pop. 25; US Rt 15. Slightly east of center of county. Carysbrook plantation acquired for Miles Cary (under age) by his mother; built 1725. Named after Cary Brook Castle in England. Community has Fluvanna High School for entire county.

VaVCo 5-1952

Cohasset (RR Fork Union): Ry C&O; Pop. 50. In mid-southern portion. In 1907, when Virginia Air line built, a Mrs. Dicky from Cohasset, Mass. named it for her home town. An Indian name.

Columbia: Ry C&O; Pop. 86; incorporated 1897. Near mid-eastern county boundary. Columbia was Point of Fork until 1788; point formed by Rivanna into James. Products floated on Rivanna as early as 1756. General Assembly named town Columbia. Water supply, well.

WP: Va 621

Dixie: Pop. ———. In southeast portion of county. Dixie, rural postoffice, junction US Rt 15 and Va. 6. One explanation: young men gathered here and sang "Dixie". Another explanation: A Miss Wood driving from Chatham to Bremo stopped at Dixie and learned of her uncle's death. Soldiers mustered out here.

LRI

Fork Union: elev. 368; Pop. 200; US Rt 15; in southeast portion of county. Three or four denominations worshipped in church built 1824. Nearby is fork of James and Rivanna. Fork Union name evolved. Water supply, three wells; one chlorinated.

TD 12-9-1951

Fork Union Military Academy; began 1898 as community school. Baptist ownership after 1912. Military training introduced in 1902.

Snead 32

Kent Branch in northeast portion, flows into Byrd Creek. Named for Kent family. LRI

Kents Store: Pop. 20. In northeast portion. Chapel Hill, then Holland's Store. James M. Kent had store in 1845; postoffice in store. Snead 41

Palmyra: Ry C&O; elev. 274; Pop. 350; US Rt 15. In central portion of county. Formed around courthouse in 1830. Named for ancient city in Greece. Water supply, two wells. LRI

Stage Junction: Pop. 15. In mid-eastern portion. A stage settlement where two roads meet. Steeles 1177

Troy: Ry C&O; Pop. 40. In northeast portion. Named for Capt. T. O. Troy, a promoter of Virginia Air line in 1907. LRI

Venable Creek in northeast portion of county; with Kent Creek forms Byrd Creek. Named for Fluvanna family. LRI

Wilmington: Pop. 25. In east central portion of county. DU

FRANKLIN COUNTY

Formed 1785; named for Benjamin Franklin, then governor of Pennsylvania; many early settlers had come from Pennsylvania. Settlement started about 1760. Area: 718 sq.mi.; Pop. 25,925; Pop. per sq.mi., 36.1; increase Pop. 1950-60, 5.6%. 63.5% area of county wooded. Rank occupational groups: construction, agriculture, trade. Rank agricultural income: field crops, dairy, poultry.

Roads 61

Blackwater River with tributaries drains northern third of county. tributary of Roanoke River. Name derived from color of water; inky appearance from walnuts from many trees falling in stream. LRI

Boones Mill (census name Boone Mill): Ry N&W; elev. 1,128; Pop. 371; increase Pop. 1950-60, 10.7%; US Rt 220. In mid-northern portion of county. Jacob Boone, cousin of Daniel Boone, arrived 1782, built mill. WP: Va 608.

Callaway: elev. 1,205; Pop. 130. Near to middle of county west boundary. Col. James Callaway gave land for court house. VaVCo 4-1952

Ferrum: Ry N&W; elev. 1,235; Pop. 400. In southern portion near edge western third of county. Ferrum village began 1889 when railroad built. Railroad surveyors interested in iron mine near present station; *ferrum* is Latin for iron.

Wingfield 26

Ferrum Junior College was Training School established Sept. 1914. In 1936, expanded to junior college level; confers Associate in Arts degree. Related to Methodist Church. Co-educational; work scholarships help deserving but financially handicapped youth. Ann.Bul.

Gladehill: Pop. 50. In east-central portion of county. DU

Henry: Ry N&W; elev. 882; Pop. 125. About middle of county's south boundary. Formerly Alumine. Railway station named Henry because of Henry County line, but postoffice in Franklin County. LRI

Maggotty Creek in north central portion, tributary of Blackwater River. Name used 200 years ago. Diary, Nov. 4, 1753, Maggodi (Maggoty) Creek mentioned. 12 V 273

Penhook: Pop. 45. In mid-eastern portion of county. DU

Redwood: Pop. 100. In central portion of county. DU

Rocky Mount: Ry N&W; elev. 1,091; Pop. 1,412; US Rt 220. Two villages for 100 years. Rocky Mount and Mount Pleasant. In 1873, became one village. Settlement began about 1760. Rocky Mount became county seat in 1786. Name of town derived from abrupt precipice in vicinty. Munitons for Revolutionary army made nearby. Water supply from Pigg River; filtered, chlorinated.

Wingfield 18; WP: Va 608.

Snow Creek drains southeastern portion of county. Decisions, July 14, 1769, referring to chapel on Snow Creek. Probably for family by name of Snow. LRI

Union Hall: Pop. 50. In northeast portion of county. DU

Waidsboro (RR Lanahan) Ry N&W; Pop. 100. In southwest portion of county. Waid was large land-owner in first half of century. LRI

Booker T. Washington's Birthplace: National Monument, 164.50 acres. Birthplace on Burroughs Plantation in Hale's Ford area; Hales Ford in northeastern portion of county. Born probably in 1858; graduate Hampton Institute 1875; in 1881, principal of Tuskegee Institute, Alabama. Became orator and leader of Negroes educationally and economically. Died Nov. 14, 1915. Interesting item in inventory, November 23, 1861: "One Negro boy, 'Booker', value $400.00." Com Va 4-1952; WP: Va 608

Wirtz: Ry N&W; elev. 1,140; Pop. 75. A German name. Near center of north half of county. VaVCo 4-1952

FREDERICK COUNTY

Formed 1738; named for Frederick, Prince of Wales, father of King George III. Early settlement in 1732. Area: 433 sq.mi.; Pop. 21,941; Pop. per sq.mi., 50.7; increase Pop. 1950-60, 25.1%. First railway train into Winchester from Harpers Ferry in 1836. In 1871, planting first commercial orchard on large scale. Expansion to nearly 600,000 trees at present. Virginia's leading apple producing county. About half total county area wooded. 1.6% county area in George Washington National Forest. State's leading county in number peach trees of bearing age. State's leading county in terms of tonnage and product value of stone production. Rank occupational groups: manufacturing, trade, agriculture. Rank agricultural income: livestock, fruits and nuts, dairy.   Roads 89

Apple Blossom Festival, since 1924, festive event each spring in Winchester, attracts nation-wide interest. Although the event in Virginia, four Appalachian states — Pennsylvania, Maryland, West Virginia, and Virginia — are interested in the colorful event.   EcD county

Brucetown: Pop. 200. Earliest settler of town named Bruce; named for family.   ESS county 37

Gore: Ry W&W; elev. 703; Pop. 200; US Rt 50. Near Gainesboro. Named years, known as Cross Junction; when postoffice established, took name of community.   LRI

Gainesboro: Pop. 100; elev. 642; US Rt 522. In south portion of northwest one-fourth of county. Formerly, Pughtown; laid out as town in 1798.
          ESS county 38

Gore: Ry W&W; elev. 703; Pop. 200; US Rt 50. Near Gainsboro. Named for Gore family; probably more in honor of Mrs. S. S. Gore, active church-woman and unusual neighbor.   ESS county 37

Hayfield: Pop. 150; US Rt 50. About mid-point of west half of county. Soon after French and Indian War, two or three men were mowing native grass close to present location of the postoffice; Indians massacred the men. Believed there is connection between massacre and postoffice name.   LRI

Hogue Creek. (See page 236.)

Hopewell Meeting organized 1734, still active, so oldest organization of any denomination in Virginia west of Blue Ridge; congregation of the Society of Friends. It is five miles north of Winchester on Opequon River.
          37 V 23; Wayland SV 24

Middletown: Ry B&O; elev. 660; Pop. 378; US Rt 11. Near mid-point of southern boundary of county. Dr. Peter Senseny applied for charter 1796; long called Senseny Town. On main highway between county seats, Winchester and

Woodstock, influenced name Middletown. Nearby fort built about 1755. Water supply from Winchester development. Wayland SV 40; Couper II, 1113.

Mountain Falls: Pop. 50. In southwest portion of county. Beautiful falls on North Mountain about 1½ miles distant gave name to postoffice. LRI

Opequon Presbyterian Church receives name from Opequon Creek in present Frederick County; was first Presbyterian congregation in the Valley. 30 V 176

Shenandoah College and Conservatory of Music: founded 1875; came under control of United Brethren in Christ in 1887; denomination later joined in Evangelical United Brethren Church; in 1968, the denomination merged in the United Methodist Church. College was located in Dayton until moved to Winchester in 1960. Conservatory of Music grants bachelor degrees. Shenandoah College is junior college. Ann.Bul.

Star Tannery: Pop. 250. In southwest portion of county. Tannery established early in 1880's; operated about 20 years, name became Star Tannery.
ESS county 33

Stephens City: Ry B&O; elev. 770; Pop. 879; US Rt 11. Laid out on land of Lewis Stephens, whose father, Peter Stephens, settled 1732. Established 1758, Stephensburg. Often called "New Town" because Winchester was "Old Town". Name became Stephens City. Water supply from Winchester. V HSSA 10

Stephenson: Ry B&O; Pop. 60; US Rt 11. In northwest portion of county. Stephenson family owned much land in vicinity at earlier time. LRI

Sunnyside: Pop. 200. On hill sloping south. First home builder placed sign in front, "Sunnyside". Others built, and sign was moved to roadside. Postal station in 1955 used same name. LRI

Whitacre: elev. 993; Pop. 50. Near state line and near middle in northwest portion of county. Whitacre, successful family; merchant in Gainesboro.
Norris 596

Winchester (independent city): Ry B&O; PA; W&W; elev. 711; Pop. 15,500; increase Pop. 1950-60, 9.24%; Area 3 sq.mi.; US Rts 11, 50, 340, 522. Interstate 81. Believed first white residents 1738. First name settlement Opequon; then Old Town and Fredericktown; name Winchester in 1752 in honor of English home of founder, James Wood. John Handley School, an endowed public school, on 75-acre tract. Shawnee-Land ski nearby. Water supply from North Fork of Shenandoah River; filtered, chlorinated.
Willis-Walker 26; V HSSA 9, TD 12-11-1966

Winchester Research Station includes 16 acres. Purpose to investigate diseases and insects attacking tree fruits. Com Va 9-1953

GILES COUNTY

Formed 1806; named for William Branch Giles, United States Senator and Governor of Virginia, 1827-1830. Area 356 sq.mi.; Pop. 17,219; Pop. per sq.mi., 48.4. Probably explored in Rich Creek in 1671. 22.7% county area in Jefferson National Forest. State's leading county in limestone calcining. Rank occupational groups: manufacturing, trade, agriculture. Rank agricultural income: livestock, fruit, dairy.   Roads 74; EcD county

Bald Knob of Salt Pond Mountain (4,380 ft.); in eastern part of county. Vegetation scarce on summit; partly bare rock, so had bald appearance.   McCl

Butt Mountain in eastern section (elev. 4,195 ft.). Mountain butts out from ridge and ends abruptly.   McCl

Doe Creek. In central section. Suggestion that may have been named for a doe.   LRI

Doe Mountain in central section (alt. 4,200+). Suggestion that may have been named for a doe.   LRI

Eggleston: Ry N&W; elev. 1,747; Pop. 300. Near middle southern half of county. Called Gunpowder Springs because water has taste and odor resembling gunpowder. Then, became Eggleston Springs for pioneer settler. Then, name became Eggleston.   VaVCo Dec 1950; EcD county

Flat Mountain (4,100 ft.) in southeastern section. In 1748, Dr. Thomas Walker saw this mountain's flat top and gave it the name.   McCl

Fork Mountain (4,000+ ft.) in north eastern section. Name given because the divisions in the mountain slope make a fork.   McCl

Glen Lyn: Ry N&W; elev. 1,520; Pop. 222; US Rts 219, 460. Near state line in northwest portion. Earlier names, Parkinson Shumate's Ferry; then called Hell's Gate by workmen building N&W Railway. Name became Glen Lyn in 1883, meaning lovely glen. Appalachian Electric plant built in 1919; plant capacity 400,000 kilowatts. John Toney settled here in 1750; called the place Montreal; later called Mouth of East River.   McCl

Goldbond: Pop. 200. In north portion about between eastern and middle thirds of county. Was Olean earlier; changed to Goldbond in 1945 when National Gypsum Company came; Goldbond is company's trade name.   McCl

Kimballton: Ry N&W; Pop. 350. In northeast portion of middle section of county. In 1881, E. J. Kimballton, President N&W Railway, visited section, interested in building railroad to coal fields; a branch line went up to Kimballton.
                                                                            McCl

Mountain Lake: elev. 3,934; summer Pop. 500. Near center of eastern third of county. Lake on Salt Pond Mountain discovered 1751; three-fourths mile in length; one-fourth mile in width. Water so transparent that lake bottom can be seen in every part.   McCl

Narrows: Ry N&W; elev. 1,599; Pop. 2,508; US Rt 460. In northwest part of middle portion of county. Previously known as The Narrows of New River from deep gorge which New River cuts through Alleghenies; town one mile south of gorge. Became The Narrows, later shortened to Narrows.
                                                                ESS county

Newport: elev. 1,937; Pop. 100. Near county line in southeast section. During migration century, it was place of entrance to large frontier country. In 1858, mail, travelers came by stage to this place and then on other routes in different directions. As a portal or point of entrance, it was called Newport.   McCl

Pearisburg: Ry N&W; elev. 1,804; Pop. 2,268; increase Pop. 1950-60, 13%; US Rt 460. Near center of county. Captain George Pearis established ferry across New River in 1782; offered land for county courthouse; town created 1808. Celanese Corporation of North America opened 1939; produces acetate flake, yarn, and fiber.   CWHM 42+; WP: Va 447; EcD county

Pembroke: Ry N&W; elev. 1,620; Pop. 1,038; increase Pop. 1950-60, 2.7%; US Rt 460. About middle east edge of middle section of county. Lybrooks, early residents; first four postmasters, Lybrooks. Reported one early settler, Pem Lybrook; suggested Pembroke from his name. May have been influenced by Pembroke, Pembrokeshire, in Wales.   LRI

Rich Creek: Ry N&W; elev. 1,520; Pop. 748; US Rts 219, 469. In northwest portion of middle section of county. The five large springs at source of stream flowed unusually cold water; one is bottled as having medicinal benefits. The unusual springs gave the name Rich Creek to the stream, which in turn became the name of the town.   McCl

Ripplemeade: Ry N&W; elev. 1,605; Pop. 300. Near center of county. Rippling waters of New River and meadows along banks gave the community its name.   McCl

Salt Pond Mountain: 4,327 ft. Early settlers took cattle to depression for salting; they reported continuous tramping of cattle closed outlet in floor of depression and spring water filled depression forming Mountain Lake. This report led to mountain name.   McCl

Staffordville: elev. 1,731; Pop. 50. In southeast portion of middle section of county. Named for families of Staffords living in community.   McCl

Stony Creek in northeast section of county. Has many stones in its bed.
                                                                     McCl

Walker Creek in central and southwestern sections of county. Named for Dr. Thomas J. Walker in years 1748-50 while an explorer in area.   McCl

Wolf Creek in northwest section of county. Many wolves found at Big Spring, source of creek, and nearby, so name given to Wolf Creek.   McCl

GLOUCESTER COUNTY

Formed 1651; named for Gloucester, England. Area: 225 sq.mi.; Pop. 11,919; Pop. per sq.mi., 53.0; increase Pop. 1950-60, 15.2%. Land patents date from 1640. Perhaps most well-known crop daffodils, raised both for blossoms and bulbs; blossoms shipped to large eastern markets. Rank occupational groups: manufacturing, trade, public administration. Rank agricultural income: field crops, poultry, livestock. Roads 77; EcD county.

Achilles: Pop. 540; elev. 6. In extreme eastern part. From given name of local merchant. Nich

Ark: Pop. 75; elev. 9. Near central part of county. Named for Old Ark Farm, located nearby. Nich

Bena: Pop. 50. In southern portion of county. DU

Cash: Pop. 5. In northern edge western third of county. DU

Dutton: elev. 70; Pop. 25. In northeast corner of county. Named for local family. Nich

Glass: Pop. 170. Named for Mr. Henry Glass, local merchant and postmaster. Has boatyard, stopping place for semi-annual north-south hegira of large and small yatchs and cruisers. Nich

Glenns: Pop. ——; US Rt 17. In northeast area. Named for a local family. Nich

Gloucester, county seat: elev. 76; Pop. 500; US Rt 17. Has courthouse built in 1766. Was Botetourt Towne for Lord Boutetourt before became Gloucester Court House.

Gloucester Point was Tyndall's Point in colonial days, and later as Gloucester Town. A fort was built here in 1607. Was outpost of Cornwallis at Yorktown, 1781.

Hayes: Pop. 100; US Rt 17. Near York River in eastern third of county. Formerly called the 'Hook', then Hayes Store. Named for family of store-owner, Mr. Hayes. Nich

James Store: elev. 80; Pop. 15. At middle of eastern edge of northeast fourth of county. Named for Dr. Rickard James, retired physician, operated store. Nich

Maryus: Pop. 200. In extreme southeast area of county. Named for distinguished Gloucester County citizen by name of Maryus Jones. LRI

Naxera: elev. 10; Pop. 250. In northern part. Name, a coined word, to be entirely different from other postoffice names. LRI

Ordinary: Pop. 100. In west center of southeast portion. Long Bridge Ordinary built before 1730. Named for Seawell's Ordinary, colonial ordinary on stage route to and from Yorktown. Nich

Perrin: elev. 5; Pop. 300. On coast in extreme southeast part of county. Captain John Perrin built "Little England" in early 17th century. Perrin River named by General Assembly March 1, 1916. LRI

Petsworth Church at Gloucester is mentioned by a resident of Petsworth parish in 1676. It has the oldest organ in a Virginia church dating from 1737.
9 V 197; TD 9-24-1967

Pinero: Pop. 50. In central western third of county. DU

Schley: elev. 5; Pop. 175. At middle of eastern part of county. Named for Admiral Winfield Scott Schley, Spanish American war hero. Nich

Severn: elev. 8; Pop. 300. In northern part of eastern third of county.

Severn River named after Severn River in Gloucestershire, England. July 8, 1702: List of navigable rivers included Severne. Flows east across eastern third of county. LRI

Tidemill: Pop. 100. At extreme southwest corner of county. Named for a grist mill which once stood nearby and was operated by the rising and falling of the tides. The huge wooden wheel turned one way when the tide flowed into the cove, the other way when it ebbed out. Records indicate that it ground grain for Washington's army during the siege of Yorktown in 1781. Nich

Virginia Institute of Marine Science at Gloucester Point conducts biological, chemical, geological, and physical studies of the marine environment, investigates problems of the commercial and sport fishing industries, gathers information for use, development and conservation of all marine resources including fisheries, and engages in research in all marine sciences. Va Govt (1966) 55.

Ware Neck: elev. 10; Pop. 150. In north eastern central part of county. Named for peninsula or neck of land on which located. Nich

Ware River flows east in mid-eastern part of county; named for Ware River in England. Will in 1689 mentioned large estates on Ware Creek. Listed as navigable river, July 8, 1702. 5 W (1) 25; 1 V 363

White Marsh: Pop. 80. Name of ante-revolutionary and colonial residence. Record of land patent, August 24, 1637. 3 W (1) 24, 48.

Wicomico: Pop. 300. Near York River in extreme southwest area of county.

Pronounced Y kom eye ko. Indian settlement Werowocomoco. Wicocomoco, name of tribe belonging to confederacy of Powhatan. Last part of name, *moco,* a stockaded village. Said to be site where Pocohontas saved life of John Smith.

V HSSA 40

Woods Cross Roads: Pop. 16; US Rt 17. In western third of county. Named for cross roads, location of Wood's Ordinary. John Woods operated ordinary and nearby grist mill. Nich

Zanoni: Pop. 100. In east central portion of county. DU

GOOCHLAND COUNTY

Formed 1727; named for Sir William Gooch, governor of colony 1727-1749. Area: 289 sq.mi.; Pop. 9,206; Pop. per sq.mi., 31.9; increase Pop. 1950-60, 3.0%. First gold produced in Virginia in 1829; gold from placer deposits. In 1836, Louisa Railroad constructed; now part of C&O. Rank occupational groups: manufacturing, agriculture, trade. Rank agricultural income: livestock, poultry, field crops.   Roads 63

Beaverdam Creek flows along eastern edge of middle portion of county; tributary of James. Stream mentioned in earliest land grants of its area; a beaverdam causes flooding of large areas of creek bottomlands.   Weeks

Big Licking Creek flows south across the west part of the middle portion of county; tributary of James. Stream was named because springs brought salt and other minerals to surface; native animals came to lick the earth, so it was called a "lick".   Weeks

Cardwell: Pop. 30. In center near western edge of eastern third of county. Judge Richard Henry Cardwell, Confederate veteran, outstanding legislator and jurist, spoke in local areas; audience so moved by his address, that proposed his name be given to postoffice.   Weeks

Crozier: Pop. 100. In southern part of eastern third of county. Sgt. John Abbott, many years in U. S. Army, when appointed postmaster proposed name because of high regard for a former commanding officer.   Weeks

Dover Creek flows south into James and in earliest Royal land grants, the stream has this name. French Hugenots arrived in 1700 and gave the name "Calais" to south side of river; then north side was "Dover" across the channel.
                                                                     Weeks

Elk Hill (plantation) was once owned by Thomas Jefferson. Ry C&O; Pop. 25. In southern part of western third of county. A second Elk Hill plantation is nearer to the C&O station, which may have influenced the naming of the station.   Weeks

Fife: Pop. 50. In middle of southern area of west fourth of county. The Rev. James Fife, Baptist minister, led in having postoffice established.   LRI

Goochland, county seat. Pop. 400; US Rt 522.

Hadensville, named for prominent family. Pop. 10. Near county line in north portion of western third of county.   Wright 38

Irwin: Ry C&O; Pop. 5. On James in central third of county. Members of Irwin family are reported as influencing the location chosen for the railway station. The Irwin family lived at "Blythwood".   Weeks

Maidens: Ry C&O; Pop. 25; US Rt 522. In central third on James. Originally Maiden's Adventure, received name from legend that young girl crossed James to rescue her lover from Indian marauders.   Wright 30

Manakin-Sabot: Ry C&O; Pop. 250. Near James in mid-area of eastern third of county. Manakin has name from home of Monacans or Manocons, land given to Hugenot colony; in earliest years Manakintown. The *town* part of the name was dropped. Sabot Island nearby has shape resembling the wooden shoe of the French peasantry.   24 V 122; 2 V 87

Oilville: Pop. 25; US Rt 250. In northwest area of east one-third of county. A sassafras oil pressing business was conducted at this location in the latter part of 19th century, but name persists for postoffice.   Weeks

Pemberton: Ry C&O; Pop. 50. On James near middle of west third of county. Named for Captain John Pemberton who lived at "Clover Forrest".
                Weeks

Rock Castle: Ry C&O; Pop. 50. On James in southeast corner in west third of county. Takes its name from house built in 1732 on rocky bluff above James.
                Com Va 12-1957

Sandy Hook: Pop. 25; US Rt 522. In northwest portion of middle third of county. Probably named for nearby "Sandy Bottom" plus bend in road near the postoffice.   Weeks

State Farm: Ry C&O; area, 1,240 acres; Penal Institution, 1,300 residents. In eastern part of central third of county. Short term and well-behaved long term convicts; also misdemeanants to benefit by reforms rather than being confined in county jails of section of state.   WP: Va 619

State Industrial Farm for Women, 368 acres, dates from 1931; institution for rehabilitation and academic training including vocational training. Handicraft center of institution well known.   Agee 191

Tuckahoe Creek has an Indian name for Indian truffles. There may have been many of these growths. Other influences on its name may include the copying from the plantation name of Thomas Randolph (1689-1730). Besides, Tidewater Virginians spoke disparagingly of persons living between the Fall Area and the Blue Ridge as "Tuckahoes".   Weeks

GRAYSON COUNTY

Formed 1792; named for William Grayson, member Virginia Convention which adopted Federal Constitution, and one of first senators. Area: 450 sq.mi.; Pop. 17,390; Pop. per sq.mi., 38.6. Nearly one-half total area wooded. 4.5% county area in federally-owned lands. Rank occupational groups: manufacturing, agriculture, trade. Rank agricultural income: livestock, dairy, field crops.

VaVCo 7-1950

Elk Creek: elev. 2,617; Pop. 100. In northeast portion of the county. First home in Grayson in Elk Creek section about 1760. Named because early settlers killed an elk there.

Steeles 1164

Elk Creek (stream) rises in northwest central area and flows northeast into New River.

Fries: Ry N&W; elev. 2,180; Pop. 1,039. Near middle of Carroll-Grayson line. Named for local resident. Water from Eagle Bottom Creek; filtered, chlorinated.

Steeles 1165

Grant: elev. 2,791; Pop. 75. In eastern area of western third of county. Named for General U. S. Grant.

Steeles 1166

Independence: elev. 2,432; Pop. 679; US Rts 21, 58, 221. During 1849, factions pulled for Old Town and Elk Creek as location of county seat. Third group did not enter discussion. Asked which place they favored, the answer was: "We're independent; we are not taking sides". This led to locating court house near where independent people lived. Named county seat Independence. Town incorporated 1934. Earlier county seat Old Town (1793-1842) near Galax. Water supply from encased springs on Point Lookout Mountain and five wells.

VaVCo 7-1950

Mouth of Wilson: elev. 2,472; Pop. 100; US Rt 58. Near eastern area of western third of county. Name from location where Wilson Creek joins New River.

WP: Va 478

Mt. Rogers, elev. 5,720 feet, highest elevation in state. In 1883, named for William Barton Rogers, Virginia's first geologist. In Pleistocene time, many thousand years ago, the northern spruce were driven south and a small vestige of Canadian fir from the Ice Age still lives on Mount Rogers.

Com Va 5-1957; VGS: Appal. Val. 514

Rugby: elev. 3,164; Pop. 65; US Rt 58. In southeast portion of western third of county. Named for rugged mountain scenery.

Steeles 1176

Trout Dale (corporate name Troutdale): elev. 3,067; Pop. 273. Near Smyth-Grayson line in northeast portion of western third of county. Village shadowed by Mt. Rogers, is in community of hills and dales with Fox Creek affording excellent trout fishing. Name from the natural dales and the trout.   LRI

Volney: elev. 2,635; Pop. 40; US Rt 58. In southeast portion of eastern third of county. E. C. Hash, instrumental in getting postoffice established, was requested to send names from which Department might choose. Among names submitted, one was Volney, his son; that one was selected by the Department.
                                                                              LRI

Whitetop in western corner of county, elev. 5,520, is second highest peak in Virginia. Formerly called Iron Mountain. 500 acres across the crest has a fine white grass which glistens like a glacier; this explains the mountain's name.
                                                                     Com Va 5-1958

Whitetop: elev. 3,300; Ry N&W; Pop. 100. In extreme southwest corner of county. Named for nearby mountain.   LRI

GREENE COUNTY

Formed 1838; named for General Nathaniel Greene, Commander of Army of South in Revolutionary War. Area: 153 sq.mi.; Pop. 4,715; Pop. per sq.mi., 30.8. 63.7% county area in forests. 14.2% county area in Shenandoah National Park. Rank occupational groups: manufacturing, agriculture, construction. Rank agricultural income: livestock, poultry, dairy, field crops.   Roads 61

Dyke: elev. 620; Pop. 100. Near middle of Albemarle-Greene boundary.
                                                                        DU

Faith Mission Home: Brother Saford Yoder, Mennonite minister, began mission work in 1961. Two associations of Mennonites have remodeled buildings in the vicinity of Mission Home and provided staff members for guiding retarded children in appropriate learning. This home opened in 1965. In southwest corner of county.   LRI

Geer: elev. 785; Pop. 25. About middle of eastern edge of west third of county. Elijah Geer active in getting postoffice established; probably named for him.   LRI

Mission Home: Pop. 100. Mission church was erected in 1901, Whittle Memorial Episcopal Church, under the leadership of Rev. Frederick W. Neve. Other day schools developed with day schools for teaching the Bible and the subjects offered in public schools. The Rev. W. Roy Mason in 1909 saw need for mail for the vicinity and persisted so a postoffice was opened at Mission Home. Improved roads and school transportation busses have made changes in the use of buildings which were needed in the early 1900's.   LRI

Quinque: elev. 685; Pop. 25; US Rt 22. In southeast portion of county. Fifth stage stop from Richmond to Harrisonburg, so given name of Latin word for five.   LRI

Ruckersville: elev. 628; Pop. 100; US Rts 29, 33. In southeast part of county. Named for Ruckers family.   LRI

South River in northeastern portion, southern tributary of Rapidan.   LRI

Stanardsville: elev. 640; Pop. 283; US Rt 33. Land for courthouse donated by Robert Stanards. Water supply from twelve mountain springs and two wells; chlorinated.   EcD county

Swift Run, stream flowing eastward on slope of Blue Ridge. Flows swiftly.
                                                                   GSW: CF

99

GREENSVILLE COUNTY

Formed 1780; named either for Sir Richard Grenville, leader of Roanoke Island settlement in 1585, or for General Nathaniel Greene of Revolutionary Army. Area: 301 sq.mi.; Pop. 16,155; Pop. per sq.mi., 53.7. 72.3% county area forested. Virginia's leading county in acreage of cotton harvested and cotton bales sold. Rank occupational groups: manufacturing, agriculture, trade. Rank agricultural income: field crops, livestock, poultry.   EcD county

Emporia: county seat: Ry ACL, NF&D; Pop. 5,535; US Rts 58, 301. Hicksford, the first community, named for Captain Robert Hix, Indian trader, developed where Fort Road crossed Meherrin River. The courthouse was erected here in 1787. In 1796, town Belfield on opposite bank. In 1887, those two villages merged as Emporia. Emporia means "center of trade". Water supply from Meherrin River; filtered, chlorinated.   EcD county

Fontaine Creek drains southern side of county. Earliest use on maps and in documents, Fountain or Fountains. Trader with Indians, George Fountain, "free Negro", drowned in stream; trading with Tuscararas as early as 1708. Another Negro trader, John Fountain, traded with Indians in South Carolina. Fontaine, fairly recent name.   LRI

Jarratt: Ry ACL, N&W; elev. 155; Pop. 608 (Pop. in Greensville County 467); increase Pop. 1950-60, 5.9%. In northeast portion on Sussex-Greensville county line. Named for William Nicholas Jarratt who gave right-of-way to Petersburg Weldon Railroad; Jarratt family came to Sussex in 1652. Jarratt's Station, half mile south, depot on old Weldon Railroad, burned by Federal cavalrymen, May 1864. In October 1939, Johns-Manville Corporation opened world's largest plant for manufacturing insulating board.

LRI; EcD county; WP: Sussex 104

Purdy: Ry N&W; Pop 120. In northwest corner of county. Named for Wm. Purdy, large land-owner, when railroad built in community.   LRI

Skippers: Ry ACL; Pop. 75; US Rt 301. In south central portion of county. Two explanations of name. One, signalman for railroad, nicknamed "Skippers". Other, Mrs. Skipwith lived near; her name corrupted to Skippers.   LRI

HALIFAX COUNTY

Formed 1752; named for George Montaga Dunk, Earl of Halifax, British statesman. Area: 800 sq.mi.; Pop. 33,637; Pop. per sq.mi., 42.0. 49.9% county area forested. 20,600 acres of county in Buggs Island Lake. In county, first bagged, granulated tobacco called ."Bull Doze". Tobacco interests purchased and centered production in Durham, and name of product became "Bull Durham". State's leading county in pounds of flue-cured tobacco produced. Rank occupational groups: agriculture, manufacturing, trade. Rank agricultural income: field crops, livestock, poultry.   Roads 70; Va VCo 7-1952

Alton: Ry NF&D; Pop. 80. Near southern boundary in southwest fourth of county. Earlier name, Warren's Shop. Name Alton probably taken from railroad name, Atlantic and Danville.   Wooding

Buckskin Creek in southwest portion, tributary of Dan River. Land grant mentions Nov. 5, 1729.   15 V 273

Buffalo Creek in northwest portion of county. Will proved April 13, 1776, refers to land on Buffalo Creek.   17 V 72

Clover: Ry SOU; elev. 485; Pop. 261; US Rt 360. In northeast corner of county. Believed named for Clover Creek.   Wooding

Cluster Springs: Ry N&W; elev. 475; Pop. 150; US Rt 501. In south central portion of county. Early name, Black Walnut. In early twentieth century, Cluster Springs Military Academy. In approximately three mile radius, about 75 to 100 springs flowing different kinds of mineral waters.   LRI

Crystal Hill: Ry N&W; Pop. 150. In mid-center of north half of county. Large spring near village influenced name.   Wooding

Denniston: Ry N&W, NF&D; elev. 395; Pop. 50. Near middle of south boundary of county. A family by name of Denniston were the first to settle in the community.   LRI

Difficult Creek flows in the northeast portion, tributary of Dan River. Land grant mentions in 1746.   25 V 299

Halifax: Ry N&W; elev. 370; Pop. 792; US Rts 360, 501. Originally Banister, county seat in 1792. National Tobacco Festival in town. Natives of Halifax opened Craddock-Terry factory in Lynchburg in 1901; opened factory to make girls' shoes in Halifax in 1946. Water supply, two wells; chlorinated.   VaVCo 7-1952

Harmony: Ry NF&D; Pop. 40. Near middle of south boundary of county.   DU

Ingram: Pop. 40; US Rt 360. Near west county line in southwest portion. Named for first family which settled there. Jordan Lafayette Ingram, store and water mill grist owner.   Wooding

Lennig: Ry N&W; Pop. 60. Near center of north half of county. Named for daughter of railroad official.   Wooding

Mayo: Ry NF&D; Pop. 50. Near middle of extreme south half of county. Named for Mayo Creek, formerly Sugar Tree Creek.   Wooding

Nathalie: Ry N&W; Pop. 125. Near center in north fourth of county. Woman gave land for right-of-way and depot to railroad; in return she was allowed to name the station. She chose name Nathalie in honor of daughter of Major Otey, President, Lynchburg & Durham Railway Division.   LRI

Paces (RR Pace): Ry SOU; Pop. 25. In extreme southwest portion of county. Mr. Pace gave two acres for depot; station named Pace. The Postoffice Department added "s", so postoffice name is Paces.   LRI

Republican Grove: Pop. 65. In extreme northwest portion of county. First church was an all denomination building, named Republican Church; believed Republican Grove originated from that. Another tradition: one Republican here was hung in large grove; name developed.   LRI

Sandy Creek in west central portion, tributary of Dan River. Has sandy stream bed. Land survey mentions stream, February 25, 1755.
5 W (2) 190; Wooding

Scottsburg: Ry SOU; elev. 335; Pop. 188. Near middle of east half of county. Named in honor John Baytop Scott, member George Washington's staff, served in War of 1812, and Vice President of Society of Cincinnati; grave in Scottsburg neighborhood.   LRI

South Boston (independent city): Ry N&W, SOU; elev. 320; Pop. 7,200; US Rts 58, 501. Name of former village Dabb's. Captain E. F. Jefferies asked for Boston as name of town; Postoffice Department objected; he then proposed South Boston. Area: 2 sq.mi.   VaVCo 7-1952

Staunton River State Park, 1,371 acres, on shore of John H. Kerr Reservoir, has facilities for variety of recreations. Wild life has increased because of protection since park developed.   EcD county

Turbeville: Pop. 75; US Rt 58. Near center of southwest fourth of county. First name Bloomsburgh; then in 1867, Turbeville Store; later Turbeville. Postmaster in 1867, Mrs. Eugene C. Turbeville.   LRI

Vernon Hill: Pop. 20; US Rt 360. Near west boundary in northwest part of southwest fourth of county. Meetinghouse erected 1836 named Mount Vernon, located on Mountain Road. Village name from name of church.   Wooding

Virgilina: Ry NF&D; Pop. 286. On state line in southeast corner of county. Old name, Tuck's Cross Roads, for an early family. On state boundary of Virginia and North Carolina. Name from *Virgi*nia and North Caro*lina*.
Mathis 11; VaVCo 7-1952

HANOVER COUNTY

Formed 1720; named for the Electorate of Hanover, province of George I of England. Area: 466 sq.mi.; Pop. 27,550; Pop. per sq.mi., 59.1; increase Pop. 1950-60, 25.3%. Settlement began 1650. Present court house erected 1735. Nearly three-fourths county wooded. County important in making Virginia leading producer excelsior in United States. Rank occupational groups: manufacturing, trade, construction. Rank agricultural income: livestock, poultry, field crops.
Roads 84.

Ashland: Ry RF&P; elev. 220; Pop. 2,773; increase Pop. 1950-60, 6.2%; US Rt 1. Named for Kentucky home of Henry Clay who in boyhood lived at 'Slash Cottage'. Selected as site of Randolph-Macon for Men, March 1867. Water supply from South Anna; coagulated, settled, filtered, chlorinated.
TD 11-10-1935; VaVCo 10-1950, 6-1952

Beaverdam (RR Beaver Dam): Ry C&O; Pop. 50. In northwest corner of county. Beavers built large dam; community name from feature. Or, named after plantation owned by Fontaine. LRI

Doswell: Ry C&O, RF&P; Pop. 150; US Rt 1. In north central portion of county. World's largest truck stop. Town named for Bernard Doswell family; he operated race track and was largest land owner in county. LRI

Hanover: Ry C&O; elev. 75; Pop. 250; US Rt 301. County seat. Named for Duke of Hanover, afterwards George I of England, or for Prussian province from which he descended. In vicinity, Jane Porter Barrett School for Girls and Hanover Industrial School, state institutions. Gannett 149

Hylas: Pop. 25. On county boundary in southwest portion of county. DU

Mechanicsville: Pop. 1,500; US Rt 360. Near southern boundary in eastern third of county. Named after wheelwright and blacksmith shop which were at forks of road here. Much of action in Seven Days' Battle in 1862 here. Page

Montpelier: Ry SOU; Pop. 150; US Rt 33. Near mid-area of extreme west portion of county. Probably named in honor of Mr. James Madison's home in Orange County (Virginia) since Mr. Madison's wife Dolly came from Scotchtown in Hanover County. Page

New Found River flows east through central western portion, tributary of South Anna. Probably an early settler stumbled upon stream unexpectedly.
Page

Noel: Ry C&O; Pop. 65. Near north boundary in northwest portion of west fourth of county. Named for John R. Noel when railroad bought right-of-way through middle of his plantation. LRI

Randolph-Macon College for Men. Chartered 1830; incorporation as oldest Methodist College in America. Begun in Boydton in 1832. Named for John Randolph and Nathaniel Macon. Liberal arts; widely known for unusually strong instruction.   Ann.Bul.

Rockville: Pop. 30. Near south boundary in middle of west fourth of county. Probably from many rocks in fields thereabout.   Page

Slash Christian Church built in 1729, possibly oldest frame structure in America. On County highway 657 to a junction with County highway 656; right here 0.2 mile to church. Like its contemporaries, has steep gabled roof with denticulated cornice. Used now by a congregation of the Christian denomination since 1942; it was formerly church of St. Paul parish. Surroundings called "The Slashes" because of swampy nature.   WP:Va 366; TD 7-17-1955

Studley: Pop. 40. Near center at west edge of eastern third of county. Named after English town of same name by ancestry of Patrick Henry.   Page

Taylors Creek, tributary of South Anna. Named after Taylor family who intermarried with Morris family by whom its nearby area was originally owned.
                                                                         Page

HENRICO COUNTY

Formed 1634; named for Henricopolis, founded 1611, which was named for Henry, Prince of Wales; name shortened to Henrico. Area: 232 sq.mi.; Pop. 117,339; Pop. per sq.mi., 505.8; increase Pop. 1950-60, 20.8%. Battles in 1862 and 1864 in county. About half county wooded. Rank occupational groups: manufacturing, trade, public utilities. Rank agricultural income: poultry, livestock, dairy.

Stewart 58; Roads 84

Bosher Dam, on James, eight miles above Richmond, named for Bosher family. Constructed as part of James River-Kanawha Canal system to turn water from James into canal then carrying freight and passengers. Present use to develop electric power and manufacture of paper; also, auxiliary source of municipal water for City of Richmond.

LRI

Richard E. Byrd Flying Field: named for American naval officer and polar explorer (1888-1957). Port located about four miles east of Richmond; served by leading airlines. Dedicated April 1, 1950. Popularly known as Byrd Airport.

LRI

Deep Creek along south portion of west boundary of county; tributary of James. Land grant mentions Deep Creek, August 5, 1751.

2 V 319

Glen Allen: Ry RF&P; elev. 855; Pop. 900. Near north boundary in west third of county. Glen Allen, resort built in late seventies. Name received from Benjamin B. Allen.

Lutz: RA 132

Highland Springs: Pop. 7,000; US Rt 33. In north portion near boundary of east and middle thirds of county. High area in Fall Zone with many springs trickling down hills and slopes. These features caused town's founder to give name Highland Springs. Water from six wells.

LRI

Laburnum Manor: Pop. 2,500. Laburnum was the lovely estate of Mr. and Mrs. Bryan; its name became the name of a street and a district.

Munford 43; LRI

Lakeside: Pop. 21,000. Lakeside Park, now Lakeside Country Club.

Munford 130

Laurel: elev. 220; Pop. 500. In east area of western third of county. Name of street links with community name.

LRI

Metro (sub-station postoffice): Pop. ———.

DU

Pine Dell: Pop. ———.

DU

Richmond National Battlefield Park: eight tracts totaling 684 acres include locations of Battles of 1862 and 1864. Markers along 55-miles Battlefield Park Route. Placed under National Park Service 1933. Markers indicate trenches, fortifications, houses used as headquarters, field hospital, and small museum.

EcD county; Harrison 32.

Ridge: Pop. 23,000. Takes name from Ridge Road, a principal thoroughfare west of the city limits.   LRI

Sandston: Pop. 6,000; US Rt 60. In north portion about boundary of east and middle thirds of county. Named in honor of Oliver J. Sands, important leader in forming village. Location had large munition plant in World War I. Water from four wells.   LRI

Tuckahoe: Pop. ———. The old Randolph plantation. *Tockawhougha,* root of Indian turnip.   Stanard 220; Com Va 3-1935

Turkey Island named in 1607 by Captain Christopher Newport on voyage of discovery up James River. In 1604, became property of William Randolph, founder of Randolph family.   SCWSHM 9; Cavalcade 42

Varina, county seat until 1752. In southeast portion about boundary of east and middle thirds of county. Varina parish mentioned regarding lease, March 21, 1633.   2 V 312

Westwood: Pop. 1,400. Westwood was name of Brockenborough plantation.

Stanard 192

HENRY COUNTY

Formed 1776; named for Patrick Henry, advocate of independence, elected governor four times. First county along southern boundary to take an American name. Named for first governor of Virginia as an independent state. Area: 384 sq.mi.; Pop. 40,335; Pop. per sq.mi., 105.0. 65.2% county area forested. County ranks second as furniture manufacture in the United States. Rank occupational groups: manufacturing, trade, construction. Rank agricultural income: field crops, livestock, dairy.   Roads 72; VGb 25; VaVCo 9-1947

Axton: Ry N&W; Pop. 200; elev. 1,020; US Rt 58. Near mid-area of county's east boundary. Earlier name, Old Center. Nearby family house, Axton Lodge, home of Congressman; received request regarding naming of postoffice; promptly replied proposing Axton. Said to be only postoffice in United States having Axton name.   LRI

Bassett (census name Bassetts): Ry N&W; elev. 740; Pop. 3,700. Unincorporated. Named for John H. Bassett family, descendants of colonial family, whose chair factory was nucleus of village. In northwest portion of county.
WP: Va 610

Collinsville: Pop. 4,300; US Rt 220. In southwest portion of northeast fourth of county. In 1931, a Mr. Collins opened a non-battery flash light plant. In 1945, postoffice established and given name Collinsville. Now thriving shopping and residential unincorporated community.   LRI

Fieldale: Ry C&NW, N&W; Pop. 1,499; increase Pop. 1950-60, 15.7%. In southwest area of northwest fourth of county. Field interests built model community three miles upstream from Martinsville on Smith River; Fieldcrest Mills, one of three leading towel manufacturers in United States. Built 1919.
WP: Va 610; VaVCo 9-1947

Martinsville (independent city): Area: 10 sq.mi.; Ry C&NW, N&W; elev. 1,025; Pop. 20,000; increase Pop. 1950-60, 9.0%; US Rts 58, 220. Town established 1791, named for Joseph Martin, pioneer. Became county seat 1793. General Joseph Martin, Indian fighter and brigadier general of state militia in 1793. Incorporated 1873; independent city 1928. City has largest nylon plant in world. Standard Garment Company, greatest pants makers in world. Water supply, reservoir on Beaver Creek; filtered, chlorinated.   EcD county; VaVCo 9-1950

Patrick Henry College opened 1962; two-year community college. In Martinsville.   EcD county

Ridgeway: Ry N&W; elev. 3,550; Pop. 524; increase Pop. 1950-60, 19.0%; US Rt 220. Near state boundary in south central part of county. Named by

Samuel Sheffield, early store keeper. Formerly tobacco market. Water supply, five wells. Steeles 1175; WP: Va 611

South Martinsville: (has branch postoffice): (part of Martinsville).

Spencer: elev. 900; Pop. 200; US Rt 58. Near western part of southwest fourth of county. Early family of Spencer in community; important in business.
Hill: History Henry County, 263+.

Stanleytown: elev. 1,065; Pop. 500. Near central in northwest fourth of county. Thomas Bohnson Stanley built furniture plant near Bassett; village sprang up and the name "Stanleytown" was assumed. Pedigo 253

HIGHLAND COUNTY

Formed 1847; has highest mean altitude of Virginia's counties which explains its name; has sometimes been called "Little Switzerland of America". Area: 416 sq.mi.; Pop. 3,221; Pop. per sq.mi., 7.7. Nearly three-fourths county area in forests. Annual Maple Sugar Festival in early March. Occupational groups rank: farming, manufacturing, construction. Agricultural income rank: livestock, poultry, field crops.   EcD county; Roads 92

Blue Grass: elev. 2,464; Pop. 75. In north portion near West Virginia. Earliest name, Hull's Store; later Crabbottom. Was given present name by U. S. Board of Geographic Names in early 1950's.   Morton: High 161

Doe Hill: elev. 2,514; Pop. 50. Near mid-point of West Virginia line. Near sources of Bullpasture; name links to foothill ridges where doe were formerly seen. Had store earlier than 1850.   Morton: High 161

Headwaters at beginning of tributary of Calfpasture River. Elev. 2,081; Pop. 10. In southwest portion of northeast one-fourth of county.   Steeles 1167

Hightown: elev. 3,200; Pop. 20; US Rt 250. In north portion about four miles east of West Virginia line. Located close to source of tributaries of James flowing south; and source of tributaries of Potomac flowing north.   LRI

Jack Mt., alt. 4,400+; two miles east of Monterey. Pioneer Jackson's name was reported to have been shortened to Jack.   LRI

Lantz Mt., alt. 4,000+, crosses county three or four miles from West Virginia line, 5½ miles northeast of Monterey. Was probably named for Bernard Lantz, a farmer in the early 1700's.   LRI

McDowell: elev. 2,107; Pop. 127; increase Pop. 1950-60, 18.6%; US Rt 250. About center of southeast half of county. Named for James McDowell, former governor of Virginia. Oldest village in Highland County; earliest name Sugar Tree Bottom; then Crab Run. Stonewall Jackson successfully beat off advance under Milroy, May 8, 1862, his position on hills just south of town.
Gannett 194; SCWHM 17.

Mill Gap: elev. 2,344; Pop. 50. In extreme west part of county. Name suggested by presence of Schultz's Mill at gap in mountains.   Steeles 1172

Monterey: elev. 2,881; Pop. 270; increase Pop. 1950-60, 3.0%; US Rt 250. An early name was Bell's Place, from first settler at site in 1774. County seat, was Highland, but when General Zachary Taylor became president, name changed to honor his Mexican victory at Monterey. In Spanish, name means "mountain of the king".   Gannett 213; EcD county

Monterey Mountain, elev. 4,100+; 1½ miles northwest of Monterey; name from nearby village.

Mustoe: elev. 2,391; Pop. 25; US Rt 220. Near center of west one-fourth of county. Named for local family.   Steeles 1172.

Ramshorn (mountain), alt. 4,530 ft., on Virginia-West Virginia line, 8½ miles southwest of Monterey. Name of formation arose from its appearance.
Kenny: West Virginia Place Names, 519.

Riven Rocks, alt. 4,381, 4½ miles northwest of Monterey, lightning strikes quite often. Probably "riven" refers to broken cliff or crags.   HR 1-25-1966

Sounding Knob, alt. 4,400+, five miles south of Monterey, the name from "hollow sound produced by footfalls on a certain limited spot", probably the roof of a cavern.   HR 1-25-1966

South Branch of Potomac flows north from center of county into West Virginia.

Tamarack Ridge, alt. 4,400, on Virginia-West Virginia line, northwest of Monterey, was probably named for larch species known as Tamarack pine.
HR 1-25-1966

Vanderpool: Pop. 25; elev. 2,595. Is east of center of west one-fourth of county. Was formerly Gaul Town, for first settler; then Woodsborough. A nearby mountain pass was used as Indian Trail; first man to pass through on horseback, Vanderpool.   Steeles 1179

North Branch of the Potomac rises near Hightown and flows to the northeast into West Virginia.

ISLE OF WIGHT COUNTY

Formed 1634; Warrascoyak, first name of shire, named for Indians living there. In 1637, name changed to Isle of Wight after island in British Channel. First settlement on Lowne's Creek, northeast boundary of county. Area: 319 sq.mi.; Pop. 17,164; Pop. per sq.mi., 53.8; increase Pop. 1950-60, 15.1%. First court house on Glebe Farm. One-half county area forested. Rank occupational groups: manufacturing, agriculture, trade. Rank agricultural income: field crops, livestock, dairy.   Huntley 351; EcD county

Battery Park: Pop. 240. In southeast portion on James. Earlier names Patesville, Newport, and then in 1787 Old Town. "Todd's Battery" located in either 1812 or 1861-65. As memorial to coastal battery units, name became Battery Park in 1891. Shipping point for water freight and harbor for fishing boats.
                                                              LRI

Carrolltown: Pop. 70; US Rt 258. In southeast corner of county. In early 1870's, a Mr. Carroll owned small store, Carroll's Shop. Purchaser of store saw need for mail service and petitioned for postoffice. Store owner was appointed postmaster at Carrollton in 1877.   LRI

Carrsville: Ry SAL; Pop. 200; US Rt 58. In southwest corner of county. Named for resident of vicinity when railroad was built through community.
                                                              LRI

Isle of Wight CH, county seat since 1800. Named for English island. Pop. 60; US Rt 258.

Pagan River drains eastern side of county; tributary of James. Given name from unChristianized Indians.

Rescue: Pop. 325. In southeast area near James. Earlier name, Smith's Neck, from land grant to William Smith in 1645. One explanation of present name: first postmaster, William T. Carter, given privilege of naming postoffice. Man riding a mule had been bringing mail from a distant postoffice. Carter's statement was: "The mail was rescued from the mule's back." Another explanation was the Methodists established a church; the founders stressed that they were rescuing people from sin.   LRI

Rushmere: Pop. 125. In northeast area near James. Earlier name, Ferguson's Wharf. Another postoffice in Virginia had the same name. Daughter of prominent citizen suggested Rushmere after town in Scotland, meaning "running water".   LRI

St. Luke's Church, four miles southeast of Smithfield on Virginia highway 10, is said to be the oldest English-constructed building now standing in America;

the original wall supports the present structure. It is believed it was erected in 1632 so it is contemporary with Jamestown colony; it is Gothic in design.

EcD county; VGb 9.

Smithfield begun 1662 on land owned by an Arthur Smith, an early colonial. Pop. 917; US Rt 258. Had been settlement more than 100 years before incorporated in 1752. Original county seat. Old Masonic Hall at Smithfield, second oldest in America, built 1787. Smithfield hams processed from hogs raised in peanut belt of Virginia and North Carolina. Municipal water supply from wells.

Roads 30; VGb 9; VaVCo 9-1950

Walters: Ry N&W; Pop. 125. About mid-point near west boundary of south half of county. Earlier name, Fraiser's Siding. Another station on railroad was named Joyners. About 1909, Mr. Walter Joyner, native of community, persistently worked for depot at location, so railroad named station Walters to avoid confusion.   LRI

Windsor: Ry N&W; elev. 85; Pop. 579; increase Pop. 1950-60, 28.3%; US Rt 259. In eastern part of west third of county. Name selected by Mrs. Mahone from novel of Sir Walter Scott. Water supply from wells.   VaVCo 9-1953

Zuni: Ry N&W; Pop. 155; US Rt 460. On Blackwater River about mid-point west county boundary. One explanation of name was from Scott novel.

VaVCo, Sept 1953, 58.

JAMES CITY COUNTY

Formed as one of the original shires in 1654; James City was original name of Jamestown, named for James I, whose commission gives the well-known King James translation of the Bible. Area: 148 sq.mi.; Pop. 11,539; Pop. per sq.mi., 78.0; increase Pop. 1950-60, 82.7%. 71.2% county area forested. Rank occupational groups: trade, manufacturing, public administration. Rank agricultural income: field crops, livestock, dairy, poultry.   Roads 86

Common Glory: Drama blends history, romance, music, and high comedy. Story includes from 1774 to 1781. Means common glory to all man. 12-acre wooded tract; provides reflection of wooded hills in placid water. Includes Matoaka Lake; Matoaka is real name of Pocohontas.
                              VaVCO 7-1949; Kibler: VHL 118

Eastern State Hospital at Dunbar, three miles west of Williamsburg. First building erected at Williamsburg 1773. Oldest institution for mentally ill in America.   Kibler 75

Jamestown: Pop. 5. Name in honor of King James I of England. Early colonists found water six fathoms in depth near shore so ships were moored to trees; became first site permanent English settlement May 13, 1607. Built stockade; became town; colonial capital until burned in Bacon's Rebellion in 1676. Site of first legislative assembly, July 30, 1619. Site where first Negroes landed in 1619. Seat of government until moved to Williamsburg in April 1699. Sea wall built 1901-1905 protects from continued wearing away by river.
                              Huntley 134; VGb 63; Tate 148.

Lightfoot: Ry C&O; Pop. 300. About mid-point near east boundary of county. Named for Philip Lightfoot, lawyer-merchant, prior to 1748.
                              Huntley 166

Norge: Ry C&O; Pop. 100; US Rt 60. Near southwest part of northwest fourth of county. Name honors ancestral homeland of Norway; farmers from Dakotas and Wisconsin moved to community to live in less rigorous surroundings.
                              VaVCo 11-1946

Toano: Ry C&O; elev. 100; Pop. 250; US Rt 60. Near center of northwest fourth of county. Was Burnt Ordinary after ordinary burned. An Indian name thought to have originated from chief Powhatan's tribe.   LRI

College of William and Mary: Cornerstone laid August 8, 1693. Second oldest in America; first royal college in America; chartered by King William and Queen Mary. In 1779, became a university; in 1906, became a state institution.

Among list of firsts: first and only American university to receive its charter from the Crown. Became co-educational in 1918.

First and only American college to receive a Coat of Arms from the College of Heralds, 1694.

First college in the United States to have a full faculty: President, six professors, 1729.

First to establish an intercollegiate fraternity, the Phi Beta Kappa, December 5, 1776.

First college to have the Honor System, 1779.

First college to have elective system of studies.

First college to have a school of Modern Languages, 1779.

First college to have a School of Municipal and Constitutional Law, 1779.

First college to teach Political Economy, 1784.

First college to have a School of Modern History, 1803.   Ann.Bul.

Williamsburg: Ry C&O; elev. 90; Pop. 10,000; increase Pop. 1950-60, 43.4%; US Rt 60. Oldest incorporated city in America; restoration of Colonial Williamsburg by John D. Rockefeller, Jr., attempts to restore accurately and preserve permanently most significant portions of this historical and typical city of America's colonial period. Settled about 1632; first called Middle Plantation; served as outpost against Indian invasion. When became capital in 1699, renamed Williamsburg in honor of William III of England. Received royal charter as "city incorporate"; today is an independent city. Capital of Virginia 1699-1780. Assembly of Virginia one day each session meets in Capital at Williamsburg as oldest legislative body in America, dating from August 9, 1619.

Among firsts in Williamsburg:

Wren Building built in 1695 is oldest academic structure in America.

Bruton Parish Church has served continuously longer than any other Episcopalian Church in America; present building erected 1710 and 1715. (Bruton Parish name from Bruton in Somersetshire, England.)

Old Masonic Hall, torn down in 1912, location of first Grand Lodge of Virginia established.

First printing office south of Potomac in 1730.

Water supply: impounding reservoir; filtered, chlorinated.
            Va Doc 25, 28++; EcD county; Kibler CVS 25; Kibler HL 59

KING AND QUEEN COUNTY

Formed 1691; named for King William and Queen Mary. Settlement began 1625. Area: 318 sq.mi.; Pop. 5,889; Pop. per sq.mi., 18.5. About 77 percent county area forested. Rank occupational groups: manufacturing, agriculture, trade. Rank agricultural income: poultry products, vegetables, field crops.

EcD county

Bruington: Pop. 50. Mid-point in east part of west third of county. Named for Bruington family who lived in community years ago. LRI

Cauthornville: Pop. 50. In northwest part of west third of county. George Cauthorn lived here; *ville* from *villa* meaning residence. Mr. Cauthorn buried on his property. LRI

Cologne: Pop. 25. Near mid-point in extreme east part of county. Store-owner saw bottles Hoyt's cologne on shelf; so proposed that as name of post-office. LRI

Crouch: Pop. 40. Slightly north of middle of county. DU

Cumnor: Pop. 35. In center of county. DU

Dragonsville: Pop. 100. In northeast portion of county near Dragon Run. February 5, 1765, agreement regarding 800 acres adjoining Dragon Plantation or Green Branch. 37 V 366

Gressitt: Pop. 300. Near extreme south part of county. Named for two brothers, operators of crossroads store. Community had been known as Gressitt's Corner; became Gressitt. LRI

Helmet: Pop. 40. In northern portion of county. DU

Indian Neck: Pop. 22. In northwest part of west fourth of county. Named from Indian Neck Woods. LRI

Ino: Pop. 75. About middle and near northeast boundary of county. DU

King and Queen Courthouse: Pop. 65.

Little Plymouth: Pop. 75. Near western part of eastern third of county.
DU

Mascot: Pop. 50. On Dragon Run near northeast corner of county. DU

Mattaponi means "Bad Bread"; small Indian tribe. Elev. 11; Pop. 300. Near York River in east fourth of county. Oldest church building in county built in 1690; in church yard are tombs of Carter Bruxton, signer of Declaration of Independence. Governor of Virginia granted to Baptists colonial church in 1824, and they have used it ever since.

VaVCo 2-1953; Roads 39; Bagby 64

Newtown: Pop. 65. Central location near west boundary of county. Named because present village grew about one-half mile from older village, so name applied.   ESS county

Owenton: Pop. 150. About mid-point in west fourth of county.   DU

Plainview: Pop. 50. In southern part of extreme east part of county. Named because of a plain view over wide and open fields.   ESS county 19

Saint Stephens Church: Pop. 50; US Rt 360. In southeast part of west third of county. Colonial county had three parishes; one was St. Stephens. When Baptist congregation organized in 1842, from parish name, became St. Stephens Baptist Church. Later, postoffice opened and named Saint Stephens Church.

LRI

Shackelfords (Centreville): Pop. 80. Central location near east boundary of county. In earlier years, prominent family named Shackelford lived here.   LRI

Shanghai: Pop. 100; elev. 101. In southeast portion of eastern third of county. Reported that postoffice name was chosen from list of names submitted by Post Office Department.   LRI

Stevensville: Pop. 150. Near center of county. Named for Stevens family among first to patent land in area, in late 1600's. A large state-operated fish hatchery is nearby.   LRI; EcD county

Walkerton: Pop. 200. On Mattaponi River in southwest portion of middle third of county. Named for family who settled there in 1663; Dr. Thomas Walker is most distinguished of family.   LRI

KING GEORGE COUNTY

Formed 1720; named for King George I. Settlement began in late 1600's. Area: 178 sq.mi.; Pop. 7,243; Pop. per sq.mi., 40.7; increase Pop. 1950-60, 7.9%. James Madison, author of American Constitution and President of United States, was born in county. 65% county area forested. Rank occupational groups: manufacturing, public administration, trade. Rank agricultural income: livestock, field crops, poultry.   Roads 60

Dahlgren: Pop. 475. In northeast portion on Potomac. U. S. Naval Proving Ground on Virginia shore named for Admiral Dahlgren. Proving ground includes 4.3% county area.   Wilstach 346

Dogue: Pop. 25. In southwest portion near Rappahannock. Named for tribe of Indians which once had camp on river in area.   LRI

Goby: Pop. 35. Near Potomac in northwest portion of county. Report that name was picked at random.   LRI

Index: Pop. 100. Near extreme southeast corner of county. First postmaster looking in book for names to consider, saw *index* at top of page; chose that name.   LRI

Jersey: Pop. 30. Near center southeast fourth of county. Named for most popular cattle in area at time of naming.   LRI

King George, county seat: Pop. 240.

Ninde: Pop. 35. In east central part of county. Nindes Store was named for local merchant.   Steeles 1173

Owens: Pop. 70; US Rt 301. On Potomac in northeast part of county. Choctanack, first King George meeting place, became Owens Post Office. Owens was named for local merchant in whose store postoffice was located.

Steeles 1173

Rollins Fork: Pop. 25. In extreme southeast area. Was named for local merchant.   Steeles 1176

Sealston: Pop. 150. In extreme southwest corner of county.   DU

Shiloh: Pop. 40. Near middle of southwest fourth of county. Named for an early Baptist Church.   Steeles 1176

Tetotum: Pop. 40. Near Potomac in southeast part of northeast fourth of county. Named for an Indian tribe in area.   LRI

KING WILLIAM COUNTY

Formed 1701; named for King William III. Area: 278 sq.mi.; Pop. 7,563; Pop. per sq.mi., 27.2. Eastern tip of county had settlers in 1653; courthouse built about 1725 has been in continuous use. Carter Braxton, Signer of Declaration of Independence, lived here. 63.6% county area wooded. Rank occupational groups: manufacturing, agriculture, trade. Rank agricultural income: dairy, livestock, field crops.   Roads 85; EcD county

Aylett: Pop. 60; US Rt 360. On Mattaponi River in northeast portion of west half of county. Original grant to Aylett family, Hugenots, by King Charles II.   Clarke 15

Epworth: Pop. 25. Epworth Methodist Church was about 100 yards from earlier location of postoffice.   LRI

King William, county seat. Pop. 40. Courthouse built about 1725.

Lanesville: Pop. 40. Formerly known as The Bonnet. Early family named Lane.   LRI

Mangohick: Pop. 50. In extreme western part. A drunken man had hiccoughs. Indian said: "Man-go-hick".   LRI

Manquin: Pop. 100; US Rt 360. In south central portion of county. Earlier name Brandywine postoffice. Nearby stream, Moncurin Creek; postoffice name derived from stream name.   LRI

Mattaponi Indian Reservation in northeastern corner of county. Located in 1668; 65 acres. List Virginia Indians, 1670 included Mattaponeys.
                                                        WP: Va 601; 14 V 289

Pamunkey Indian Reservation in southeastern part of county. Located in 1677. Pamunkey is derived from *pam* which means sloping or slanting, and *anki* which means hill or rising upland. Reservation of 875 acres almost surrounded by curves of York River; State of Virginia exercises a kindly supervision over the government of the tribe. Both Mattaponi and Pamunkey tribes are remnants of the Powhatan Confederacy. Pottery is an interesting commercial enterprise of the Pamunkeys.   Gottmann 601; Pendleton 377

Port Richmond: elev. 23; Pop. 400; incorporated 1924. Located on Southern Railway and on Pamunkey and York Rivers so anticipated would become the Port of Richmond; development did not materialize. Town now a part of West Point. This farm town has developed since 1920; intensive experimental truck-farming is conducted on 10-acre farms.   LRI

Sweet Hall: Ry SOU; elev. 40; Pop. 50. Sweet Hall, colonial home, built 1720. Old Sweet Hall Ferry established about same year.   Clarke 22

West Point: Ry SOU; elev. 16; Pop. 1,676. First name, King and Queen; next Delaware; in 1691, port of entry; named Delaware in 1705. Grant of land to Captain John West. In 18th century, the town was called The Point. Local citizens added the West family name. Chesapeake Corporation organized in 1916; has large pulp mill; company program includes fire control, tree planting, planned harvesting; and improved products.   Com Va 1-1954; WP: Va 465

LANCASTER COUNTY

Formed 1652; named for Lancaster, England. Area: 142 sq.mi.; Pop. 9,174; Pop. per sq.mi., 64.6; Pop. increase 1950-60, 6.2%. Settled shortly after 1640. Millenbeck on west side Corotoman River in southwest corner of county, first county seat. Queenstown, early port on Rappahannock River. Epping Forest, birthplace of Washington's mother, in county. Rank occupational groups: manufacturing, trade, agriculture. Rank agricultural income: field crops, poultry, livestock. Roads 59; VaVCo 9-1952

Alfonso: Pop. 55. In northern part of western third of county. Named for Alfonso Barrack. Clarence E. Barrack was postmaster after office re-established September 1899. Peirce

Antipoison Creek. John Smith stung by stingray; Indians treated wound; name of stream became Antipoison Creek. LRI

Christ Church, three miles north of Irvington, built in 1732, on site of older church erected 1669-1675; least meddled with of all old Virginia churches. Considered probably the finest Greek-cruciform colonial church building in America. Roads 24; VaVCo 9-1952; EcD county

Corrotoman River. Corotoman Indians lived on stream until 1790, so named for them. Listed as navigable river, July 8, 1702. Pronounced: curry-tomon. Peirce; 1 V 363

Foxwells: Pop. 100. On peninsula in southeastern part of county. Was Fisherman until 1919. Name changed to Foxwells, February 4, 1919, when Susie E. Foxwell became postmistress. Peirce

Indian Creek. May 22, 1650: Grant tract 600 acres lying on north side Rappahannock beginning at "Gum tree standing on a poynt nigh ye mouth of Indian Creeke". 38 V 389

Irvington: Pop. 570. In southern portion of county. Name Carters Creek, 1873-1891. Became Irvington 1891. Name derived from early family named Irving. Has summer recreations; packing houses of seafood; also plants extracting menhaden oil and manufacturing fertilizer. WP: Va 553; LRI

Kilmarnock: Pop. 927; elev. 89; increase Pop. 1950-60, 34.5%. In central area of east boundary of county. Named for town in Scotland. Steeles 1169

Lancaster: Pop. 100. County seat.

Lively: Pop. 300. Near mid-eastern part of western third of county. Many large oak trees nearby so village named Lively Oak. Later, shortened to Lively; probably oaks were dying. LRI

Merry Point: Pop. 60. On West Branch of Corotoman River in southwest portion of county. Mary's Mount (present Merry Point) was settled by Daniel Cockin, Jr., before 1630. Report of marriage of resident of Merry Point, Nov. 12, 1748.   Roads 52; 31 V 380

Mollusk: Pop. 325. Near southeastern part of western third of county. DU

Morattico: Pop. 250. In northeastern portion of county. Name of Indians; location at mouth of Morattico Creek.   Peirce

Nuttsville: Pop. 150. Near center of northwest portion of county. Name originated from Col. Wm. O. Nutt, resident of Northumberland County. Peirce

Ottoman: Pop. 75. In western part of southwest portion of county. Name proposed Corotoman; P. O. Department cut name to Ottoman.   Peirce

Palmer: Pop. 75. On isthmus in southeastern part. Named for first postmaster, John A. Palmer, Jr.   Peirce

Regina: Pop. 25. Near northeast corner of county.   DU

Tabbs Creek: Father Tabb was early explorer of stream.   LRI

Weems: Pop. 250. In north central portion of county, near Rappahannock. Disposing of "Corotoman" estate in 1886, commissioner persuaded the steamboat "Mason L. Weems" to stop if a wharf was built and named in honor of steamboat line.   Rappahannock Herald, 4-20-1967

White Stone: Pop. 395. In eastern third of county. Location was called The White Stone. John Andrew Twigg Bridge (Rappahannock Bridge) connects to Gray's Point in Middlesex. Near White Stone Beach, fishing and salt-water swimming. Noted for sea industries.   Peirce

Windmill Point Creek in extreme southeast part of county. Name probably from windmills in early day.   LRI

LEE COUNTY

Formed 1792; named for Henry (Light-Horse Harry) Lee, Revolutionary soldier and Governor of Virginia, 1791-1794. Area: 434 sq.mi.; Pop. 25,824; Pop. per sq.mi., 59.5. About 45% county area wooded. 6.3% county area in Jefferson National Forest and Cumberland Gap National Historical Park. Has distinction that its county seat is nearer to capital city in six other states than to Richmond. State's leading county in bushels grain yield per acre of corn. Rank occupational groups: agriculture, trade, educational services. Rank agricultural income: field crops, livestock, dairy. Roads 95

Ben Hur: Ry L&N; Pop. 400. In northwest part of east third of county. Named for Lew Wallace's book, Ben Hur, by friend of author. Laningham

Blackwater: Pop. 500. In southeast part of middle third of county. Sawdust from sawmills on stream washed into stream and turned water black.
Laningham

Cumberland Gap, where Virginia, Tennessee, and Kentucky join was named, April 13, 1750, by Dr. Thomas Walker for Duke of Cumberland, son of George II. Was route through which pioneers passed on way to Kentucky. US Rts 25E, 58. SCVSHM 21

Cumberland Gap National Historical Park — Nation's largest historical park, 20,184 acres; 7,400 acres in Virginia. Dedicated July 4, 1959. Gabriel Arthur passed through in 1673. Cudjo's Cave and the Pinnacle in park are in Lee County. Pinnacle has observation tower overlooking several states.
Com Va 6-1959, 17, 72.

Dryden: Ry L&N; elev. 1,430; Pop. 500. Near center of east third of county. Named for an early settler. Laningham

Ewing: Ry L&N; elev. 1,390; Pop. 500; US Rt 58. Near east edge of west third of county. Named for early settlers, two Ewing families.
Laningham

Gibson Station (RR Gibsons Station): Ry L&N; Pop. 100; US Rt 58. In extreme southwest part of county. Named for Gibson families, early settlers.
Laningham

Jonesville: elev. 1,530; Pop. 711; increase Pop. 1950-60, 17.7%; US Rt 58. Established as county seat in 1792. Named for Frederick Jones who donated land for site of Jonesville. Water supply from spring; chlorinated. Laningham

Keokee: Ry SOU; Pop. 500. In extreme northeast part of county. Was Crab Orchard until 1905. Land leased by coal company, mine opened 1905. The wife of one of the officials of coal company, Mr. Perrin, had name Keokee; she was of Indian descent. The company was Keokee Coal and Coke Company, and village became Keokee, a modern coal-mining village. Water supply from watershed in Kentucky, carried by tunnel through Black Mountain; chlorinated. LRI

Newman Ridge in extreme southeast part of county. Named in winter 1761-62 for Walter Newman, who was Long Hunter. VaVCo 11-1949

Niggerhead Rock, near Pennington Gap, shows profile of neck and head.
Bodine 138

Pennington Gap (RR Pennington): Ry L&N; elev. 1,380; Pop. 1,799; US Rt 421. In central west part of east third of county. A Pennington family settled early near the gap in the mountain. Laningham

Rose Hill: Ry L&N; elev. 1,445; Pop. 600. In northeast part of west third of county. Nearby hill over-run with wild roses led to name. LRI

St. Charles: Ry L&N, SOU; Pop. 368. In northwest part of east third of county. Named for Charles Bondurant, an early coal operator and promoter.
Laningham

Wallen Creek rises in northern portion of county near Scott County boundary and flows southwest and becomes tributary of Powell River. Elisha Wallen organized company of hunters about 1776; stream received name after him.
Summers 76

Wallen Ridge named for Elisha Wallen, Long Hunter, in winter 1761-62.
VaVCo 11-1949

Woodway: elev. 1,459; Pop. 400. Near central west part of east third of county. Named for Mr. Woods, first postmaster. Laningham

LOUDOUN COUNTY

Formed 1758; named for Lord Loudoun, titular governor of Virginia. Area: 517 sq.mi.; Pop. 24,549; Pop. per sq.mi., 47.5; increase Pop. 1950-60, 2.5%. Earliest settlers about 1700. Scotch Irish and Welsh settlers about 1730. German settlers about 1730. Forests cover one-third county area. Value of dairy products and livestock make county rank first among Virginia counties. County leads state in acres harvested and bushels winter wheat produced. Rank occupational groups: agriculture, trade, construction. Rank agricultural income: livestock, dairy, poultry.   Roads 87; VaVCo 1-1953

Aldie: Pop. 100; US Rt 50. In mid-center southern portion of county. Name in tribute Aldie Castle in Scotland, the seat of that Mercer family from which Charles Fenton Mercer believed himself descended. In 1810, Charles F. Mercer, prominent citizen, laid out the town.

Williams: Legends of Loudoun, 167

Arcola: Pop. 40. In southeast corner of county.   DU

Ashburn: Ry W&OD; elev. 298; Pop. 200. Near mid-center northern portion of county. Earlier name Farmville. Dr. Lee granted right-of-way and donated land for station in 1869; station given name of his farm.

ESS county 35

Bluemont: elev. 793; Pop. 225. Near mid-point of west boundary in southwest quarter of county. Was Snickersville, from landowner, Edward Snickers. In 1900, named Bluemont, situated at southeastern base of Blue Ridge.

ESS county 30+

Broad Run Farms in east third of county. Broad Run rises in Rappahannock Range, is tributary of Occoquan. Broad Run Farms border creek which gives development its name. Broad Run mentioned in land grant about 1725. Bridge across Broad Run in 1755. Development in eastern part of county affected by metropolitan overflow from National Capital vicinity.

VaVCo 1-1953

Catoctin Creek and branches drain northwestern portion of county; tributary of Potomac. Name is Indian for Great Village.   Steeles 1161

Foxcroft School for Girls. Established 1914. Rigorously regimented military life with high academic standards provided by healthy outdoor life with carefully planned study. Miss Charlotte H. Noland was student at Oxford, England, in 1910 and one afternoon saw name, Major Foxcroft, which seemed ideal name for school she planned to establish on property of her home at Middleburg.   LRI

Goose Creek with branches drains southeastern and central parts of county, tributary of Potomac. Translation of Indian name *Gokongoloto* means Goose Creek; name as early as 1712. "Goes Flug" was and is Goose Creek. Bass fishing in Goose Creek. Wayland SV 117; Fauquier Bicentennial Com. 49

Hamilton: Ry W&OD; elev. 455; Pop. 403. Near center western half of county. Hamilton postoffice established March 27, 1827, with Charles B. Hamilton as postmaster. Town incorporated 1875. Water supply, one spring.
VaVCo 1-1963

Hillsboro: Pop. 124. In southwest area of north third of county. Founded 1805. Catoctin breaks through Short Hill Mountain; named from location in gap of Short Hill Mountain. Town incorporated 1930. Water supply, one spring.
Gannett 157

Leesburg: Pop. 2,869; increase Pop. 1950-60, 62.5%; US Rt 15. A settlement known as Georgetown before county was formed. Town laid out 1758 and named for Frances Lightfoot Lee. Earliest town surrounded by stockades. Deed May 11, 1766, to lot on which Old Stone Church built; site owned by Virginia Conference Historical Society; first Methodist property in America. "Colonial Leesburg, Inc." maintain older buildings as nearly to original form as possible; when new buildings erected, encourage architectural form which preserves harmony with old. County seat. Water supply: three springs, one well; chlorinated. VaVCo 1-1953; TD 5-15-1966

Lincoln: Pop. 150. In mid-center of north part southwest fourth of county. In heart of Quaker settlement. Earlier name, Goose Creek, from Goose Creek Quaker Church there. In April 1861, postoffice approved, and named for president, Abraham Lincoln. LRI

Lovettsville: Pop. 217. Near mid-point of north boundary of west half of county. In 1820, laid out on land of David Lovett. Incorporated 1876.
ESS county, 30.

Middleburg: Pop. 761; increase Pop. 1950-60, 14.7%; US Rt 50. On south boundary in west third of county. Earliest name, Chinn's Crossroads; in early years, surrounding land owned by Joseph Chinn family. Name Middleburg because about halfway between Alexandria and Winchester. Red Fox Tavern claims to be oldest tavern in the U.S.A. Street advertisement on porch wall, The OLDEST TAVERN in the U.S.A. Middleburg, first Virginia town to have license plate, running red fox over town name. Area peculiarly adapted to fox-hunting or riding-to-hounds, and became widely known as the "Leicestershire of America". Water supply from Little River; filtered, chlorinated.
VGb 30; TD 11-13-1966

Northern Virginia Pasture Management Research Station, 425-acre tract near Middleburg, investigates grazing management, variety of grass and legume, and other factors affecting quality and productivity of pasture. Com Va 9-1953

Oak Hill, President James Monroe's home in this county. Here, he wrote message to Congress, delivered December 1823, known throughout the world as the "Monroe Doctrine". The estate took its name from a group of oaks planted on the lawn, one each from the then existing states, each tree presented to President Monroe by a congressman from the state represented.   Samuel 33

Paeonian Springs: Ry W&OD; Pop. 300. In southwest part of northern third of county. Paeonian Springs signifies health giving.   ESS county 35

Philomont: Pop. 100. Near center of southwest fourth of county. Quaker settlement.   DU

Point of Rocks. Mid-point of north boundary of county. Point of Rocks Ferry established in 1739. Original Point of Rocks bridge constructed across Potomac in 1850.   Mead: Legend Loudoun, 42, 196.

Purcellville: Ry W&OD; elev. 554; Pop. 1,419; increase Pop. 1950-60, 50.1%. First settlement 1764. In 1832, first store and postoffice operated by Purcell family; named for Valentine Purcell. Incorporated March 8, 1908. Water supply: springs, headwaters North Fork Catoctin Creek; chlorinated.
VaVCo 1-1953

Round Hill: elev. 551; Pop. 430; increase Pop. 1950-60, 6.7%. In northwest part of southwest fourth of county. Settled about 1735. Postoffice started Jan. 6, 1868. A large conical hill projects from base of Blue Ridge, served as landmark for early hunters and travelers; name derived from hill. Water supply from springs on Blue Ridge; chlorinated.   VaVCo 1-1953

Sterling: Ry W&OD; elev. 272; Pop. 300. In northeast part of eastern portion of county. Earliest name, Guilford; confusion with two Guilford postoffices in Virginia. Ben Cockerill, a miller, proposed Sterling as name; there was a Sterling Farm near village, which led to village name.   LRI

Waterford: Pop. 247. Near mid-point of north third of county. Settlement 1733 called Milltown. Oldest town in county. Enterprising citizen from Waterford, Ireland, named for his former home. Was busy trading and manufacturing center; thriving Quaker settlement. "Waterford Foundation, Inc." formed about 1943. Washington commuters and old residents encourage restoration of old properties, revive old industries, arrange annual exhibits of arts and crafts.
ESS county 29; Bodie 24, 50, 116.

LOUISA COUNTY

Formed 1742; named for Queen of Denmark, daughter of King George II. Area: 514 sq.mi.; Pop. 12,959; Pop. per sq.mi., 25.3; Increase Pop. 1950-60, 1%. About 70% area forested. Classical School (1752) grew into Presbyterian Seminary which later became Hampden-Sydney College. Rank occupational groups: manufacturing, agriculture, trade. Rank agricultural income: livestock, field crops, poultry.   Roads 88; EcD county

Bumpass: Ry C&O; Pop. 50. In northeast corner of county. Named for early settler. Store not far from Bumpass Turnout; now Bumpass Station.
                                        Steeles 1160; Harris LC 128

Dabney's: Pop. 15. In southeast corner of county. Millsite, first known as Todd's; later as Dabneys, and more recently as Payne's. Named for a Mr. Dabney who moved to Texas shortly after the postoffice was founded.

Ferncliff. (See page 236.)   Harris LC 113; LRI

Fredericks Hall: Ry C&O; Pop. 45. Frederick Overton Harris, first president Louisa Railroad, from whom Fredericks Hall named. Near center northeast fourth of county.   Gwathmay 252

Gum Spring: Pop. 40; US Rts 250, 522. On county line in southeast portion of county. Spring with gum tree nearby on old Three Chopt Road; many frequently stopped to water horses; name developed.   LRI

Louisa: Ry C&O; elev. 437; Pop. 576; increase Pop. 1950-60, 67.4%; US Rt 33. First courthouse of county at Talley Place on Beaver Creek (now Tanyard Branch) about one mile from present courthouse. Byrd Mills have been in continuous use since 1740. Municipal water supply, two wells and one spring; chlorinated.   Gwathmay 264; Harris LC 26

Mineral: Ry C&O; elev. 465; Pop. 366; US Rt 522. Near mid-point west part of east half of county. Community, first Tolersville, after Adam Toler, who kept store until 1810. Name changed to Davis Turnout; name until late 1850's. When became railroad station, name Mineral, because variety of minerals found nearby. Iron pyrites, found nearby, source of sulphur from 1860's to 1900. Town incorporated 1902.   Harris LC 133+; WP: Va 499

Orchid: Pop. 40. South of mid-point of southeast portion of county. Patrons discussing postoffice name saw wild orchid growing by door; agreed name Orchid.   LRI

Pendletons (Pendleton RR): Ry C&O; Pop. 50. Near mid-point west part of east half of county. Name from 18th century family.   Harris LC 133

Trevilians: Pop. 50. In center of west half of county.   DU

LUNENBURG COUNTY

Formed 1746; named for King George II, who was Duke of Brunswick-Lunenberg. Settlement in 1720's and 1730's. Area: 443 sq.mi.; Pop. 12,523; Pop. per sq.mi., 28.3. 70.7% county area forested. Rank occupational groups: agriculture, manufacturing, trade. Rank agricultural income: fields crops, livestock, dairy.   Roads 66

Bagley's Mills: Pop. 10. In southern portion on Meherrin River. Named for mills on early Bagley Farm.   Steeles 1159.

Dry Creek drains north central portion of county; tributary of Nottoway River. Land grant on Dry Creek, June 14, 1739.   14 V 343

Dundas: Ry N&W; Pop. 200. In east central portion. Report that colored railroad worker when Virginian Railroad being built remarked, "We have dun dis". Apparently, this was said at the close of a day's work. When station built at that place, it was named Dundas.   Marable

Fort Mitchell: Ry SOU; Pop. 150. In extreme southwest portion. More than century ago, popular lady by name of Mitchell lived in community. Asking about her favorite admirer at a given time, people would say, "Who is holding the fort now?" This led to place name.   Marable

Kenbridge: Ry N&W; Pop. 1,188; increase Pop. 1950-60, 1.0%. In east central portion. Formerly Tinkling Spring. Land platted on land formerly owned by Kennedy and Bridgeforth families. Town name from two owners' names. Incorporated 1908. Water from Flat Creek: treated, filtered, chlorinated.   Steeles 1169

Lunenburg: Pop. 40. In east central portion. Earlier name, Lewiston; became Lunenburg Court House.   WP: Va 595

Meherrin (in Prince Edward and Lunenburg): Rys N&W, SOU; elev. 585; Pop. 300. On northeast boundary of Lunenburg County. Indian word, meaning "island".   Gannett 204

Middle Meherrin Creek in southwest portion, tributary of South Meherrin River.

North Meherrin River crosses county from northwest portion to south central area of county, tributary of Meherrin River.

Rehoboth: Pop. 25. In southwest portion. Took its name from Rehoboth Methodist Church, which discontinued in 1920's.   Marable

Victoria: Pop. 1,737; Ry N&W; increase Pop. 1950-60, 8.0%. In central portion of county. Named for Queen Victoria of Great Britain. Water from Modest Creek; coagulated, filtered, chlorinated.   Marable

MADISON COUNTY

Formed 1792; named for James Madison, "Father of the American Constitution" and President two terms. Area: 327 sq.mi.; Pop. 8,187; Pop. per sq.mi., 25.0. Explorations began 1670; first settlement about 1725 from German colony. 15% county area in Shenandoah National Park. 57.2% county area forested. Rank occupational groups: manufacturing, agriculture, trade. Rank agricultural income: livestock, dairy, poultry.   Roads 60; EcD county

Aroda: Pop. 80. In south central portion. In colonial times was called White Shop, for a local blacksmith. Postoffice established June 15, 1922; named by U. S. P. O. Dept.   Steeles 1159; Yowell 114

Ashsah: Pop. 35. In south central portion. Postoffice established April 7, 1905; named by P. O. Dept.   Yowell 144

Aylor: Pop. 60. Postoffice established Sept. 28, 1904; named for Aylor family. Near center of east edge of west one-half of county.   Yowell 61, 144.

Banco: In east central portion on Robinson River. Pop. 25. Postoffice established Oct. 10, 1901; named by U. S. P. O. Dept.   Yowell 164

Brightwood: Pop. 150; US Rt 29. Formerly Fleshman's Shop, because a Fleshman owned a shop. Then, Dulinsville for a local family. Postoffice established March 6, 1885; named by Postoffice Department. In east central portion. Has factory specializing in manufacture of hickory-rod chicken coops.
                         Yowell 144

Criglersville: Pop. 100. In central portion on Robinson River. Postoffice established Jan. 2, 1833. Named for Crigler family, among first settlers, owned one of first tanneries in county.   Yowell 61, 144.

Etlan: elev. 670; Pop. 100. Near northeast boundary. Postoffice established Oct. 18, 1899; named by P. O. Dept.   Yowell 144

Graves Mill: elev. 810; Pop. 50. In west central portion on Rapidan River. Named for mill owned by Graves family. Postoffice established Feb. 9, 1841.
                         Yowell 144

Haywood: elev. 627; Pop. 25. In east central portion. Postoffice established Aug. 4, 1880; named by P. O. Dept.   Yowell 145

Hood: Pop. 40; elev. 659. In southwest portion. Named for Hood family.
                         Yowell 145

Hebron Lutheran Church building, dating from 1740, is the oldest built by and still used by Lutherans in America. Congregation's records of 1733 include treasurer's report having list of men's names. Supported early free school, started between 1730 and 1740.   EcD county; Yowell 105

Leon: Pop. 10. In east central portion. Formerly called James City, taking name from James family, of which Jesse and Frank were members, was established October 1, 1810. Name changed by P. O. Dept. to Leon, November 24, 1840, second postoffice established in county.   Yowell 61, 145.

Locust Dale: Pop. 25; US Rt 15. In southeast portion. Took its name from being established in grove locust trees. Earliest name Locust Grove; changed to Locust Dale.   Yowell 61, 145

Madison: Pop. 301; elev. 589; US Rt 29. In central portion. First postoffice in county, Madison Court House, Jan. 1, 1801, named for county. Town incorporated Mar. 20, 1875. Water supply, three drilled wells.   Yowell 60.

Madison Center is community institution from the School of General Studies of the University of Virginia offering college level courses. It was inaugurated in 1962; is located on a five acre plot at Madison.   Ann.Bul.

Madison Mills: Pop. 60; US Rt 15. On Rapidan River; in southern portion. Named for flour mill built there by Madison family. Postoffice established Jan. 20, 1848.   Yowell 61, 145.

Oakpark: Pop. 300. In southeastern portion. Name from being in grove of oaks. Postoffice established Apr. 25, 1854.   Yowell 61, 145

Old Rag Mountain, alt. 3,291 ft., spectacular mass of huge rugged stones, cliffs and precariously balanced boulders.   Lambert 18, 66; Yowell 28

Pratts: elev. 587; Pop. 100. In south central portion. Named for local merchant. Postoffice established November 13, 1883.   Steeles 1174

Radiant: Pop. 85. In south central portion. Postoffice established Mar. 18, 1865; named by P. O. Dept.   Yowell 61, 145

Robinson River crosses county from northwest to southeast; tributary of Crooked Run, which is tributary of Rapidan. Takes name from Robinson family. Colony on Robinson River 1724-25. March 3, 1729, constable's orders to serve "in fork of the Robinson". In 1735, patent to tract of land on Robinson River.   13 V 132, 366; 33 V 329

Rochelle: elev. 598; Pop. 125. In south central portion. Formerly called Jack's Shop from storekeeper Jack living there. Name from French La Rochelle. Postoffice established March 25, 1854.   Yowell 61, 145.

Syria: elev. 693; Pop. 200. In northwest portion. Postoffice established Dec. 19, 1898; named by P. O. Dept.   Yowell 61, 145.

Twymans Mill: Pop. 25. Postoffice established 1868. Named for Twyman family. Near center southeast one-fourth of county.   Yowell 145.

Uno: Pop. 80. In southern portion. Earlier name Kingdom. Named by P. O. Dept. in 1891.   Steeles 1179

Ward-Rue Wildlife Management Area receives its name from timber dealers, Ward and Rue, one-time owners of land. From later owners, the Commonwealth of Virginia purchased and then deeded to Department of Interior.   LRI

Woodberry Forest. In southeastern portion. William Madison built Woodberry Forest in 1793. The Madisons spelled the name Woodbury, name of an old English Manor House. Woodberry Forest School, nationally recognized private school for boys, established in 1888, campus was Woodberry Forest plantation, owned by brother of president. "The Residence" as old home is now called, is the home of the headmaster. Postoffice name comes from the name of school.   EcD county; 32 V 204; WP: Va 395; Yowell 61, 145.

Wolftown: Pop. 100. In central area of northwestern section of county. Fourth postoffice established in county in 1828, called Rapidan; this name from nearby Baptist Church. Name changed to Wolftown in 1857; not known why given Wolftown.   Yowell 61, 145.

MATHEWS COUNTY

Formed 1790; named for Colonel Thomas Mathews, Revolutionary soldier. Area: 67 sq.mi.; Pop. 7,121; Pop. per sq.mi., 81.9. Courthouse built 1792. 52.9% county area forested. Lively business in boats for hire to visitors whose interests are in sport fishing by hook, line, and trolling. Commercial fishing provides employment for greatest number of men. Other occupational groups rank: manufacturing, trade, and transportation, communication and facilities. Rank agricultural income: poultry, soy beans, corn.

Roads 77; EcD county; VaVCo 9-1951

Bavon: Pop. 100. In extreme southeastern portion of county. From list of names, the postoffice name was chosen. LRI

Beaverlett: Pop. 130. In central eastern part of county. Nearby canal, Beaverdam. Another Virginia postoffice, Beaverdam; postoffice named Beaverlett. LRI

Billups Creek in northwest portion, flows into Milford Haven. Land grant given to George Billups in 1653 was on both sides of stream which has since been known by owner's name; now owned by ninth generation. LRI

Blakes: Pop. 200. DU

Bohannon: Pop. 150. In mid-southwest portion of county. Tradition that named for early resident. LRI

Cardinal: Pop. 100. Near center west half of county. DU

Cobbs Creek: Pop. 65. DU

Diggs: Pop. 35. DU

East River flows south in central portion of county. In years before 1791, Mathews was included in Gloucester County. Then, East River was the easternmost river in Gloucester County. This may account for its name. LRI

Foster: Pop. 25; elev. 15. In center of western third of county. William T. Foster, storekeeper, started postoffice. TD 12-12-1951

Grimstead: Pop. 300. On Gwynn Island. Named for first postmaster, J. B. Grimstead. LRI

Gwynn: Pop. 400; (summer Pop. 1,200). Gwynn's Island, named for Hugh Gwynn, representative in House of Burgesses. Gwynn Island in northeastern part of county. Lord Dunsmore driven from Gwynn's Island in 1776.

WP: Va 456

Hallieford: elev. 13; Pop. 200. In mid northern portion of county. Man named Hallie had postoffice; ford was added; this made name of postoffice.

LRI

Horn Harbor. Land patented on Horn Harbor in 1651. 2 V 384

Hudgins: elev. 13; Pop. 25. In east north central. Named for family having large tract of land. LRI

Laban: elev. 5; Pop. 200. In mid-eastern portion of county. Named for Laban Hudgins, storekeeper and first postmaster. LRI

Mathews: elev. 8; Pop. 500. County seat. Major Thomas Mathews made resolution in Virginia House of Delegates for formation of county.

EcD county

Miles (Hicks Wharf): Pop. 150. In mid-southern portion of county. Hicks Wharf was steamboat landing in steamboat days until in early 1930's. Then was local postoffice. Miles operated general store; Hicks Wharf postoffice discontinued and Miles postoffice created. LRI

Mobjack: elev. 6; Pop. 200. Near outlet of East River into Mobjack Bay. Name believed to be corruption of Indian word. (See Mobjack Bay).

Gannett 211

Moon: elev. 10; Pop. 70. In northeast portion. Many proposed names rejected because duplicated other postoffices in state. Prospective postmaster saw unusually bright moon; sent in Moon as name and it was accepted. LRI

Motorun: Pop. 100. DU

New Point: Pop. 100. In southeast portion. New Point Comfort Light House established several years before postoffice; seemingly, name came from light house nearby. LRI

North: Pop. 150; elev. 12. In central western part. Name North chosen because North River nearby. LRI

Onemo: Pop. 80. In mid-eastern portion of county. Onemo is from the words "one more". LRI

Peary: elev. 5; Pop. 125. In southeast portion. Postoffice established in 1910; report that Robert Edwin Peary had discovered North Pole; station named for him. LRI

Port Haywood: elev. 5; Pop. 100. In east central part. Storm; man brought boat into harbor of East River; he was Capt. Haywood; he commended the safe harbor; from then called Port Haywood. LRI

Redart: Pop. 30. In northeast portion. An old settler's name was Trader. The postoffice name is his name spelled backwards. LRI

U. S. Coast Guard and Rescue Station (Milford Haven Station) for search and rescue operations and for maintenance of navigation aids in the area.

TD 2-19-1967

Shadow: Pop. 35. DU

Susan: Pop. 350. Near center southeast one-fourth of county. DU

MECKLENBURG COUNTY

Formed 1764; named for Princess Charlotte of Mecklenburg-Strelitz, Queen of George III. Area: 626 sq.mi.; Pop. 31,428; Pop. per sq.mi., 50.2. About three-fifths county area forested. Rank occupational groups: agriculture, manufacturing, public utilities. Rank agricultural income: field crops, livestock, dairy.   Roads 66

Allens Creek flows northeast in central portion of county; tributary of Roanoke River. Named for Allen family who lived here before county was formed.   Hutcheson

Baskerville: Ry NF&D; Pop. 70. In central part of west area of east one-half of county. Postoffice established 1898. Named for Baskerville family.   Hutcheson

Blackridge: Pop. 40. Near Brunswick line in southeast area of county. Located on ridge on Black's Road leading to Black's Ferry crossing Roanoke River, hence Blackridge.   Hutcheson

Boydton: Ry NF&D; Pop. 449; US Rt 58. Slightly west of county center. County seat since 1765; laid out in 1812; named for Alexander Boyd, county judge who died in 1801 while holding court; was also Scotch immigrant and wealthy merchant. Randolph-Macon founded at Boydton, opened 1832; moved to Ashland 1867. Old Elm Hill farm, near Boydton, had pioneer herd of Brahman cattle in Southside Virginia.   WP: Va 475; VaVCo 9-1952

Bracey: Ry SAL; Pop. 100. In southeast portion of county. Named for Bracey family in 1901.   Hutcheson

Buffalo Junction: Ry NF&D; Pop. 100. In southwest portion of county. Buffalo Springs early resort. After railroad constructed, spur line from station to springs. Postoffice named Buffalo Junction.   Hutcheson

Buggs Island in Roanoke River was named for Bugg family who owned property which was sold to Sir Peyton Skipwith.   Hutcheson

Butchers Creek flows south in western part of Mecklenburg County; tributary of Roanoke River. Named for John Butcher who resided there at time William Byrd II established Virginia-North Carolina boundary.   Hutcheson

Chase City: Ry SOU; elev. 535; Pop. 3,207; increase Pop. 1950-60, 27.3%. Until 1870, village Christiansville; newcomers led in adoption of new name. Name changed to Chase City after Chief Justice Chase of United States Supreme Court. Incorporated 1873. Water supply, nine wells; one chlorinated.   Hutcheson

Clarksville: Rys NF&D, SOU; Pop. 1,530; increase Pop. 1950-60, 47.8%; US Rts 15, 58. In southwest portion on Buggs Island Lake. Named for Clark Royster, property on west bank of Roanoke River. In 1669, John Lederer visited; found Indians trading corn, pelts, and dried tobacco leaves, oldest continuous tobacco market in world. Incorporated as a town April 19, 1818. Water supply from John H. Kerr reservoir; filtered, chlorinated. Hutcheson

Flat Creek drains east central area of county; when flooded, the low lands were called a flat creek. Earlier name, Flat Rock Creek. Hutcheson

Forksville (RR Skelton): Ry SAL; Pop. 120. In northeast corner of county. Derivation: forks of the road. Hutcheson

LaCrosse: Ry NF&D; SAL; elev. 726; Pop. 435; increase Pop. 1950-60, 7.5%; US Rt 58. In northeast area of county. Earlier name was Old Piney Road at intersection of Piney Road and St. Tammany's Ferry Road. Name after game LaCrosse; a Miss Northington fancied the name. Water supply, two wells. Hutcheson

Little Bluestone Creek like other streams having Bluestone name trace back to William Byrd II's land grant, whereon he constructed an edifice, called Bluestone Castle. Hutcheson

Miles Creek drains the central area of the east half of the county. It takes its name from the Miles family residing thereon in the early days. Hutcheson

Nelson: Ry NF&D; Pop. 120. In the extreme southwest corner of county. Named for Nelson family. Hutcheson

Palmer Springs: Pop. 75. Near state line in southwest portion of east half of county. Named for Palmer family; Amasa Palmer believed in medicinal value of waters of his spring. Hutcheson

Radcliffe (Smiths Cross Roads): Pop. 50. Near center east one-fourth of county. DU

Skipwith: Ry SOU; Pop. 85. In center of west fourth of county. Skipwith family owned tract during four generations. Sir Peyton Skipwith built "Prestwould". VaVCo 9-1952

South Hill: Ry NF&D; Pop. 2,500; increase Pop. 1950-60, 19.3%; US Rts 1, 58. In northeast portion of county. Around 1800, four miles northwest of present town, there was a South Hill Methodist Church and school. Big knoll or hill about two miles directly north, rare in area. Name chosen meant south of the hill. In 1814, postoffice at same spot took name South Hill. Boydton-Petersburg Plank Road built through county; Binford's Store became coach stop. In 1867, postoffice moved to coach stop Inn on through road to Richmond;

postoffice retained its name. Incorporated 1900. Water from Meherrin River; filtered, chlorinated.   Hutcheson

Union Level: Ry NF&D; Pop. 100. In center near west edge of east one-third of county. Stages on Plank Road crossed the level between Miles and Allens Creeks. Stage coach drivers had expression: "The wheel horses would brake the stage to Miles Creek, the lead team would get them over the hump of the level; then with my feet on the spatterboard, I blow my horses on the level." This explains the second part of the name; Union is not explained.

Hutcheson

MIDDLESEX COUNTY

Formed 1673; named for an English County. Area: 132 sq.mi.; Pop. 6,319; Pop. per sq.mi., 47.9. Settlement of county developed about 1640. Increasing popular water sports in summer months. Rank occupational groups: trade, manufacturing, agriculture. Rank agricultural income: field crops, livestock, poultry.   Roads 77; VaVCo 9-1961

Amburg: Pop. 350. In extreme eastern portion of county.   DU

Butylo: Pop. 25. In extreme north part on Rappahannock.   DU

Christchurch: Pop. 136. In center of county. Established 1666. Christ Church built 1712-1714; restored in 1800's. Christchurch School is an Episcopal boarding school for boys; adjoins churchyard.   WP: Va 454; EcD county

Church View: Pop. 100; US Rt 17. In southwest part of northern third of county.   DU

Deltaville, (Sandy Bottom): Pop. 800. (Summer Pop. 1000). In extreme east part of county. Was Unionville from union of two churches. Postoffice moved because land forms a delta on the Chesapeake Bay. Waters around town have become year round harbor of pleasure boats.   Revere 22

Fishing Bay in southeastern corner of county and waters upstream of Piankatank have become year round harbors of pleasure boats.

Hardyville: Pop. 40. In extreme east part of county. Named for George Lofton Hardy, merchant and first postmaster.   LRI

Hartfield: Pop. 200. Originally Lot; named after family of J. A. Hart. About center of eastern third of county.   LRI

Healys: Pop. 100. Near southern edge in eastern third of county. Named for Healys family.   LRI

Jamaica: Pop. 15. Near center of western third of county.   DU

Lagrange Creek borders on peninsula of productive land which had farm known as "Lagrange Farm". Lagrange in French applies to an extensive well-improved farm. Later, Lagrange Farm was known as Kilmer Hall when owned by Willis Sharpe Kilmer. Stream took name from earlier farm name. In east part of west one-third of county.   LRI

Locust Hill: Pop. 35. Near eastern edge of middle third of county.   DU

Parrotts Creek drains middle area of west one-third of county. Has name from a family. Oct. 24, 1701, land grant on branch of Parrott's Creek.
                                                                  16 V 192

Remlik: Pop. 15. In east central part of west one-third of county. Remlik was training station for race horses owned by Willis Sharpe Kilmer. Station name is Kilmer spelled backwards.   LRI

Saluda: Pop. 300; US Rt 17. County seat; courthouse records date from 1673. Name probably derived from corruption of Indian name. Small Indian tribe formerly living in South Carolina; reported they moved to Pennsylvania early in 18th century.   WP: Va 453; Revere 2

Samos: Pop. 50. Near center of northwestern third of county. Named for Greek island in Aegean Sea by Mr. John Callis.   LRI

Stormont: Pop. 50. Near center of county.   DU

Syringa: Pop. 150. In central part of east half of county. When post-office established, the postmaster proposed the name of the flowering shrub, syringa.   LRI

Topping: Pop. 35. Near southern edge of eastern third of county. Named for a family.   LRI

Urbanna: Pop. 512; increase Pop. 1950-60, 1%. On Rappahannock, mid-point county. Urbanna Creek, formerly Indian name Nimcock Creek. Town named Nimcock. Established 1705. About 50 years later, named to honor Queen Anne. Urbanna Creek near Urbanna, year round harbor of pleasure boats.
                    Revere 21; WP: Va 453

Wake: Pop. 100. Near center of eastern third of county. Named for a family.   LRI

Warner: Pop. 50. Along western edge middle third of county. Reported that Mr. Robert Warner Allsworth was first postmaster and his middle name became postoffice name.   LRI

Water View: Pop. 150. In western one-third of county on Rappahannock River. Formerly located on Rappahannock River and named because of view of the water.   LRI

MONTGOMERY COUNTY

Formed 1776; named for General Richard Montgomery, killed at Quebec, 1775. Area: 395 sq.mi.; Pop. 32,923; Pop. per sq.mi., 83.3; Pop. increase 1950-60, 10.6%. Early settlement in county in 1748; massacred during French and Indian War. 61.8% county area forested. 7% in Jefferson National Forest. Rank occupational groups: manufacturing, educational services, trade. Rank agricultural income: dairy, livestock, poultry, vegetables.   Roads 74

Blacksburg: Ry N&W; Pop. 8,800; increase Pop. 1950-60, 162.0%; elev. 2,083; US Rt 460. Named for William Black who gave land for town; incorporated 1798. Was site Draper Meadows settled in 1745 led by Colonel Patton; wiped out by Shawnees massacre July 8, 1755.   Crush 4, 14; WP: Va 445

Cambria consolidated with Christiansburg 1964. Was Bangs (Christiansburg Depot) incorporated by Virginia legislature in 1878. Legislature changed name to Cambria in 1878; more euphonious name. Town's beginning when right-of-way offered free to location of railroad station over the hill just out-of-sight and hearing from objecting residents of Christiansburg.   Crush 144

Christiansburg: Ry N&W; elev. 2,089; Pop. 4,375; increase Pop. 1950-60, 47.7%; US Rts 11, 460. Near center of south one-half of county. Originally called "Hans' Meadows", established 1792. Named for Colonial William Christian, Indian fighter. County seat. Friends Freedman's Association of Philadelphia organized Christiansburg Industrial Institute for Negroes; operated until 1933, when conveyed to county schools.   WP: Va 434; VaVCo 8-1951

Elliston: Ry N&W; elev. 1,300; Pop. 600. Near mid-center of east boundary of county. Was Big Springs; in boom of 1880, proposed steel center for short time, "Carnegie City"; about 1890, named for Major Ellis, who married daughter of President Tyler. Water supply, springs; chlorinated.
Crush 141; Steeles 1164

Ironto: Ry N&W; Pop. 300. Near center of east one-half of county. Named for adopted daughter of Dabney Burkett in 1911.   Steeles 1168

Lafayette: Pop. 300; elev. 1,300; US Rts 11, 460. Mid-center of east boundary of county. Delightful village. Oldest settlement in county; named for the General.
Steeles 1167

McCoy: Ry N&W; Pop. 420. In northwest corner of county. Named for a local family in 1908. Had coal mining.   VaVCo 8-1951; Steeles 1170

Pilot: elev. 2,267; Pop. 60. Near center of south boundary of county. Named for local merchant early in 19th century.   Steeles 1174

Radford (independent city): Ry N&W; elev. 1,775; Pop. 10,000; increase Pop. 1950-60, 10.7%; US Rt 11. Names have been Ingle's Ferry; Lovely Mount; Central Depot. Dr. John Bane Radford was owner of property. Incorporated 1887. Railroad came 1856. Water supply, New River; filtered, chlorinated, fluorinated.   WP: Va 435; EcD county

Radford College, Women's Division of VPI until 1964. Established 1910 State Normal and Industrial School for Women; opened 1913. State Teachers College in 1924. Became Radford College in 1944; conferred B. A. in 1935. Made separate institution in 1964, and authorized to confer M. S. degree. Has 75 acre campus.   Ann.Bul.

Riner: Pop. 125; elev. 2,080. Near center of southwest fourth of county. Early name Auburn. Named for David Riner about 1800.
                                                        Crush 141; Steeles 1175

Shawsville: Ry N&W; elev. 1,458; Pop. 300; US Rts 11, 460. Is east of center of southeast fourth of county. In spring 1756, Mary Draper Ingles and husband went to Ft. Vaux (Vass), a fort built upon the plantation of Captain Ephraim Vaux in present village of Shawsville. Present name of village for a railroad construction engineer.   Crush 4; Steeles 1176

Toms Creek along west half of northern portion; tributary of New River. Earlier name Jones Creek. One suggestion, the man's name was Thomas Jones; this led to referring to Tom's Creek.   LRI

Virginia Polytechnic Institute had its first session in 1872. Its name was Virginia Agricultural and Mechanical College. In 1896, by Act of General Assembly, the name became Virginia Agricultural and Mechanical College and Polytechnic Institute; in general usage, it was Virginia Polytechnic Institute. In 1944, the General Assembly gave the institution the legal name, Virginia Polytechnic Institute; popularly, it is Virginia Tech. It has become a university conferring Masters and Doctors degrees.   Ann.Bul.

VPI (branch station postoffice). Payment of $20,000 raised by Montgomery County in 1872 led to transfer of Preston and Olin Institute to become Virginia Agricultural and Mechanical College. Preston and Olin Institute had been founded by Baltimore Methodist Episcopal Conference in 1854. Now Virginia Polytechnic Institute.   Crush 139

Whitethorne: Ry N&W; Pop. 30. On New River in northwest portion of county. Named for a local farm.   Steeles 1180

NANSEMOND COUNTY

Formed 1637; first called Upper Norfolk County; in 1642 named Nansemond for an Indian tribe (Indian name Nansimum) which means "fishing point or angle". Area: 402 sq.mi.; Pop. 31,366; Pop. per sq.mi., 78.0; increase Pop. 1950-60, 24.3%. Permanent settlement in 1618. 63.7 percent county area forested. Leading peanut-growing county of nation. Rank occupational groups: manufacturing, trade, agriculture. Rank agricultural income: field crops, livestock, poultry.

EcD county; VaVCo 9-1950

Bennetts Creek: Pop. 500. Will dated Sept. 18, 1731, income from land bequeathed on Bennett's Creek to support Glebe school in Lower Parish of Nansemond County.

5 W(2)30.

Chuckatuck Creek in northwest portion of county, flows into Hampton Roads. Name Indian origin. Land grant mentions stream, 1635. In list navigable streams, July 1702.

LRI; 3 V 183; 1 V 362.

Lake Cohoon, impounded headwaters of Nansemond River. In west central part of county. Name for Cahoon family who owned land around it. Former spelling Cahoon, now Cohoon.

LRI

Crittenden: elev. 21; Pop. 250; US Rt 17. In northwest corner of county. Named for Captain Crittenden, a local resident about 1880. Water supply, two wells.

Steeles 1163

Driver: Ry ACL; elev. 20; Pop. 160. In northeastern portion of county. Named for Col. Driver, a local resident in 1888. One mile north was a free school, established by will of John Yeats, September 1731. Glebe Church built 1736. In 1775, parish minister driven from church for preaching loyalty to the king; building repaired 1854.

Steeles 1163; Roads 32

Dundalow: now part of Suffolk; named posthumously for Marvin Dundalow.

LRI

Eclipse: Pop. 290. In northwest corner of county. Named about 1900 for an eclipse of the sun.

Steeles 1164

Frederick College in northern Nansemond; co-educational; established as four-year liberal arts. Address, Portsmouth. Name honors Frederick T. Beazley, ancestor of benefactors of college. In 1960, 800 acres bordering on Hampton Roads acquired as campus. College opened 1961. In 1968, property given to State of Virginia to be two-year community college.

Ann.Bul.

Hobson: Pop. 250. Near northwest corner of county. Named for Lieutenant Commander Hobson, of Santiago fame.

Steeles 1167

Holland: Ry NF&D, SOU; Pop. 338; US Rt 58. Near Isle of Wight line in southwest fourth of county. Named for Z. T. Holland, first merchant. First Ruritan Club was formed in Holland, May 21, 1928. At least 50 percent of membership of each Ruritan Club must be farmers, having purpose of striving through community service, fellowship and good will to make a rural community a better place in which to live.   Steeles 1167; VaVCo 9-1950

Lake Prince: impounded water of Exchange Creek; southern edge of northern third of county. Named in 1920 for a resident of Norfolk.   Steeles 1169

Somerton Creek drains southwest portion of county; tributary of Blackwater River after stream enters North Carolina; Blackwater River along western boundary. Somerton Creek mentioned, September 21, 1710.   5 V 8.

Suffolk: Rys ACL, N&W, NF&D, SAL; elev. 55; Pop. 12,300; increase Pop. 1950-60, 2.2%; US Rts 13, 58, 460. In colonial beginnings, Sleepy Hole; in 1742, Constance's Warehouse; named Suffolk for county in England. City has largest tea processing plant of the United States. Leading peanut market of world so known as "Peanut Capital". Independent city in 1910. Water supply from Portsmouth system; filtered, chlorinated, fluorinated.

Com Va 12-1965; WP: Va 571; Gannett 293

Tidewater Field Station established near Holland in 1914. Investigations regarding production of peanuts, cotton, soy beans, other crops, and hogs; pasture management.   VaVCo 9-1950; Com Va 9-1953

Whaleyville: Pop. 402. In south central area of county. S. M. Whaley founded Whaleyville. Incorporated 1950. Water supply, well.   VaVCo 4-1949

NELSON COUNTY

Formed 1807; named for General Thomas Nelson, Jr., third governor of Virginia. Area: 468 sq.mi.; Pop. 12,752; Pop. per sq.mi., 27.2. Sportsman's paradise; fishing in mountain streams. Federally-owned lands include 5.2% county area. Rank occupational groups: manufacturing, agriculture, trade. Rank agricultural income: livestock, fruit, field crops. EcD county

Afton: Ry C&O; elev. 1,407; Pop. 75. In northeast corner. Named by Mrs. David Hansbrough, wife of first postmaster, native of Scotland, for she saw close resemblance to her homeland. LRI

Arrington: Ry SOU; elev. 800; Pop. 250. Near mid-center of west boundary of southwest fourth of county. Named for family; Wm. Arrington and then his wife were station agents on railroad for years. LRI

Buffalo River in southwest corner of county. Early settlement, Jan. 2, 1737. Land willed on Buffalo River, July 25, 1774. 22 V 193, 445

Crabtree Falls starts from top of Pinnacle Peak and descends over broken and shelving rocks 3,000 feet in going a horizontal distance of 2,000 feet. The "Grand Cataract" makes a fall of 500 feet. In a setting of wild sylvan beauty, stream descends in a series of five beautiful falls. Highest waterfall east of Mississippi; stream flows into Tye River. Federal government acquired ownership in 1968. Near Montebello. EcD county; Claiborne 3

Faber: Ry SOU; elev. 622; Pop. 80. In east central portion. Mr. Faber, early settler, had feed and sawmill. Early name "Faber Mills"; then "Orlando"; then "Faber". LRI

Gladstone: Ry C&O; elev. 400; Pop. 150; US Rt 50. On James River in southwest corner of county. Town named for William Ewart Gladstone of England. Water works system owned by C&O Ry; water from large spring flows by gravity to distribution system. Steeles 1166; EcD county

Hat Creek flows southwest as tributary of Tye River; in northwest fourth of county. Col. Joseph Barnett lived on Hat Creek 1750. 4 W (2) 185

Lovingston: elev. 734; Pop. 375; US Rt 29. County seat. Named for original owners of land. Water supply from three wells. Steeles 1170

Massie Mill: Ry VBR; elev. 702; Pop. 250. In southern part of northwest portion of county. Named for early family who owned most of nearby land. Steeles 1171

Montebello: Pop. 50. In extreme northwest corner of county. Named by great-grandfather of William R. Massie; ancestor had his summer home there. LRI

Nellysford: elev. 673; Pop. 140. In northeast portion. Girl named Nelly drowned in nearby ford; hence name Nellysford. LRI

Piney River (Canody): Ry VBR; elev. 652; Pop. 300. Near mid-point of west boundary of county. Named for stream which in turn flows through an area known as Piney Woods — an unusual growth of pines in this valley. American Cyanid Company (Piney River) produces fine white powder; ilmenite (locally Nelsonite) processed. LRI

Rockfish: Ry SOU; Pop. 60; elev. 446. In southeast portion. Located on Rockfish River. Probable connection in name. Board on Geographic Names

Rockfish River. Land grant on branches of Rockfish River, October 24, 1728. 14 V 30

Roseland (Fleetwood): Pop. 35. Near mid-point of southern part of northwest one-fourth of county. Named for "Rose's Land"; a section once owned by "parson" Robert Rose. Tate 81

Schuyler: elev. 311; Pop. 450. Schuyler Walker operated grist mill here many years ago; town name from his first name. Alberene is a soapstone mined at Schuyler; company-owned railroad, Nelson-Albemarle Railway, serves mills and connects with C&O at Esmont. Alberene, coined name, from Albemarle and last syllable of name of promoter, James Serene. Marketed as Alberene since 1870. Schuyler water supply from small mountain stream; chlorinated. LRI; VaVCo 6-1954

Shipman: Ry SOU; Pop. 500. In south central portion. Originally was Montreal. Later named Oak Ridge. Was named Shipman after John Shipman, former resident. LRI

Tye River drains west area of southwest fourth of county. Stream discovered by Allen Tye in 1735; named for him. Percy ACS, 5.

Tye River (village): Rys SOU, VBR; elev. 600; Pop. 130. Mid-point of county boundary of southwest fourth of county. Named for stream. EcD county

Tyro: elev. 834; Pop. 150. In central northwest portion of county. Tyro is a beginner; Tyro was name of home of William E. Massie; probably was beginning in local area. LRI

Virginia Blue Ridge Railway: Name from Blue Ridge of Virginia. Originally 16 miles in length began operation in 1916; first ten miles completed in 1915. Now operates between Tye River and Piney River. Products from titanium, copperas (sulphate of iron), and aplite are important in outbound traffic. Heavy products are significant in inbound traffic. Was the last steam railroad in Virginia when began using diesels in 1963. LRI

Wingina: Ry C&O; Pop. 25. About mid-point on southern boundary. Wingina was supposed to be an Indian chief, son-in-law of Powhatan. There was an Indian village at this location on the James River. LRI

NEW KENT COUNTY

Formed in 1654; there are two explanations of the county name. One, that it was named for an English county. The other, that Colonel William Claiborne selected the name after Kent Island, in upper waters of Chesapeake Bay, after Lord Baltimore drove Claiborne from there. Area: 212 sq.mi.; Pop. 4,504; Pop. per sq.mi., 21.2; increase Pop. 1950-60, 12.7%. Over four-fifths of county wooded. Rank occupational groups: manufacturing, trade, public administration and agriculture. Rank agricultural income: field crops, livestock, dairy.

Roads 86; Gwathmey 370.

Barhamsville: Pop. 50. In southeast corner near county's southern boundary. Named after family who settled here about 1654. Establishment of postoffice reported in mid-18th century. Pronounced: bear' ams ville.   LRI

Lanexa: Ry C&O; Pop. 70. In extreme southeast corner.   DU

New Kent: Pop. 25. County seat.

New Kent Forest Tree Nursery. 876 acres. Three miles east of Providence Forge on former State Game Farm property. Forty-five to fifty acres are planted each year to supply twenty million seedlings distributed annually. Seedlings raised for distribution throughout the state for reforestation program.

EcD county; Gottmann 275

Providence Forge: Ry C&O; Pop. 130; US Rt 60. A Presbyterian colony settled here about 1770; built a forge for making farm implements; this led to name of village. Some remains of old forge on estate having the name.

Roads 48; Kibler HVI 133

Quinton: Ry SOU; Pop. 30. In northwest corner of county. In late 1860's, a traveler by name of Quinton had horse taken sick, which died at roadside pond. Pond became Quinton Pond. First name of railroad station, Summit; confused with another station having same name. Station took name from pond, so is Quinton.   LRI

Tunstall: Ry SOU; Pop. 10. In north portion, near Pamunkey River. One report was named from Robert W. Tunstall, principal, Norfolk Academy. Another, Tunstall family owned land at time postoffice established near Southern Railway.   LRI

NORTHAMPTON COUNTY

Formed 1634; named Accomac; in 1643, name changed to Northampton for an English shire. Area: 226 sq.mi.; Pop. 16,966; Pop. per sq.mi., 75.1. 26.3% county area forested. Among the state's counties, ranks first in acreage harvested for each: sweet corn, cucumbers, snap beans, cabbage, sweet peppers; is the state's leader in value of vegetables for sale. In the county, one farm in each six has annual income of $40,000. Rank occupational groups: manufacturing, trade, agriculture. Rank agricultural income: field crops, vegetables, livestock.   Roads 58

Bayford: Pop. 35. Near mid-point northwest one-fourth of county. Bayford Park, recreation area, period 1880-1890. At present, local recreation. Formerly, when shipping to Baltimore by boat, was big shipping point; now oysters shipped.
Hamilton

Bayview (RR Bay View): Ry PA; Pop. 130. About mid-point of southern half of county. Lovely view from earlier plantation home overlooking Chesapeake Bay; now believed this may have influenced choosing Bayview as an appropriate name.   LRI

Birdsnest: Ry PA; Pop. 125; US Rt 13. Near mid-point of north one-half of county. Bridgetown Station became Birdsnest to get postoffice name approved. Birdsnest name from low room in middle three-story building. Another explanation is property sold in 1842 called Birdsnest, several miles from station, but may have influenced choice of name.   ESS county 24; Whitelaw 376

Bridgetown: Pop. 25. New church built on Hungars Creek was called Nassawaddox, now Bridgetown. Nassawaddox, Indian tribe in vicinity, name means "a stream between two streams". (Hungars Creek between Chesapeake Bay and the ocean.) After bridge across creek, name changed to Bridgetown.
ESS county 16; Wood 40

Cape Charles: Ry PA; elev. 12; Pop. 2,041. At extreme southern point of county. Harbor built in 1884; used by large steamships, wharf facilities spacious and substantial. Town named for cape, which had been named in honor of Duke of Yorke. Water from two wells; treated.   Wood 48; Turman 199

Cape Charles Air Force Station: Pop. ———.

Capeville: Ry PA; Pop. 200. Near mid-point of southern half of county. Midway between Cape Charles (town) and Kiptopeke.

Cheriton: Ry PA; elev. 35; Pop. 761; US Rt 13. Near northern part of south half of county. First county seat was Townfield, near present Cheriton. Another early name was Sunnyside, from being a sunny spot. Cheriton name chosen by landowner, Dr. William Stratton Stockley. Original name ,"Cherry Stones", from which name Cheriton.   ESS county 19, 21; Whitelaw 80

Cobbs: Ry PA; Pop. 100. Near northern part of south half of county. Land owned by H. W. Cobb; early 19th century. Railroad station called Cobbs Station. Postoffice was Chesapeake until city of Chesapeake formed; then name relinquished, and became Cobbs Rural Station.   Hamilton

Cobbs Island mideastern portion of county. Borders on Atlantic. Has lifeboat station.

Eastville: elev. 35; Pop. 261; US Rt 13. Courthouse since 1680, has oldest continuous records in United States, dating to 1632. Peachburg was earlier name. Another name, "The Horns", from two branches of Hungar's Creek forming 'horns'. Present name explained because settlement then east of other settlements. Town incoporated 1896.   ESS county 8, 17; Woods 42

Eastville Station: Ry PA; Pop. 150. Eastville Station has postoffice although only one mile east of Eastville, the county seat.   Turman 203

Exmore: Ry PA; elev. 35; Pop. 1,566; US Rt 13. In extreme north part of county. Tradition, name because tenth station on railroad south of Delaware. Important shipping point of farm and sea products. Water supply from well.   Turman 204

Fisherman's Island in 18th century or earlier was known as Linen Bar as name of shoal formed by a storm-wrecked ship with a cargo of linen. The island in the 19th century was known by either name, Linen Bar or Fisherman's Island; eventually it became Fisherman's Island. It now supports northern end of Chesapeake Bay Bridge.   Hamilton

Fort Custis named for John Custis (1676-1749). Kiptopeke, co-heir with Debedeacon, met and welcomed Capt. John Smith here.   Allen 5; ESS county 14

Franktown: Pop. 125. Near mid-point of north half of county. Name in 1764, "New Towne"; village grew, Frank Andrews opened store in 1764; soon became "Frank's Towne"; name became Franktown. Important truck-farming center.   Whitelaw (I), 459

Hog Island, northern portion of county; has two lifeboat stations. Patent 1687 for Hogg Island.   Hamilton

Jamesville: Pop. 100. In northwest part of county. Land acquired by James in 1671. Present village on tract inherited from earlier owner.   Hamilton

Little Inlet north of Smith Island, entrance to Mink Island Bay. Severe storm in 1851 cut channel through Smith Island; northern part now Myrtle Island; channel is Little Inlet.   Hamilton

Little Machipongo is lifeboat station. Little Machipongo Inlet is between Hog Island and southeastern Accomack County.

Machipongo: Ry PA; Pop. 100; US Rt 13. In mid-point of southern one-third of county. Matchapungoes were large tribe and had several villages. Name means "bad dust" or "much dust".   Whitelaw 18; Turman 110

Marionville: Pop. 75. About southern edge of northwest one-fourth of county and near coast. In earlier years, important inlet for sailing vessels. Francis Marion Sturgis secured postoffice; thus given name Marionville.
ESS county 23

Mockhorn Island is in southern portion near to mainland of county. In 1657, patent for acreage on Mockon Island. In 1683, patent recorded Machone Island. Now wildlife refuge. Local people still pronounce name as though spelled Mockon.   Hamilton

Nassawaddox: Ry PA; elev. 35; Pop. 650; US Rt 13; incorporated 1958. Is south of mid-point of north one-fourth of county. Settled 1656. Meaning, "a stream between two streams".   Wood 38

New Inlet between Wreck Islands and Ship Shoal Island in southern third of county. Atlantic storm cut the inlet.   Hamilton

Oyster: Pop. 250. In northeast portion of south half of county. Vicinity supplies enormous volume of oysters and clams. Location several packing houses, from which oysters, fish and clams are shipped to distant markets.
Allen 24; Wood 47

Sand Shoal Inlet between Cobbs Island and Wreck Islands, mid-eastern islands. Very shallow inlet due to sandy bottom; hence name given. Is extremely shallow at low tide; local fishermen must be very careful in navigating inlet.
Hamilton

Ship Shoal Island borders on Atlantic in southern one-third of county. Shoal means "shallow". Island slopes off very gradually under water and water appears deeper than actually is; too shallow for ships to approach.   Hamilton

Smith Island borders Atlantic in southern portion of county. Has life boat station. Named for Captain John Smith in 1608.   Hamilton

Townsend: Ry PA; Pop. 120. Is south of mid-point in southern half of county. Named for first postmaster, Samuel Townsend, who came to community in 1869.   LRI

Wardtown: Pop. 50. Near mid-point of extreme northwest area of county. House built about 1820 called Ward House, home of Alexander Wales Ward. Postoffice at crossroads intersection which has this house; name derived.
Hamilton.

Weirwood: Ry PA; Pop. 100. Near center of north half of county. Location Kellam Airfield, Eastern Shore Air Service.   DU

Willis Wharf: Pop. 400. In extreme northeast area of county. Before 1890, name was Bigelow's Wharf. In 1854, Edward L. Willis purchased land; name became Willis Wharf. Has largest deep sea trap fishing on the Atlantic Coast.
Whitelaw (I), 482; VHSSA 45.

Wreck Islands borders Atlantic about midway of county; seven miles east of Oyster. Part of Wreck Islands above Shell Creek is locally called Bone Island. Patent 1687, patent for area of "Rack Island". In 1877, state warrant for Wreck Island. Many shipwrecks on island have given it the name.   Hamilton

Wreck Islands Natural Area on the low-lying reef of 1,380 acres provides conditions for its contribution of undisturbed native life development.
Com Va 10-1964

NORTHUMBERLAND COUNTY

Formed 1648; named for an English county; was originally an Indian district called Chickacoan. Area: 200 sq.mi.; Pop. 10,185; Pop. per sq.mi., 50.9; increase Pop. 1950-60, 1.7%. Located at mouth of Potomac; 15% county area is water. First English colonist settled 1640. Soy beans is most important crop. Rank occupational groups: manufacturing, trade, agriculture. Rank agricultural income: field crops, livestock.   Roads 59; EcD county

Beverlyville: Pop. 150. In extreme northeast portion of county.   DU

Browns Store: Pop. 10. At southern edge of middle portion of county. Named for a Brown family about 1860.   LRI

Burgess: Pop. 570; US Rt 360. In northern portion of eastern third of county. Burgess was name of first four postmasters; name was Burgess Store until 1950.   LRI

Callao: Pop. 150; US Rt 360. In western third of county. Jacob H. Callaway, store owner, established postoffice, wished name Callaway. There was an office in Franklin County having that name; then Callao was approved as name.   LRI

Coan River in northeastern part. Name from Indian tribe called Chicacoan. Pronounced, cone.   LRI; Com Va 3-1935

Ditchley: Pop. 60. Near coast in southeastern part. Ditchley, old estate, established by Hancock Lee about 1725.   EcD county; VaVCo 8-1950

Edwardsville: Pop. 60. Near west boundary of northeast fourth of county. Received name from Paget Edwards.   LRI

Fairport (Timbs): Pop. 300. On coast in southeastern part of county. On Cockrell's Creek where meets Great Wicimico River. In earlier years, was a good port and harbor for boats, which gave it the name Fairport.   LRI

Gonyon: Pop. 15. Near mid-point of east half on Potomac River. Name picked from story in Christian Herald; five names submitted to P. O. Dept.; Gonyon was selected.   LRI

Heathville: Pop. 225; elev. 102; US Rt 360. Near center of middle third of county. Named for family of John Heath, earlier called Hughlet's Tavern; then Heath's Store; became county seat in 1706.   WP: Va 559; EcD county

Hyacinth: Pop. 60. Midway in extreme western portion of county.   DU

Lewisetta: Pop. 160 (summer Pop. 300). In northeastern part of county, on half-moon shaped peninsula of Potomac. Had first wharf and warehouse on peninsula.   LRI

Lilian: Pop. 5; US Rt 360. In northeast area of county. Postoffice established 1885. Named for Lilian Cockrell who married George N. Reed, son of Elijah Reed. Earlier spelling was Lillian, but Postoffice Dept. cut out one of the "l's".   LRI

Lottsburg: Pop. 90. Near center of north third of county. Family by name of Lot lived in community around 1695. Reported that postoffice when established in 1840 was given name from early family.   LRI

Miskomin: Pop. 100. On southwest boundary near mid-point of county. Named for Methodist minister, the Rev. H. E. Miskomin, in 1865.   LRI

Mundy Point: Pop. 10. In extreme northwest area of county.   DU

Rainswood: Pop. 50. Near county boundary in west half of county. Surrounding land in woods, owned by Rain family. Then Rain's woods became Rainswood.   LRI

Reedsville: Pop. 400. In northeast part, on narrow peninsula, sprung up since 1875. Prominent fishing port; most important fish oil, fish meal, and scrap center on the coast. Named for Elijah Reed who came from Maine and settled here; the first postmaster in 1888 was George N. Reed, son of Elijah Reed.
LRI; VaVCo 8-1950

Sunnybank: Pop. 95. In northeast corner of county. Admirer of writer, Albert Payson Terhune, whose home was named Sunnybank, so chose name for postoffice.   LRI

Walmsley: Pop. 30. In extreme southwest area of western part. Original name Swanton; confusion with Swanton, Vt. Present name from Methodist minister preaching in area about 1850.   LRI

Wicomico Church. (Pron. Y-kom-eye-ko). Pop. 350. In southern part of eastern third of county. Village takes its name from an early chapel, first church of the first Lees to settle in Virginia. Originally spelled "Wicocomico" church; later, in 1653, became Lee Parish.   VaVCo 8-1950; WP: Va 552

NOTTOWAY COUNTY

Formed 1788; named for Indian tribe Mangoac or Nadowa, Anglicized into Nottoway; name meant "snake" or "enemy". Area: 308 sq.mi.; Pop. 15,141; Pop. per sq.mi., 49.2. First courthouse at Hendersonville, named for proprietor of store. 72.1% county area forested. 12.3% county area in Camp Pickett. Rank occupational groups: trade, manufacturing, agriculture. Rank agricultural income: field crops, livestock, dairy. Gannett 327

Blackstone: Ry N&W; elev. 425; Pop. 3,659; increase Pop. 1950-60, 3.4%; US Rt 460. In mid-point of southeastern fourth of county. Original name, "Blacks and Whites"; two taverns, Mr. Schwartz (Black in German) and Mr. White, operators. Chose Bellefonte; too similar to Bellefonte, Pa. Renamed for English jurist, Sir William Blackstone, in 1885. Incorporated 1888. Blackstone College operated 1892-1950. Water supply, Pickett reservoir on Nottoway River; filtered, chlorinated. VaVCo 12-1950; 11-1952

Burkeville: Rys N&W, SOU; elev. 515; Pop. 705; increase Pop. 1950-60, 1.4%; US Rts 360, 460. At mid-point near west county boundary. Burke's Junction was early name railroad stop. Burkeville named for Colonel Samuel Dabney Burke (1794-1880). WP: Va 594; Turner 170

Crewe: Ry N&W; Pop. 2,012; US Rt 460. Crewe began 1886 when railway roundhouse erected, halfway between Norfolk and Roanoke; named for Crewe, English railroad center. Water, Little Nottoway River; filtered, chlorinated. VaVCo 12-1950

Nottoway: Ry N&W; elev. 420; Pop. 100; US Rt 460. In center of county. County seat. Name meaning "rattlesnake" or "adder".

Piedmont State Hospital for mentally ill uses buildings of former sanitarium for tuberculosis patients, founded in 1918. Located near Burkeville.
— Va Govt 59

Sweathouse Creek flows north in northeastern portion of county. Land grant on Sweat House Branch, Nov. 1729. 35 V 273

ORANGE COUNTY

Formed 1734; named for Prince of Orange, who that year had married Princess Anne, daughter of George II. Area: 354 sq.mi.; Pop. 12,900; Pop. per sq.mi., 36.4. Rank occupational groups: manufacturing, agriculture, trade. Rank agricultural income: livestock, dairy, poultry.   Roads 89

Barboursville: Ry SOU; elev. 537; Pop. 150; US Rt 33. In southern area of southwest portion of county. Historic home Barboursville near; James Barbour served as Virginia Governor, United States senator, Secretary of War, Minister of England. Home burned Christmas Day, 1884; never rebuilt.

Chr.-Mas 413; EcD county

Burr Hill: Pop. 100. In northern portion of eastern third of county.   DU

Germanna, location on Rapidan River, on which colony of Germans settled in 1714; brought there by Governor Spotswood to mine and smelt iron. Between 1721 and 1726, many left to claim and settle on lands farther inland.

VaVCo 5-1952; Gottmann 79

Gordonsville: Ry C&O; elev. 440; Pop. 1,109; US Rts 15, 33. Beale Tavern at what now junction of Routes 15, 33. Nathaniel Gordon purchased 1,350 acres April 1787; built Gordon Inn; community came to be known as Gordonsville. Louisa Railroad reached Gordonsville, 1840. Water supply from springs; chlorinated.   TD 9-23-1951; VaVCo 5-1952

Grassland: Pop. 27. Near mid-point of west area of east half of county. Virginia Central Railroad in 1877 constructed through bluegrass field of Hawfield estate. Green grassy field suggested name Grassland.   LRI

Lahore: Pop. 15. In center of southeast portion of county. Was Woolfolk. In 1881, request to change name to more unusual.   TD 9-28-1951

Locustgrove: Pop. 50. In east area of northwest fourth of county. Large groves of locust trees were here formerly; which gave community its name. LRI

Mine Run (Tender): Pop. 40. Near mid-point Spotsylvania line. Never failing spring near postoffice, a source of stream which flows through area having gold mining many years ago; believed this gave name to stream, which later became name of postoffice.   LRI

Montpelier (RR Montpelier Station): Ry SOU; Pop. 150. In northwest part of east third of county. Montpelier, home of the Madisons, built 1741.

EcD county

Orange: Rys C&O, SOU; elev. 525; Pop. 2,955; increase Pop. 1950-60, 11.0%; US Rt 15. In 1749, county seat at present location. Village first incorporated 1834; charter repealed; again incorporated 1885; present charter 1896. Water supply, Rapidan River; treated, coagulated, settled, chlorinated.

EcD county; Scott 40

Piedmont Research Station; 33 acres. Investigation of field crop production.

Com Va 9-1953

Rhoadsville P.O.; Lafayette Station. Pop. 78. Near center of east third of county. Lafayette, station on Narrow Gauge Railroad, named in honor of the Marquis. Here he camped for a night, his headquarters under a large tree.

Scott 175

Seigen Forest, named for the German city from which the Germanna colonists came, includes 270 acres owned by the Germanna Foundation. Here, descendants of the early colonists gather annually and report progress in their preservation of history.　　　　　　　DNR; Wayland: Germanna 21, 87.

Somerset: Ry SOU; Pop. 100. In northeast part of east third of county. President Madison's sister's home, Somerset, built 1802. Nearby railroad station named for that home.　　　　　　　　　　　　　　　　　Scott 212

Unionville: Ry SOU; Pop. 250. At mid-point in east middle third of county. Named for first church in the community.　　　　　　　　ESS county 38

PAGE COUNTY

Formed 1831; named for John Page, governor of Virginia, 1802-1805. Area: 316 sq.mi.; Pop. 15,572; Pop. per sq.mi., 49.3; increase Pop. 1950-60, 1.1%. Settlement began 1726. 63.7% county area forested. 31.2% area owned by federal government. Rank occupational groups: manufacturing, trade, construction. Rank agricultural income: livestock, poultry, dairy.   Roads 88

Big Meadows received name from large, nearly level, panoramic view area on summit of Blue Ridge in Shenandoah National Park. Alt. 3,500. Picnic and camp grounds; lodge and tourist attractions.   GSW: CF

Luray: Ry N&W; elev. 820; Pop. 3,014; increase Pop. 1950-60, 10.3%; US Rts 211, 340. Four suppositions regarding the origin of the name. 1. Lewis Ray, early blacksmith, had popular stopping place for travelers, and place name was coined from his name, Lew Ray's. 2. Luray is a corruption of Lorraine. 3. Marye family came from Luray, France. 4. Name given by William Staige Marye, an Indian name. Water supply from two mountain sources and spring; chlorinated.   VGb 38; Strickler: PC 108-111.

Luray Caverns were discovered 1878. Spectacular array of formations made by flowstone and dripstone in columns and draperies. Lofty stone campanile, Belle Brown Northcott Singing Tower, having forty-seven bells, given by the late T. C. Northcott. Tower erected 1937 and presented to the town of Luray.
                    Com Va 6-1936; Stevens 95; VGb 38

Marys Rock Mountain, alt. 3,514, is near mid-point of southern boundary of county. Lower part penetrated by tunnel 700 feet in length; Skyline Drive passes through. One explanation of name: Mary, wife of Frances Thornton, a large landowner thereabout. Another explanation: William Randolph Barbee, a sculptor, named rock for his wife, Mary McKay.   Wayland SV 9; Lambert 16

Overall: elev. 665; Pop. 15. At northern edge of county, near mouth of Overall Run, formerly Milford, was named for a family.   Strickler PC 136

Rileyville: Ry N&W; elev. 744; Pop. 250; US Rt 340. In northeast part of county. Was earlier Cedar Postoffice; was given present name in 1885; named for a local family. Three boats loaded with plank to be sold at Riverton in 1888 were last three boats with that kind of load and started from Rileyville.
                    Steeles 1175; Wayland: Hist Shenandoah Co. 349

Shenandoah: Ry N&W; elev. 1,079; Pop. 1,839; US Rt 340. On southwest boundary of county. Town incorporated February 12, 1884, under name Milnes; William Milnes, manufacturer of pig iron. Name changed to Shenandoah, Febru-

ary 1890. Water supply from South Fork Shenandoah River; filtered, chlorinated.   Strickler PC 224

Skyland was "dude ranch" called Stony Man Camp; to avoid Stony Man
Postoffice at base of ridge, Skyland chosen as camp name. While living here,
Pollock fought to protect forests, develop system of trails, built a swimming
pool, and staged unusual and stupendous shows. Elev. 3,350. At eastern edge of
county.   Lambert 40; Pollock: Skyland 55

Stanley: Ry N&W; elev. 1,060; Pop. 1,039; increase Pop. 1950-60, 160.4%;
US Rt 340. In center of southwest half of county. Assembly incorporated Stanley, February 1900; named for Stanley McNider, son of president land development company.   Strickler PC 232

Stony Man, alt. 4,031 ft., east central edge of county, has spectacular cliffs
of weathered greenstone rock forming profile of a man. Second highest peak in
Park.   Lambert 66

PATRICK COUNTY

Formed 1790; named for Patrick Henry, who thus had two counties named for him. Area: 469 sq.mi.; Pop. 15,282; Pop. per sq.mi., 32.6. Nearly three-fourths county area forested. 3.5% county area included in Philpott Reservoir, Blue Ridge Parkway, and Fairy Stone Park. Rank occupational groups: manufacturing, agriculture, trade. Rank agricultural income: field crops, livestock, dairy.   Roads 72

Ararat (Blue Ridge Academy): Pop. 300. In southwest portion of county. Named for River; village one mile east of river.   Steeles 1159

Ararat River given name by Bible informed settlers. Stream flows from a mountain; naming seemed quite obvious.   LRI

Claudville: Pop. 15. In southwest portion of county. Probably named for local landowner.   LRI

Critz: Pop. 75. In southwest portion of county. Name from family.   LRI

Meadows of Dan: elev. 2,900; Pop. 30; US Rt 58. In northwest portion of county. Named because meadows along Dan River.   Steeles 1171

North Mayo River named for early settlers; highly regarded in area. One of Mayos was member Byrd Surveying party in 1700's.   LRI

Patrick Springs: Pop. 500. Near center of southeast fourth of county. Formerly mineral springs were an attractive summer resort hotel, which later burned. Now Bible Conference location.   LRI

South Mayo River

Stuart: elev. 1,450; Pop. 974; US Rt 58. Near mid-point of south half of county. Early name Taylorville; often called Patrick Court House, county seat established 1792. Named Stuart in honor of General J. E. B. Stuart; incorporated November 22, 1884. Water supply: mountain watersheds and wells; chlorinated.   LRI

Vesta: Pop. 120. In northwest part of west half of county. Probably named for daughter of leading citizen.   LRI

Woolwine: Pop. 100. In northwest portion of county. Name from family.   LRI

PITTSYLVANIA COUNTY

Formed 1766; named for William Pitt, Earl of Chatham, British statesman. Largest county in Virginia; area: 1,012 sq.mi.; Pop. 58,296; Pop. per sq.mi., 57.5. Two-thirds county area wooded. Virginia's leading producer flue-cured tobacco. Rank occupational groups: manufacturing, farming, trade. Rank agricultural income: field crops, livestock, poultry.   Roads 70

Ajax: Pop. ———. On county boundary in northwest portion.   DU

Averett College: Began 1859, Union Female College. Became Roanoke College, 1864. Named Averett in 1917 in affectionate recognition of two men. Two-year college, operated under Baptist General Association of Virginia. In Danville.
                    Ann.Bul.

Blairs: Ry SOU; elev. 660; Pop. 150. Near mid-point of south half of county. Mr. John Blair, contributor of railroad station land, prominent citizen, member Virginia House of Delegates. Name had "S" added to distinguish from Blair, West Virginia.   LRI

Bright Tobacco Research Station at Chatham. 144 acres for investigating disease-resistant varieties.   Com Va, Sept 1953

Callands: Pop. 20. Near mid-point of west boundary of county. Named for Samuel Callands, store keeper. Was county seat until 1777, town named Chatham. When county seat moved to Sandy River location, that location was first known as Competition.   Clement 101

Chatham, was Competition until 1874, when named Chatham for William Pitt, Earl of Chatham. Ry SOU; elev. 830; Pop. 1,822; increase Pop. 1950-60, 25.1%. Incorporated 1852.   Clement 210

Community College: was first branch college of VPI, established 1946. Became community college; has 50 acre campus.   Com Va 7-1965

Danville (independent city): Area: 14 sq.mi.; Pop. 48,000; increase Pop. 1950-60, 32.8%; Rys C&NW, NF&D, SOU; elev. 410; US Rts 29, 58, 360. Earliest settlement called "The Ford" at Wynn's Falls. William Wynne early settler; Wynne's Creek and Wynne's Falls received name from him. In 1793, chartered town given name Danville after the river. Town incorporated 1830. Jefferson Davis arrived April 3, 1865; for one week, capital of Confederacy. Has largest single unit textile mill in the world. Water supply, Dan River; filtered, chlorinated.   Clement 38; VHSSA 50; EcD county

Danville Technical Institute, established 1935, maintained by city. Has 110 acre campus.   Com Va 7-1965

Dry Fork: Ry SOU; elev. 625; Pop. 250. In mid-northern area of southern half of county. Two small streams or forks run together at this place; when there is a long dry spell, the two forks dry up. LRI

Galveston Mills named by native of Gretna who had returned from living in Galveston, Texas; named about 1860. Virginia's oldest grist mill dating from 1769. VaVCo 3-1953

Gretna: Ry SOU; Pop. 900; increase Pop. 1950-60, 12%. In 1879, railroad station, Franklin Junction, and postoffice Elba. In 1916, name changed to Gretna. Water supply, Georges Creek; filtered, chlorinated. VaVCo 3-1953

Hargrave Military Academy, established 1909, as Chatham Training School. In 1925, name became Hargrave Military Academy in honor of J. Hunt Hargrave, influential benefactor. Ann.Bul.

Hurt: Ry SOU; Pop. 800. At mid-point near northern boundary. Land deeded to John L. Hurt, Jr., who planned lots and financed home-building. Now incorporated. LRI

Java: Pop. 23. In mid-eastern portion of county. DU

Keeling: Pop. 30; elev. 715; US Rt 360. Near center of southeast fourth of county. A man named Keeling was owner and proprietor of store when postoffice established. LRI

Mount Herman: Pop. 100. Branch of Danville postoffice. Postal station named for its community. LRI

Pittsville: Pop. 50. In northwest portion of county. Mining of barites and other minerals flourished in 1880's. The mines were abandoned, leaving the pits; this explains Pittsville. LRI

Ringgold: Ry SOU; elev. 580; Pop. 150. In southwest portion of county. Gold was discovered there and a mine was started, but there was only enough gold to make a ring. Steeles 1175

Sandy Level: Pop. 20. In northwestern portion of county. From the community's sandy and level local conditions, it was named Sandy Level. LRI

Schoolfield (annexed to Danville since 1950). Name from R. A. Schoolfield of Riverside and Dan River Cotton Mills.
Fuller: Pittsylvania Co. Geog. Supplement, 20

Stratford College, in Danville, had beginning in 1851 as Danville Female Institute. Successor somewhat connected with Methodist Church. In 1930, local citizens fostered institution named Stratford Hall. The three predecessors became Stratford College, offering two years of liberal arts. Stratford name was chosen to link American and English cultures honoring Robert E. Lee and William Shakespeare, whose homes were called Stratford. In 1967, initiated offering four years of college work and conferring Bachelor of Arts degree.

Ann.Bul.

Sutherlin: Ry SOU; Pop. 25. Near Halifax line in southeast portion of county. Named for Major Wm. T. Sutherlin, resident of Danville, property owner, lived many years following Civil War.   LRI

Turkey Cock Mountain gets name because many flocks of wild turkeys once were there.   Clement 30

Whitethorne Creek flows in vicinity south of Gretna and is tributary of Banister River. Land grant in 1748 on Whitethorne Creek.   25 V 298

POWHATAN COUNTY

Formed 1777; named for noted Indian chief. Area: 268 sq.mi.; Pop. 6,747; Pop. per sq.mi., 25.2; Increase Pop. 1950-60, 21.4%. Three-fourths total area forested. French Hugenots arrived about 1700. Rank occupational groups: agriculture, manufacturing, trade. Rank agricultural income: dairy, field crops, livestock.

Long 167; EcD county

Ballsville: Pop. 40; elev. 397. Named for local family. Steeles 1159

Beaumont: Pop. ———. Near James in northeast part of west half of county. Beaumont Industrial School for Boys, 2,400 acres. Once large plantation owned by Mr. Beaumont, a Frenchman. Beaumont in French means "beautiful hills"; this is a lovely place along the winding James River with truly beautiful hills.

LRI

Clayville: Ry SOU; Pop. 100. In extreme southeastern part of county. Named for local clay products manufacturing company. Steeles 1162

Fine Creek: drains middle area of north part of county. Oct. 9, 1727, land sale on Fine Creek. June 11, 1729, land patent on Fine Creek.

32 V 392; 34 V 211

Jefferson, an early village. Pop. 40. Near middle of north half of county. Peter Jefferson, father of Thomas Jefferson, owned property nearby, and believed village named for him.

LRI

Jones Creek flows in north part of east half of county. Febr. 15, 1731, land sale on Jones Creek. Aug. 15, 1753, record of land sold on Jones' Creek.

2 V 195, 8.

Macon: Pop. 15; in south central portion. Family named Macon located 1753; established stage coach tavern, operated livery stable, grist mill, sawmill, and store. Part of earliest building still in use. Believed postoffice named for family.

LRI

Moseley: Ry SOU; Pop. 100. Near Chesterfield line in southeast portion. Named for local family. Steeles 1172

Powhatan Court House: Pop. 300. First court house built about 1777; village known for many years as Scottsville for Revolutionary soldier, county resident, General Charles Scott. Dunlora Academy established 1830 nearby; later moved to Richmond and developed into Richmond College, now University of Richmond. Water supply, well; aerated, filtered, treated.

Roads 68; EcD county

Powhatan Lake Fish Pond, stocked by Commission of Game and Inland Fisheries, 75 acres, was formerly Finche's Mill Pond. EcD county

Trenholm: Pop. 25. In northwest portion of county. DU

PRINCE EDWARD COUNTY

Formed 1753; named for Prince Edward, son of Frederick of Wales, and younger brother of King George II. Area: 357 sq.mi.; Pop. 14,121; Pop. per sq.mi., 39.6. Land grants date from 1730. Nearly three-fourths county area forested. Rank occupational groups: manufacturing, trade, agriculture. Rank agricultural income: field crops, dairy, livestock.   Roads 69

Briery Creek flows northeast, drains eastern part of middle portion of county, tributary of Sandy River. Land grant on Briery Creek 1739.   Bradshaw 5

Buffalo Creek flows northeast along edges of western and middle portions of county, tributary of Appomattox River. Buffaloe River deeds as early as 1740. Bridge over Buffalo, Aug. 1748.   18 V 195; Bradshaw 4

Bush River flows north across the county, drains into Appomattox River. Land grant on Bush River, Sept. 8, 1729.   Bradshaw 2

Darlington Heights: Pop. 60. In southwest portion of county. Darlington derived from place in England; Heights from rather high elevation of locality. Kyanite, an aluminum silicate, mined and processed at Baker Mountain, near Darlington Heights.   LRI; EcD county

Farmville: Ry N&W; elev. 335; Pop. 4,293; US Rts 15, 460. Earliest name, Rutledge's Ford. In 1798, Farmville founded as distributing and trading point for flat-bottomed boats on the Appomattox River. County seat; has county fair of five counties; Southside Community Hospital serves large adjacent area. Incorporated 1832. Water supply from Buffalo Creek; filtered, chlorinated.
                           62 V 466; VaVCo 7-1952; EcD county

Gallion State Forest borders southwestern portion of Prince Edward State Forest. Two forests total area, 6,000+ acres, are in southeast portion of county. Edward D. Gallion, native of Prince Edward, bequeathed property to State of Virginia to use for a forestry reservation under the management of the State Forestry Commission. State bought additional land and members of Civilian Conservation Corps worked at forestry improvement.   Bradshaw 613

Goodwin Lake in southeast portion. United States Government purchased 740 acres from Samuel Goodwin, November 12, 1936. The lake was evidently named for the earlier land-owner.   LRI

Green Bay: Ry SOU; Pop. 100; US Rt 360. In southeast portion of county. Near newly located railroad station, small lake with green moss cover. Railroad official proposed call station Green Bay; everyone agreed and name was painted on station. Postoffice automatically took that name.   LRI

Hampden-Sydney: Pop. 600. Near center of county. Location Hampden-Sydney College.

Hampden-Sydney College opened January 1, 1776. Named for two martyrs, John Hampden and Algernon Sidney. (Proposed charter name, Hampden-Sidney. — 6 W (1) 186.) Incorporated 1783; affiliated with Presbyterian Church of the United States. Four-year liberal arts; widely known because of successful alumni.   WP: Va 398; VaDoc25, p. 23.

Longwood College traces to girls' school incorporated in Farmville in 1839. In 1884, transferred to state to become State Normal School, first state institution for higher education of women in Virginia. Became State Normal School for Women in 1914. Name changed to State Teachers College at Farmville in 1924. In 1949, name became Longwood College; name from home of General Joseph E. Johnston near the town. Offers bachelors and masters degrees.
                    Va Govt 47+; Ann.Bul.

Prospect: Ry N&W; Pop. 125; US Rt 460. In northwestern portion of county.   DU

Rice: Ry N&W; elev. 438; Pop. 300; US Rts 307, 460. In northeast portion of county. About 1775, William Rice built meeting house for dissenters near present town. Originally, Rice Meeting House; town named for local church, which was named for local family.   Steeles 1175; Bradshaw 79

Sandy River flows north, drains eastern portion of county, tributary of Appomattox. Land grants on Sandy River dating 1735.   22 V 194

Worsham: Pop. 35; US Rt 15. In center of county. Charles Anderson's Tavern in 1749; became site of courthouse when county established. Place named Worsham for family; most conspicuous of family, Branch C. Worsham, county clerk, 1825-186—. Walls of old jail built in 1739 remain.
                    62 V 455+; Burrell: Hist. Pr. Ed. Co. 835; WP: Va 298.

PRINCE GEORGE COUNTY

Formed 1702; name from Prince George of Denmark, husband of Queen Anne. Area: 281 sq.mi.; Pop. 20,270; Pop. per sq.mi., 72.1; Increase Pop. 1950-60, 30.3%. Captain Christopher Newport with reconaissance party sailed past mouth of Appomattox and found clearing, May 8, 1607. 65.6% county area forested. Rank occupational groups: manufacturing, trade, agriculture. Rank agricultural income: field crops, livestock, dairy.   Roads 80; Lutz PGH 3

Disputanta: Ry N&W; elev. 115; Pop. 350; US Rt 460. Near mid-point of southeast boundary of county. Factions contended about naming of new community; some wag suggested Disputanta; name accepted.   Lutz PGH 151

Federal Reformatory at Hopewell, 1,485.80 acres of original Camp Lee, is a model prison operated by Department of Justice.

Com Va, 11-1957; EcD county

Fort Lee: Ry N&W; Pop. ———. Large military installation, named for General Robert E. Lee. 7,603 acres, 4.2% of county area. East of Petersburg and portion in area between Colonial Heights and Hopewell.   EcD county

Hopewell (independent city): Area: 7 sq.mi.; Rys N&W, SAL; elev. 50; Pop. 22,000; increase Pop. 1950-60, 75.1%. In 1635, Frances Eppes patented large tract including original Charles City Plantation. A part of this estate was called Hopewell; that name from ship *Merchant's Hope*, that had brought Eppes to the colony. Part of land named Hopewell Farms; the city's name from these names. The modern city of Hopewell traces to 1613 when Sir Thomas Dale laid out plantation Bermuda City, to distinguish from Bermuda Hundred. Name changed to Charles City Point; shortened to City Point. Massacre in 1622. Hopewell incorporated 1916; Old City Point annexed 1923. DuPont had contract for guncotton from British and French in 1914. Rank occupational groups: manufacturing, trade, public administration. Water supply from Appomattox River; filtered, chlorinated.   Lutz PGH p. xii; Com Va 9-1952; VaVCo 8-1953

Petersburg (independent city): Area 8 sq.mi.; elev. 15; Rys ACL, N&W, SAL; Pop. 37,000; increase Pop. 1950-60, 4.8%; US Rts 301, 460. Founding Fort Henry in 1645-46 marks beginning Petersburg. Indian trader, Peter Jones, settled 1675. Peter Jones Trading Station grew into village Peter's Point. In September 1732, William Byrd II, proposed naming Petersburg. In 1784, settlements at falls of Appomattox united as Petersburg. Became city in 1850.

WP: Va 274; VaVCo 7-1953

Petersburg National Military Park established by Act of Congress July 3, 1926. Gross acreage more than 1,500; thirty-two locations included in route of tour; among points of interest Crater and Battlefield Museum.

Lykes: P'burg Natl. Mil. Park, 46, 56.

Petersburg State Colony for mentally retarded and Central State Hospital for mentally ill were originally for Negroes. Central State Hospital founded in 1870. Va Govt 67, 24

Powell Creek flows north along eastern edge of central area of county, tributary of James. John Powell's Creek in land grant, July 13, 1635. 3 V 185

Prince George C. H.: Pop. 80. Courthouse building dates from 1810.

Richard Bland College named for Richard Bland whose writings prior to 1775 stirred Revolutionary opinion. Authorized 1960; two-year college; confers Associate of Arts degree. Ann. Bul.

Walnut Hill: (part of Petersburg). Fashionable suburb; summer playground. Officially part of city Jan. 1, 1956.
WP: Va 273; Scott-Wyatt: Petersburg Story, 64, 340.

Ward's Creek, in eastern portion of county, tributary of James. Captain John Ward arrived April 22, 1619, settled at Ward Creek. Land grant, July 13, 1635. 3 V 186

PRINCE WILLIAM COUNTY

Formed 1730; named for William Augusta, Duke of Cumberland, second son of King George II. Area: 345 sq.mi.; Pop. 50,164; Pop. per sq.mi., 146.4; increase Pop. 1950-60, 69.5%. First county seat on south side of Occoquan Creek; second on Cedar Run (1742-1759); third at Dumfries (1760-1822); fourth at Brentville (1822-1892); fifth at Manassas (1892-   ). About half of county wooded. 18.8% county area in federal and state-owned areas. Rank occupational groups: public administration, trade, construction. Rank agricultural income: livestock, dairy, poultry.   Roads 85

Bristow: Ry SOU; Pop. 75. A few miles west of county's center. Bristow, non-resident Englishman in Revolution; estate escheated to Commonwealth; name of community.   Harrison LPW 187

Catharpin: Pop. 20. Near Bull Run in northwest portion of county. A ship captain settled in the area.   Ratcliffe

Conway-Robinson Memorial State Forest, 400 acres in central part of western third of county, demonstrates conservation and timber production methods. Miss Agnes Conway Robinson conveyed to Commonwealth of Virginia in memory of her father, Conway Robinson (1805-1884), eminent jurist and author.
                                                                  Ratcliffe

Dumfries: Pop. 1,368; US Rt 1. In extreme southeast portion. Tobacco warehouse built 1730; town established 1749; became tobacco-shipping port. First and oldest town of earliest years of Prince William. John Graham, one of the first trustees, named town for his old home in Scotland.
                                            WPA: Pr. Will., 88; Gannett 109; Roads 17

Gainesville: Ry SOU; Pop. 150; US Rts 29, 211. In center of west half of county. Thomas Gaines (landowner) insisted name Gainesville when railroad built in 1850.   WPA: Pr.Will., 168

Haymarket: Ry SOU; Pop. 257; US Rt 15. In extreme southwest portion of the county. Was Red House in the 18th century; became Haymarket in 1799. William Skinner received large inheritance in 1752; laid out town Haymarket in 1798; named after famous race course in London.
                                                    WPA: Pr. Will., 174; Ratcliffe

Manassas: Rys C&O, SOU; elev. 310; Pop. 5,700; Pop. increase 1950-60, 215.9%. In northeast area of west half of county. Manassas Junction in 1852; incorporated as Manassas in 1873; name from Manasseh's. County seat. Water supply from five wells; chlorinated.   WPA: Pr.Will., 118

Manassas National Battlefield Park on northern boundary at about extreme corner of western third of county, northeast of Manassas. The park contains 1,670 acres and has a museum and field markers provided.

EcD county; Manassas — Historical Handbook

Manassas Park: Pop. 5,342. Residential community takes name from nearby town. Water supply, four wells.

Nebasco Creek in northeast portion of county; tributary of Potomac. Indian name, "at the point of rock".

Ratcliffe

Nokesville: Ry SOU; elev. 260; Pop. 100. In southwest area of west half of county. Named for owners of nearby site. WPA: Pr.Will., 150

Occoquan: Pop. 301. In northeast portion of county. At falls of stream, in 1729, "King Carter" built landing here to ship copper ore; town called Colchester established in 1753. Occoquan founded in 1804; incorporated 1874. Indian name means "at the end of the river." Roads 18; Sprouse 21; Ratcliffe

Powells Creek drains central eastern portion; tributary of Potomac. Originally Indian name, Yosocomico, which means "in the middle of the enclosure", but was changed to Powells River sometime between 1653-1670.

Ratcliffe

Prince William Forest Park, 12,230 acres, is southernmost unit of National Capital Park and is administered by National Park Service. Near Triangle, includes watershed of Quantico Creek branches; has hiking trails, fishing from stocked lakes, and cabin camps.

Com Va 5-1964; Folder, Prince William Forest Park

Quantico: RF&P Ry; elev. 35; Pop. 1,015. Name is an Indian word meaning "dancing" or "place of dancing". Services for vessels of Potomac Navy in Revolution. Incorporated 1874; reincorporated 1908. Training camp marines in 1917; permanent post since 1918. US Marine Corps Base includes 28,845.73 acres in Prince William County. WPA: Pr.Will., 55

Quantico Creek drains southeast portion of county; tributary of Potomac.

Quantico Marine School: The enormous size of the undeveloped landscape in the southeast area of the county makes it a major potential outdoor recreation resource, involving 57,433 acres of land, wetlands, and water, and 5 to 6 miles of shoreland along the Potomac River. The major portion of the base is covered by an oak-hickory forest on rolling lands. Potomac Valley, etc. p. 22

Triangle: Pop. 2,948; US Rt 1. Triangle, junction of highways. In southeastern portion of county. WPA: Pr.Will., 95

Woodbridge: Ry RF&P; Pop. 15,000; US Rt 1. In northeast portion of county. First called Occoquan Plantation and owned by George Mason. Woodbridge was named by his son Thomas for the wooden bridge that was built across the river in 1798; replacing the ferry across Occoquan Creek. Tolls were established. The wooden bridge was replaced in 1927. Water supply from Quantico town supply; filtered, chlorinated.   Sprouse 29; LRI; Steeles 1180

Yorkshire: Pop. 1,500. Is near Manassas. Robert Portner, practically penniless, came from Germany, made a fortune as brewer, built houses, one of which named Yorkshire. Name of community from that house. Believed house name from City of York in England, capital of Yorkshire.   Ratcliffe; LRI

PULASKI COUNTY

Formed 1839; named for Count Casimir Pulaski, killed in siege of Savannah, 1779. Area: 327 sq.mi.; Pop. 27,258; Pop. per sq.mi., 83.4. Earliest settlement at Dunkards Bottom on New River between 1745 and 1750. About 52% county area forested. 8.9% county area in Jefferson National Park. Rank occupational groups: manufacturing, trade, construction. Rank agricultural income: livestock, dairy, vegetables.

Roads 77; EcD county

Allisonia: Ry N&W; Pop. 160. In southwest corner of county. Named for family of early settlers named Allison. LRI

Back Creek flows eastward in northern part of county; tributary of New River. A creek back against a large mountain; thus Back Creek. LRI

Belspring: Ry N&W; elev. 1,770; Pop. 420. In northeastern part of northeastern fourth of county. The flow of water from large spring caused a ringing sound; the spring became known as Bell Spring; later Belspring became town name. LRI

Claytor Lake State Park on New River, eastern part of county; area 488 acres; shoreline 100 miles. Formed by Appalachian Power Company Dam; impounded New River for hydro-electric purposes; park has modern conveniences; provides bathing, boating, and fishing. Claytor Lake State Park, authorized 1947, dedicated May 29, 1948. Named for Graham Claytor, president of American Power Company, of which Appalachian Power Company is a subsidiary. LRI

Draper: Ry N&W; Pop. 233. Named for family of Mary Draper, who married an Ingles and was captured by the Indians. LRI

Dublin: Ry N&W; elev. 2,060; Pop. 1,427; increase Pop. 1950-60, 8.6%; US Rt 11. Near center of county. The first settler was William Christian from Ireland; thus Dublin. Water supply, three drilled wells; chlorinated. LRI

Fairlawn: Pop. 1,325. In northeast portion of county. Development started during outbreak of World War II; houses quickly constructed for workers in arsenal. DU

Hiwassee: Ry N&W; Pop. 400. Near center of southwest portion of county. Indian name, meaning savannah or meadow. American Pigment Corporation located in 1936, mines earth pigments; processed at Hiwassee and Pulaski. LRI

Newbern: elev. 2,135; Pop. 200. Slightly south of center of county. First county seat, 1839-1895. First settlers were Swiss people; gave name New Bern; later Newbern. Water supply, drilled well. LRI

New River: elev. 1,757; Ry N&W; Pop. 600. Near mid-eastern edge of county; New River nearby.   LRI

Parrott: Pop. 650. In extreme northeast corner of county. John Parrott opened and operated the first coal mine in this area.   LRI

Pulaski: Ry N&W; elev. 1,905; Pop. 11,600; increase Pop. 1950-60, 13.5%; US Rt 11. Martin's Tank took name from prominent local family; became Martin's in 1877. County seat name from chivalrous Polish count. Water supply, impounded reservoirs; filtered, chlorinated, fluorinated.

Snowville: elev. 1,887; Pop. 80. Founded by Asial Snow; developed industries; prospered 1830-50. First Christian Church; "mother" Christian Church of region. Near southeast corner of county.   VaVCo 9-1951

Woolwine Spring in east central area east of Newbern, flows greatest quantity of water of all springs in Virginia. Flows 10,500 gallons a minute, which totals 15,000,000 gallons per day. Name because mineral spring on the Woolwine farm. Now discharges below water level of Claytor Lake.   LRI

RAPPAHANNOCK COUNTY

Formed 1833; named for headwaters of Rappahannock River which received name from Indian tribe living along its banks. Area: 267 sq.mi.; Pop. 5,368; Pop. per sq.mi., 201. Settlement began about 1730. More than half county area forested. 18.6% county area in Shenandoah National Park. Rank occupational groups: agriculture, manufacturing, construction. Rank agricultural income: livestock, fruit and nuts, dairy.   VaVCo 10-1951; Tate 88; EcD county

Amissville: Pop. 50; US Rt 211. Near eastern corner of county. Named for family group of Joseph Amiss who received land grant in 1763.   Hite 206

Castleton: Pop. 40. Near mid-point of southeast boundary of county. Named for Castle Mountain.
LRI

Chester Gap: Pop. 100; US Rt 522; in Blue Ridge, alt. 1,320. Gap was Happy Creek Gap on 1738 map. Sept. 26, 1794, diary record of crossing Chester Gap of Blue Ridge. Gap named for early settler.
Couper II, 1118; 11 W (1) 4; 13 V 289.

Flint Hill: Pop. 200; US Rt 522. Near center of north fourth of county. Because of white flint near location of village, named Flint Hill.   Hite 193

Huntly: Pop. 25; US Rt 522. In extreme north part of county. Formerly noted for its hunting.   Steeles 1168

Laurel Mills: (Mail Castleton): Pop. 25. Near mid-point southeast boundary of county. Laurel trees bloom.   LRI

Sperryville: elev. 700; Pop. 300; US Rts 211, 522. Man named Sperry built a house, beginning of town, probably latter half of 18th century. In northeast part of southwest fourth of county. Water supply, springs.   Hite 143

Thornton River flows southeast in western and central portions of eastern part of county. Name from Thornton family, early land owners.   WP: Va 614

Viewtown: Pop. 40. In east portion of county near Rappahannock line. Located on high ground with a beautiful view.   Steeles 1179

Washington: elev. 603; Pop. 255; US Rts 211, 522; increase Pop. 1950-60, 2.4%. County seat. Surveyed, platted, and established by George Washington on July 24, 1749; named by Thomas, Lord Fairfax. Incorporated as a town, 1792. Avon Mills, 200-year-old grist mill, near town. Skyline Ski area nearby;

2,400 foot slope with drop of 500 feet. Water supply, infiltration gallery and well; chlorinated.   VaVCo 7-1949, 10-1951

Woodville: elev. 600; Pop. 60; US Rt 522. Near center of south fourth of county. Named for Rev. John Woodville, last rector of old St. Mark's parish.

Hite 80

RICHMOND COUNTY

Formed 1692; named for town Richmond, Surrey County, England. Another suggestion that name from Duke of Richmond, living when county formed. Area: 192 sq.mi.; Pop. 6,375; Pop. per sq.mi., 32.2; increase Pop. 1950-60, 3.0%. Settlement began 1640. Rank occupational groups: manufacturing, agriculture, trade. Rank agricultural income: field crops, poultry, livestock.   Roads 59; Long 67

Downings: Pop. 75. In eastern part of county. First name Ivanhoe, but another Ivanhoe in Virginia. Then, named Downings for Jerome T. Downing, postmaster, about 1889.   LRI

Eastern Virginia Research Station at Warsaw, 50 acres, makes investigations relating to the production of field crops and tomatoes.   Com Va 9-1953

Emmerton: Pop. 50. In west central area of eastern part of county.   DU

Farnham: Pop. 275. In east central part of county. Name means enclosure, or home among ferns; name for town in England. North Farnham Church, cruciform in design, dates from 1737, is frequently visited by students of colonial architecture.   Steeles 1164; Gannett 27; VaVCo 8-1950

Foneswood: Pop. 150. On northwest boundary of county.   DU

Haynesville: Pop. 300. Near mid-point of north portion of east half of county. The place was named for a gentleman and planter by the name of Corbin Haynes who lived in "Haynesville House". Postoffice established about 1890.   LRI

Robley: Pop. 125. Near mid-point south boundary of county.   DU

Sharps: Pop. 100. In east part of county. Earlier name Milden from old local home. Mr. Sharp, leading citizen and manager of steamboat wharf, had nephew who had much local property. Postoffice name changed to recognize these men. Been shipping point since colonial days. Now resort on Rappahannock.   LRI; WP: Va 550

Tidewater: Pop. 170. Near Rappahannock, in southeastern portion of county.   DU

Village: Pop. 140. Near mid-point in northern portion of east half of county. Original name Union Village because union two county lines in vicinity. Confusion regarding name so became Village.   LRI

Warsaw: elev. 200; Pop. 549; increase Pop. 1950-60, 26.2%; US Rt 360. Was originally Richmond Courthouse; renamed Warsaw for capital of Poland in 1846.   EcD county

ROANOKE COUNTY

Formed 1838; Roanoke, Roenoke, or Rawrenoke in Indian tongue means "shell money". County probably named from Roanoke River. Area: 277 sq.mi.; Pop. 61,693; Pop. per sq.mi., 222.7; increase Pop. 1950-60, 27.4%. First European visitors in 1671. About three-fourths county area wooded. Rank occupational groups: manufacturing, trade, public-serving facilities and utilities. Rank agricultural income: livestock, dairy, poultry.   Roads 72; Long 169

Back Creek flows along southern side of county; tributary of Roanoke River. In early days, residents referred to it as the back creek and the back mountain.
                                                                Steeles 1159

Bent Mountain: pop. 25; US Rt 221. In southwest corner of county. Two explanations of name: 1. Mountain has shape of horseshoe. 2. Bent Brothers came to section from Pennsylvania; did much surveying.   LRI

Catawba, name from Indian tribe. The word may be the Choctaw, *katapa,* meaning "cut off" or "separated". Elev. 1,800; Pop. 25. Near mid-point of county's north boundary.   Gannett 72

Catawba Sanitarium (State Tuberculosis Sanitarium): Pop. 25.

Clear Brook: Pop. 600. In southern part of east half of county. Name for clear stream of water nearby.   LRI

Crossroads (Shopping Center), Branch Roanoke Postoffice: Pop. ———. Takes its name from Crossroads Shopping Center at intersection of Harshbarger Road and Airport Road; a five-point intersection at northeast city limits.   LRI

Dixie Caverns, 7 miles southwest of Salem, near US Rt 11. Extreme elev. 1,170 feet; opened to public 1922. Three levels are visited; interesting rooms and formations, having a variety of colors.   McGill: Caverns 25+

Fort Lewis Mountain is in the northwestern portion of the county, two miles north of Salem, highest elevation of ridge, 3,328 feet. Named for Revolutionary fort which was named for General Andrew Lewis of French and Indian War days.   LRI

Grandin Road (substation). Name derived from location on Grandin Road, S.W.   LRI

Hollins: Ry N&W; elev. 1,169; Pop. 3,000. In northwest fourth of county near Botetourt line. Named after Mr. and Mrs. John Hollins.

Hollins College: Pop. 800. Hollins College named after Mr. and Mrs. John Hollins of Lynchburg, financial benefactors of institution in early days. Valley

Union Seminary, co-educational, began in 1842. After ten years, became Virginia's first chartered college for women; Hollins Institute in 1855. In 1911, Hollins College, conferring bachelor of arts degree since 1903; master of arts in 1958. Has 400 acres of rolling campus. Va Voc 25, p. 19; Ann.Bul.

Melrose: Ry N&W; elev. 1,005; (part of Roanoke). Station takes name from location on Melrose Avenue N.W. Name may trace to Melrose in Wales and in Massachusetts. LRI

National Business Institute, in Roanoke, founded 1886, offers higher business education leading to Associate in Arts degree. Ann.Bul.

Roanoke (independent city): Area: 26 sq.mi.; Ry N&W; elev. 905; Pop. 97,110; increase Pop. 1950-60, 5.6%; US Rts 11, 220, 221, 460; Interstate 81. Big Lick postoffice July 1, 1798. Name derived from salt marsh to which native animals came for salt. Big Lick incorporated 1874. First steam train on N&W, Nov. 1, 1852; first train to village over Shenandoah Valley Railroad, June 18, 1882. Name changed to Roanoke 1882; legislature chartered city of Roanoke, 1884. Known as "Star City of the South", man-made star on top Mill Mountain. Crystal Spring from foot of Mill Mountain flows 5,000,000 gallons daily.
EcD county; ESS county 11, 24

Roanoke College began as The Virginia Institute near Mt. Tabor Lutheran Church in Augusta County in 1842. It was incorporated in 1845; moved to Salem in 1847; name Virginia Collegiate Institute. Raised to college rank 1853, and officially named Roanoke College. Affiliated with Lutheran Church of America. First American college to grant a degree to a Korean. Ann.Bul.

Salem has name from Bryan family who migrated from Salem, New Jersey; in 1802, town laid out. Ry N&W; elev. 1,005; Pop. 17,500; increase Pop. 1950-60, 156.5%; US Rts 11, 221, 460; Interstate 81. County seat. Location Lutheran Children's Home of the South, Baptist Orphanage of Virginia, and US Veterans Administration Hospital. Municipal water from Roanoke River, deep well and spring; filtered, chlorinated. Va R 10-1956; EcD county

South Roanoke (part of Roanoke): Pop. ———.

Sugar Loaf: Pop. 3,000. Nearby mountain shaped like mound of sugar; this gave name to mountain; community takes name from mountain. New residential subdivisions in area, one part of which Sugar Loaf Estates. LRI

Tinker Mountain gets name from legend that number of deserters in Revolutionary War hid there; made pots and pans; therefore they were "tinkers".
VHSSA 19

Vinton: Ry N&W; elev. 910; Pop. 3,492. Borders on east limits of city of Roanoke. Known as Gish's Mill before 1860; started 1794; David Gish owner. Town called Gish when flag stop on Atlantic, Mississippi, and Ohio Railroad.

Name changed to Vinton in 1884. Vinyard, long-time prominent resident, and Preston, pioneer of community; the first syllable of Vinyard and the last syllable of Preston, the coined name of community is Vinton.   Va R 10-1956

Western Virginia College, two-year college, began as Roanoke Technical Institute, operated by VPI. Confers associate in applied science degrees in architectural, civil, electrical, and mechanical engineering.   TD 3-24-1967, 6-9-1968.

Williamson Road presumably was given name in bygone days from a family name. The road is a principal thoroughfare from heart of city of Roanoke into the county; it carries US Rts 11 and 220. Postoffice name from name of the **road.**   LRI

ROCKBRIDGE COUNTY

Formed 1778; named for celebrated Natural Bridge. Area: 604 sq.mi.; Pop. 24,039; Pop. per sq.mi., 39.8; increase Pop. 1950-60, 2.9%. Two-third county area wooded. 16.7% county area owned by Federal Government. Rank occupational groups: manufacturing, trade, agriculture. Rank agricultural income: livestock, dairy, field crops, poultry. Roads 73

Balcony Falls at water gap cut by James through the Blue Ridge, in south portion of the county. So named because of the terraced falls of the James River passing through "breaks" of the Blue Ridge; gives appearance of tiers of a balcony. Dam and power-plant now largely conceal the earlier appearance. LRI

Big Spring of Edgar Lackey, on Kerrs Creek, northwest of Lexington; flows 4,500 gallons per minute. The "Big Spring" on Kerrs Creek was the scene of the Shawnee raid and massacre, July 17, 1763. It has been called the Big Spring from the first settlement; a real little lake. LRI

Black Spring in the southeastern section of county, on the South Fork of Buffalo Creek; flows 5,000 gallons per minute. Name because of a farm of a man named Black; has had that name for more than 200 years. LRI

Brownsburg: elev. 1,364; Pop. 300. In north central portion of county. Petition for establishment of town in 1793; in 1798 town was Brownsburg. Prominent Brown family settled in community; the Rev. Samuel Brown, pastor of New Providence Church, 1796-1818, being founder of clan. Morton RbCo 156

Buena Vista: Rys C&O, N&W; elev. 941; Pop. 6,600; increase Pop. 1950-60, 26.9%. Iron furnace supplied cannon balls for battle of Buena Vista in Mexico; this led to name of the furnace. Town took name from Buena Vista furnace, operated many years before the town began. Name is Spanish meaning "beautiful view". Water supply from one spring, one well, three mountain sources; chlorinated. Morton: RbCo 154; Gannett 60

Buffalo Creek in southern one-third of county. Known from first deeds in 1740's because of presence of herds of buffaloes which grazed in the valley. LRI

East Lexington: Ry C&O; elev. 909; Pop. 185. One track from this station always carried all trains entering the county seat.

Fairfield: elev. 1,600; Pop. 200. Name appears early in late 1700's; evidently given because of delightful location in village. View eastward across valley of South River to Blue Ridge is unsurpassed. Interstate 81. LRI

Glasgow: Rys C&O, N&W; elev. 738; Pop. 1,091; increase Pop. 1950-60, 34.6%; US Rts 29, 501. Part of townsite developed in 1890 on Glasgow homestead; name from ancestor of famous Virginia novelist, Ellen Glasgow. James Lees & Sons employ persons already residents of county and generally engaged in part-time farming. Water supply from mountain springs and wells; chlorinated.

Morton RbCo 155; EcD county

Goshen: Ry C&O; elev. 1,396; Pop. 99. Town lies astride Mill Creek; early name of postoffice Goshen Bridge. Town name, synonym of fruitfulness and fertility.

GSW: CF; Gannett 140

Goshen Pass is in the northwestern part of county. Earlier names Dunlap's Gap and Strickler's Pass. Four-mile long gap cut by Maury River through Alleghenies. Has monument to Commodore Maury.

Bolen 151; TD 8-28-1966

Goshen Pass Natural Area, 15,954.0 acres. On rugged slopes, 900 acres of virgin forest became perpetual state forest area in 1954.

Com Va 11-1964; TD 8-28-1966

Lexington: Ry C&O; elev. 945; Pop. 7,537; increase Pop. 1950-60, 26.1%; US Rts 11, 60; Interstate 81. Named shortly after Battle of Lexington. Recumbent statue of Gen. Robert E. Lee and heroic statue of Stonewall Jackson in Lexington Cemetery are of interest to visitors. Location of Washington-Lee University and Virginia Military Institute.

VGb 43; Shen Natl Park Souvenir Bk

Maury River was formerly known as North River. Stream bears name of Matthew Fontaine Maury, often mentioned as Pathfinder of the Seas.

EcD county

Natural Bridge: Rys C&O, N&W; elev. 735; Pop. 900; US Rt 11; Interstate 81. Named for the natural wonder.

Raphine: elev. 1,855; Pop. 300. Community is birthplace of James Gibbs, inventor of sewing machine; name of community from Greek word, *raphes*, a needle.

Gordon 159

Rockbridge Baths: Pop. 200; elev. 1,121. Near center of north half of county. Formerly much patronized resort; algae applied to cutaneous afflictions; frequently report of cures. Springs flow 800 gallons per minute.

Morton RbCo 159

Southern Seminary, two year college, founded 1867, has 25 acres of campus, in Buena Vista. Seminary Preserve, wooded tract, riding trails, hikes, picnicing.

Ann.Bul.

Vesuvius: Ry N&W; elev. 1,415; Pop. 400. Near Augusta line in eastern fourth of county. Name of an iron furnace which operated here in the 1830's. "Cotopaxi", the furnace of the McCormicks was in the vicinity.

LRI

Virginia Military Institute, founded November 11, 1839, is the first state military college in the nation. In addition to military training, offers engineering and the arts and sciences. Program demands soldierly performance by cadets in all normal activities. Founded on site of state arsenal in 1836. Significant participation in Battle of New Market, May 15, 1864.   Ann.Bul.; Va Govt 51.

Walnut Grove Farm became experiment station, opened July 1956. Was McCormick Farm, 635 acres; Cyrus Hall McCormick Memorial Plot includes grist mill, blacksmith shop, brick dwelling; blacksmith shop in Augusta, brick dwelling in Rockbridge. First reaper successfully tried in 1831 at Folly farm, near Midway. Station has program for farm use to investigate insects and diseases common to man's fruits and field crops, field care and management, and research involving cattle and sheep.   VaR 1-1957; VHSSA 17

Washington and Lee University has these institutions in its history: Augusta Academy, located near Staunton, 1749-1776. This was the first mathematical and classical school in Shenandoah Valley. It became Liberty Hall (1776-1782) after the Battle of Lexington. It was Liberty Hall Academy (1782-1798). Following benefactions from President George Washington, it was Washington Academy (1798-1813). Then, Washington College (1813-1871). Became Washington and Lee University in 1871. In the interests of needed leadership, President Robert E. Lee introduced elective system, Honor-System of Self-government, added School of Law and Equity; School of Engineering; School of Journalism, first in America; and School of Commerce.

Bolen 34, 38, 41; VaVCo 10-1949; VHSSA 18

ROCKINGHAM COUNTY

Formed 1778; named for Marquis of Rockingham, British statesman. Area: 868 sq.mi.; Pop. 40,485; increase Pop. 1950-60, 15.5%. 51.3% county area in two federally-owned areas. Unusual list of co-operative associations in county. Among state's counties, ranks first in: number milk cows two years old and older, all cattle on farms, chicken eggs marketed, turkeys raised, broilers sold, and chickens on the farm. It ranks first in the acres of barley harvested for grain and in bushels produced. It ranks first for income for all products sold from the farm. Rank occupational groups: manufacturing, agriculture, trade. Rank agricultural income: poultry, livestock, dairy.   Roads 90; VaVCo 10-1949; EcD county

Bergton: elev. 1,450; Pop. 100. In northern area of county. Name means mountain town; *berg* in German means mountain; *ton* in English town. Earlier name West Gap, for man named West. Community objected to name, so became Dovesville; many persons having name Dove in area. Government found name confused with Covesville in handling mail, so from list of names, people of community chose Bergton.   LRI

Bridgewater: Ry CW; elev. 1,192; Pop. 1,815. Near mid-point of Augusta county boundary. First name Dinkletown after an early family; then Bridgeport, flatboat port on North River at bridge; Bridgewater established 1835; Bridgewater named because bridge a necessity. Covered bridge spanned North River, whence name Bridgewater. Increase in Pop. 1950-60, 18%. Wayland RC 11, 199

Bridgewater College is the oldest co-educational college in the state. Founded 1880 as Spring Creek Normal and Collegiate Institute. Moved to Bridgewater 1887 and chartered as Virginia Normal. In 1889, became Bridgewater College. Consolidation has added former institutions: Daleville at Daleville; Hebron Seminary at Nokesville; and Blue Ridge College at New Windsor, Maryland. Conferred first degrees June 1891; first college of Church of Brethren ever to grant degrees. Confers BA and BS.   Ann.Bul.; VaVCo 10-1949; Com Va 6-1936

Broadway: Ry SOU; elev. 1,033; Pop. 646; increase Pop. 1950-60, 11.5%. Near northeast corner of county. Many daredevils gathered to enjoy themselves; some objectors said they were on the "Broadway to Destruction". Broadway became the name of the gathering place. With arrival of railroad, Broadway Depot postoffice established Sept. 4, 1854. Town name became Broadway. Water supply from North Fork of Shenandoah; filtered, chlorinated.

Wayland RC 203; ESS county

Brocks Gap took name from a resident, Brocks. Brocks family were in region in 1748. North Fork of Shenandoah comes through ridge as it enters more open part of valley; a water-level gap having striking natural features as scenery; furnished route through mountains on northwest.   Wayland SV 327, 58.

Chestnut Ridge east of Harrisonburg; name from earlier wooded area covered with chestnut trees. Steeles 1162

Cook's Creek, in south central portion of county, takes name from prominent landowner along its course. Drainage area; 41 sq.mi. Wayland SV 326

Dayton: Ry CW; elev. 1,240; Pop. 930; increase Pop. 1950-60, 18%. In southwest portion of county. In early days, Rifeville or Rifetown; Daniel Rife was large landowner. Uncertain why called Dayton. Many towns named for Jonathan Dayton, ratifier of Constitution. May have been for nephew of Jonathan Dayton. Dayton water supply from Silver lake; chlorinated.
Sites-Hess: History Town of Dayton, 13+.

Dry River flows from the Alleghenies across southeastern portion of county, tributary of North River. As leaves foothills of mountain, in crossing some areas, when dry weeks, stream does not flow in wetter weather channel. Then, stream channel is seen as a depression with cobble stone bed.
Bull. 76: Va.Div. Min. Res., 157

Eastern Mennonite College had beginning as academy in 1917. Accredited as junior college 1930; in 1937, conferred Bachelor of Theology degrees; in 1947, approved to confer traditional bachelor degrees. Under auspices of Virginia Mennonite Conference. In Park View, adjoining Harrisonburg. Ann.Bul.

Elkton: Rys CW, N&W; elev. 955; Pop. 1,506; increase Pop. 1950-60, 10.6%; US Rts 33, 340. Until 1890, town name was Conrad's Store. Name Elkton from Elk Run flowing through town. Water supply from spring. In eastern portion of county. ESS county 15

Endless Caverns discovered Oct. 1879; known as Zirkle's Cave on farm of Reuben Zirkle; later Silver Hill Caverns. In 1919, the Browns purchased; installed indirect flood-lighting. Wierdly fantastic formations, many colors, underground river. Different exploring parties have never been able to find end of underground passages; this gives name of Endless Caverns. Near northern edge of county, close to US Rt 11. Douglas 409; Shen Nat. Park Souvenir Book

Fulks Run: elev. 1,175; Pop. 100. In northeast portion of county. Named for local family. Steeles 1165

German River in northern part of county, tributary of North Fork of Shenandoah. Early settlers of its area were largely of German stock. LRI

Giant's Grave is seen by a person traveling on US Rt 33 east from Rawley Springs. Earlier, the low ridge was known as Cooper's Mountain, but a guest at the summer hotel at Rawley Springs in the early 20th century said it was like a giant's grave. The name was so appropriate that it became the accepted name.
Wayland SV 327

Grottoes: early name, Mt. Vernon Forge; name became Shendun; in 1890, was changed to Grottoes, name from Grottoes of Shenandoah. Ry N&W; Pop.

969; increase Pop. 1950-60, 6.9%; US Rt 340. In south portion of county on Augusta line. Water supply from well. Elev. 1,114.

Wayland RC 206; ESS county

Harrisonburg (independent city): county seat of Rockingham County. Area: 3 sq.mi.; elev. 1,329; Pop. 13,800; increase Pop. 1950-60, 10.2%; Rys CW, SOU; US Rts 11, 33; Interstate 81. In common speech, Rocktown was name used for many years. Harrisonburg established 1780; named after Harrison family, early settlers; laid out on 50 acres by Thomas Harrison. Town incorporated 1849; independent city 1916. First annual Methodist conference west of Blue Ridge in 1794. Rockingham County Memorial Hospital, 323 beds. Water supply from 56 sq.mi. water shed on forested Allegheny Mountains; auxiliary, Silver Lake, spring-fed impoundment; chlorinated, fluorinated. Rank occupational groups: trade, manufacturing, educational services.   VaVCo 9-1951; Wayland SV 71

High Knob: elev. 4,107, near US 33, on western county boundary. This peak is one of the highest in the surrounding country.   9 V 349

Hinton: elev. 1,367; Pop. 100; US Rt 33. Near center of southwest fourth of county. Earlier name was Karicofe, for a local family. They were Northern sympathizers in the 1861-65 war. Col. Hinton of the Confederate Army lived on Muddy Creek, north of Route 33. The name of the postoffice was changed and given his name.   LRI

Keezletown: Ry CW; elev. 1,332; Pop. 175. Is mid-point of west portion of east one-third of county. Keezletown (Keisell's Town) established 1791; laid off on land of George Kiesell.   Wayland RC 193

Lacey Springs: elev. 1,172; Pop. 170; US Rt 11. In northeast portion of county. Great spring gushes from bluff; one of sources of Smith Creek; flows 4,000 gallons per minute. Known as Big Spring in 1767 and during 75 or 80 years; is near village. Lacey Spring accepted as postoffice name. Cavalry engagement, Dec. 20, 1864, opposing commanders had been roommates at West Point.   ESS county 27; Wayland SV 97; Roads 7

Linville: Ry SOU; elev. 1,193; Pop. 100. In northern third of county near Massanutten Mountain. Named for Joe Linville, early settler.   Steeles 1170

Linville Creek named for William Linville, pioneer landowner. Stream tributary of North Fork of Shenandoah.   Wayland SV 326

McGaheysville (meh gack ies ville): Ry CW; elev. 1,159; Pop. 250; US Rt 33. In central area of east third of county. Earlier name Ursulasburg in honor of Mrs. John Long. William McGaheys established first postoffice and called McGaheysville in 1802.   ESS county

Madison College: In Harrisonburg. Name honoring fourth president of United States was voted by Virginia Assembly in 1938. Established March 14, 1908, as State Normal and Industrial School for Women. In 1914, the name became the State Normal School for Women at Harrisonburg. In 1924, the official name became The State Teachers College at Harrisonburg. In 1938, it became Madison College. It is a general purpose college offering liberal arts and educational curricula; confers four different bachelor degrees and three different master degrees. The campus has expanded to 304.73 acres. In 1967, the legislature made it a co-educational institution.   Va Govt 48; Ann.Bul.

Massanetta Springs (conference church grounds) (summer branch postoffice): US Rt 33. For more than a century, known as Taylor Springs. In 1816, under ten-year lease as annual camp meeting ground of Methodists. Dr. Bruce Chrisman changed the name to Massanetta Springs; *Massan* from Massanutten, and *etta* from Henrietta, his wife's name. In 1909, J. R. Lupton purchased; summer resort until 1920. In 1921, he deeded to Presbyterian Synod of Virginia.

Com Va 7-1963

Mill Pond Spring at Dayton flows from 3,000 to 4,000 gallons per minute. It has been impounded which forms Silver Lake. The glistening of the sun rays on the lake in early morning led to a remark naming it Silver Lake. The spring and lake are owned by the city of Harrisonburg. An intake in the spring under the surface of the lake is the auxiliary water supply for Harrisonburg; it is also the water supply for Dayton.   Bull. No. 1, Springs of Va, 53

Mole Hill, from distance looks like a mole rising into view, is four miles west of Harrisonburg. Its igneous plug was evidently more resistant to erosion than the surrounding sedimentary rocks.

Steeles 1172; Bull. 76, Va. Div. Min. Res. 120

Mt. Clinton: Pop. 170. Near center of southwest one-fourth of county. Was Muddy Creek before name Mt. Clinton. About 1833, community group to decide on name; one man offered a horn of apple jack to every man who said Mt. Clinton when voting.   Wayland RC 205; ESS county 30

Mt. Crawford: elev. 1,170; Pop. 247; US Rt 11. Near midpoint of Augusta County boundary. Earlier name Mt. Pleasant and perhaps Mt. Stevens. By law, named Mt. Crawford in 1825; for a man named Crawford with Mount added because on a hill.   Steeles 1172; ESS county 29

Penn Laird: Ry CW; elev. 1,256; Pop. 100; US Rt 33. Near west portion of east third of county. The Lairds were early settlers near Massanutten Mountain in the area near Laird's Knob. Penn means "the place on a hill". The name says "Laird's place on a hill".

Steeles 1174; Eckwall: Oxford Dictionary Place Names 345

Pleasant Valley: Ry CW; Pop. 150. Near center of southeast fourth of county. Railroad named station Pleasant Valley in 1874; Postoffice named Rockingham because another Pleasant Valley postoffice in state. In 1964, other Pleasant Valley postoffice had been discontinued, so could be Pleasant Valley instead of Rockingham.   Richmond News Leader, 3-30-1964; LRI

Port Republic: Ry N&W; elev. 1,095; Pop. 500. In south portion of county near Augusta line. When Augusta County extended to the Mississippi River, this was the county seat. In early days, flatboat navigation carried products to Alexandria; this gave locality its name. Established 1802. Wayland SV 186, 189.

Singers Glen: elev. 1,565; Pop. 102. Near center of west half of county. Before 1860, name was Mountain Valley; then name to postoffice became Singers Glen. Joseph Funk, "father of song in Northern Virginia", lived there. He began teaching singing in early years of 19th century. In 1868, "Singers Glen School" for advanced students in literary studies and music located in community.
Wayland SV 266, 296+

Swiftrun (Swift Run): elev. 1,346; Pop. 40; US Rt 33. In extreme northeast portion of east area of county. Takes name from stream which tumbles down from upper part of Blue Ridge.   LRI

Swift Run (stream) was named because of its rapid flow as it tumbles down the mountain. In 1933, the U. S. Geographic Board approved the name West Swift Run to avoid confusion with stream on the east side of the Blue Ridge which is named Swift Run.   Steeles 1178; GCW: CF

Tenth Legion: US Rt 11; in northern portion. Name from Thomas Jefferson saying that the Valley was "the Tenth Legion of Democracy"; he recalled that Caesar could depend on his tenth legion.   Wayland SV 71

Tide Spring was Syphon Fountains in 1748; located 3½ miles north of Edom. Water flows at intervals; this ebbing and flowing gives the name. Waters drain into Linville Creek.   Steeles 1178; Bul. 76: Va Div Min Res, 109

Timberville: Ry SOU; elev. 1,038; Pop. 412; increase Pop. 1950-60, 52.0%. Near Shenandoah County line in central portion of county. Log house constructed in late 1700's, beginning of settlement. Village first Williamsport; store owner Abraham Williamson. Other names, Thompson's Store; Riddle's Tavern. Postoffice provided 1827; Timberland suggested because much timber nearby. Timberville incorporated 1884. Water supply, spring and well.
DNR 4-19-1966; ESS county 25

War Branch, small stream in western part of county, name from report of battle between Catawbas who lived there and an invading force of Delawares, in which the latter were defeated.   Wayland SV 61

RUSSELL COUNTY

Formed 1786; named for General William Russell, pioneer and Revolutionary soldier. Area: 483 sq.mi.; Pop. 26,290; Pop. per sq.mi., 34.4. Nearly one-half county area wooded. Rank occupational groups: agriculture, trade, construction, manufacturing. Rank agricultural income: field crops, livestock, dairy.

Beartown Mountain: alt. 4,604 ft.; highest peak in Alleghenies in Virginia counties of Great Valley.   VGS: Geol. Appalachian Valley, 515

Carbo on Clinch River in central portion, Clinchfield Coal Company's Moss #3 linked with steam generating plant having capacity of 675,000 watts.
                                             Com Va 2-1956, 5-1958

Carterton: Ry N&W; Pop. 100. Near center of west half of county.   DU

Castlewood: Ry N&W; elev. 1,475; Pop. 500. Mid-point in northern part of west third of county. Mr. Castle, hunter, early explorer of woods of area, vicinity known as "Castle's Woods". Postoffice, one-half mile south, Bickley Mills, established 1832. Water supply, limestone spring; chlorinated.
                                                  ESS county 10, 50.

Cedar Creek in south central, tributary of Clinch River. Many cedars in vicinity probably gave name. Many settlers came from Rockbridge County and may have given name from stream flowing under Natural Bridge.   LRI

Cleveland: Ry N&W; elev. 1,425; Pop. 415. Mid-point west edge of middle third of county. Owner of plat suggested Cleveland as town name in honor President Grover Cleveland; postoffice opened 1890. Water supply: limestone spring and well; chlorinated.   ESS county 49

Clinch Mountain Wildlife Management Area in eastern corner of county.

Coulwood: (RR name Finney) Ry N&W; Pop. 125. In north central portion of county.   DU

Dante: Ry Clinchfield; elev. 1,704; Pop. 1,436. In extreme northwest part of county. Named in honor W. J. Dante, secretary of development organization. Postoffice established 1903. Water supply, well and abandoned mine; filtered; chlorinated.   ESS county 47

Drill: elev. 2,290; Pop. 250. In northeastern section of county.   DU

Honaker: Ry N&W; elev. 1,960; Pop. 851. At west edge of north part of east third of county. Local settlement, New Garden, had postoffice in 1849.

Railway officials named station in honor Squire Harve Honaker, postmaster of settlement. Water supply, limestone spring with auxiliary well; chlorinated.

ESS county 48

Lebanon: elev. 2,130; Pop. 2,130; increase Pop. 1950-60 210.2%; US Rt 19. In middle of south part of central third of county. Twenty acres in deed May 10, 1816, for town as county seat. Name Lebanon selected April 6, 1819; many cedars of vicinity suggested name from Biblical locality. Water supply, limestone springs; chlorinated.   ESS county 46

Rosedale: elev. 2,329; Pop. 25. Near center of northeast fourth of county. Rosedale was name of plantation on which postoffice located; land in family 150 years. Changed to Elway in 1897; changed back to Rosedale, Oct. 1, 1941.

Communication, Bd Geographic Names

Swords Creek: Ry N&W; elev. 1,861; Pop. 300. Near center of east third of county. Number of families named Swords lived here. There is creek running through community and name of village derived from stream.   LRI

SCOTT COUNTY

Formed 1814; named for General Winfield Scott, later commander of the American Army. Area: 539 sq.mi.; Pop. 25,813; Pop. per sq.mi., 47.9. 8.9% of county area in Jefferson National Forest. Rank occupational groups: agriculture, manufacturing, trade. Rank agricultural income: field crops, livestock.

Roads 77

Bellamy: Pop. ———. On Copper Creek, in south central part of county. Church named for minister who donated building; community name from church.

LRI

Clinchport: Ry SOU; elev. 1,425; Pop. 302; US Rts 58, 421. In center southwestern fourth of county. At confluence of Stock Creek and Clinch River, probably named in anticipation that Clinch would be a navigable stream.

Addington 11

Copper Creek flows east across south central of east two-thirds of county. Named for copperhead snakes many years ago.

LRI

Duffield: Ry SOU; elev. 1,365; Pop. 97; US Rts 23, 58, 421. Near mid-point of county boundary of southwest one-fourth of county. Duff family were first settlers; named for them. Near the village, a plant produces lithium, a metallic element used as a base for oils, paints, and enamels.

LRI

Dungannon: Ry CLIN; elev. 1,315; Pop. 444. In north central part of county. Named by Capt. Patrick Hagan for his old home in Ireland.

Tate 27

Fort Blackmore: Ry CLIN; elev. 1,280; Pop. 250. In north central part of county. Received name from Capt. John Blackmore, prominent member of family who settled at mouth of Stony Creek on Clinch River in 1774.

Addington 43, 46.

Gate City: Ry SOU; elev. 1,340; Pop. 2,142; US Rts 23, 58, 421. In south central part of county. Was Winfield; then Estillville, after Judge Estill of Abingdon. Changed from Estillville to Gate City to rid of confusion with Esselville in Wise County when railroad came in 1880's. Name is linked to Moccasin Gap nearby and it was gate way to coal fields farther west.

VaVCo 11-1949; LRI

Hiltons: Ry SOU; Pop. ———; US Rts 58, 421. In southeastern part of county. Named in honor of Hilton family, has railroad name Hilton.

Addington 11

Moccasin Creek was named from tracks in soft mud by Indians wearing moccasins. Big Moccasin Gap cuts through Clinch Mountain; Daniel Boone came through Big Moccasin Gap in 1769.

Addington 13, 39

Natural Tunnel, under Powell's Mountain, 900 feet long, 365 feet from top of tunnel to bed of stream flowing through it; 150 feet wide. Stock Creek flows through. Southern Railway claims it is the only Natural Tunnel in the world used by a railroad. US Rts 58, 421 located through.

Tate 27; VaVCo 11-1949

Natural Tunnel State Park includes 800 acres; features Natural Tunnel, "lovers leap" on the pinnacle and several large erosional "chimneys".

DNR5-11-1967

Nickelsville: Pop. 291. At mid-point near east boundary of county. Baptist Church at Nickelsville organized some time prior to February 1807.

Addington 257

Snowflake: elev. 1,600; Pop. 50. In central southeast one-fourth of county. Postoffice Big Branch moved to present location; while moving, there was a big snow storm; some one suggested call new postoffice Snowflake.   LRI

Weber City (railroad name Moccasin Gap): Ry SOU; Pop. 1,274; US Rts 23, 58, 421. In central part of county. Owner of filling station wanted to attract business; Amos and Andy program had Weber City. Owner painted sign Weber City on each side of station; area grew and name stuck.   LRI

SHENANDOAH COUNTY

Formed 1772; named Dunmore in honor of last colonial governor of Virginia. In 1777, name changed to Shenandoah, meaning "Beautiful daughter of the stars." Area: 507 sq.mi.; Pop. 21,825; Pop. per sq.mi., 43.0; increase Pop. 1950-60, 3.1%. About half county area forested. 23.3% county area in George Washington National Forest. Several chinchilla farms in county. Rank occupational groups: manufacturing, agriculture, trade. Rank agricultural income: poultry, livestock, dairy.   Long 169

Basye: elev. 1,336; pop. 80. Named for Basye family; long time residents. Near southwest corner of county.   Painter

Battlefield-Crystal Caverns at Strasburg. Nearby are breastworks on hilltop constructed by General Banks in campaign of 1862. George F. Hupp owned Hupp's plantation which included Hupp's Cave. After electrification, constructing concrete steps, bridges and walks, opened to public May 30, 1922.
                                              Wayland HSC 130, 451; VHSSA 11

Bird Haven: elev. 1,400; Pop. 42. Shenandoah Community Workers has craftsmen producing wooden products and rugs and quilts from patterns evolved by their ancestors. Philanthropist built factory and because there was a variety of birds, he gave name Bird Haven.   Painter; WPA: Va 422

Ski Bryce, near Basye, on Supin Lick Mountain. Machine at foot ski slope can hose down as many as five inches of new snow in single evening over entire slope; claims to have largest snow-maker available in world. Location been mountain resort since 1908.   DNR 3-9-1967

Columbia Furnace: Pop. 40. In northeast part of south half of county. Dates to 1803, when name Columbia was applied to many ventures; furnace active during more than 80 years. Destroyed by Federals twice in 1861-1865.
                                              Painter; Wayland SV 297

Conicville: elev. 1,256; Pop. 45. In center of north part of southern half of county. Formerly "Cabin Hill"; name changed to Conicville in 1892 to reduce confusion with postoffice having similar name.   Wayland SV 157, 159.

Edinburg: Ry SOU; elev. 845; Pop. 517; US Rt 11; Interstate 81. In northeast part of south half of county. In 1828, a man named Shryock owned land included in part present town; name of community then Shryock. In 1845, the postoffice was Stony Creek; at mouth of energetic stream. Incorporated May 24, 1852, as Edinburg. Early settlers agreed that they had found second Garden of Eden; instead of Eden-burg, name became Edinburg. Edinburg Mills was spared in burning of buildings during the 1860's. Water supply, two mountain streams and wells; chlorinated.   Wayland SV 142-144; VHSSA 11

Fishers Hill: Ry SOU; elev. 680; Pop. 150. In southeast fourth of county. Fisher home, northeast side Fisher's Hill near stream and pike, source of name.
Wayland HSC 326

Lebanon Church: Pop. 100. In extreme northern part of county. Former name Cottontown; probably after Cotton family in vicinity; just north of village is Cottontown Run. Another explanation is children had flaxen or white hair. Lebanon Church dedicated October 22, 1871. Lebanon because of many cedars on nearby hills.
Wayland HSC 24, 124; Painter

Massanutten Academy, Woodstock, opened to students in 1899; established by the Reformed Church in America (now included in United Church of Christ). Military training is used to aid in organizing discipline.

Mauertown: Ry SOU; elev. 800; Pop. 225; US Rt 11; Interstate 81. Near center of north half of county. Named for early resident. Locally, name is pronounced "Morry Town".
WPA: Va 429; Wayland HSC 156

Meem's Bottoms; Meem family were early owners of 3000 acres of mountain and farm land in 1841. (pronounced "Mims Bottoms"). Had been Allen's Bottoms. Wide lowland north of North Branch of Shenandoah River as seen along US Rt 11.
Cavalcade, Autumn 1963

Mount Jackson: Ry SOU; elev. 917; Pop. 722; US Rt 11; Interstate 81; in south central part of south half of county. In 1746, surveyors of Fairfax Line designated stream coming down from the west as "Benjamin Allen's Mill Creek". In 1812 and later, deeds to town lots had town name of Mt. Pleasant. In 1826, the name became Mt. Jackson to commemorate times and virtues of "Old Hickory". Water supply: mountain stream and well.
Wayland HSC 522; Wayland SV 65

Narrow Passage: narrow erosional remnant between North Fork of the Shenandoah and Narrow Passage Creek. In early north-south travel in the Valley, it was location of trail and road. Tree growth limited to single trail not wide enough for two wagons to pass. US Rt 11 crosses.
Wayland SV 62

New Market: elev. 1,060; Pop. 783; increase Pop. 1950-60, 11%; US Rts 11, 211; Interstate 81. In southeast corner of county. Earlier name, Crossroads, location where two trails intersect. New Market laid out in 1784; named for famous racing center in England; had been started as town by General John Sevier, noted Indian fighter, Revolutionary patriot, founder and first governor of Tennessee. Incorporated Dec. 14, 1796. Has Henkel Press, one of America's oldest publishing houses, since 1816. Water supply: mountain stream; filtered, chlorinated.
Wayland HSC 143; V Gb 39

New Market Battlefield Memorial commemorates the 250 VMI cadets who, fighting the Union threat, made the famous charge in capturing a battery, May 15, 1864; ten cadets were killed and forty-seven were wounded.
DNR 6-17-1967; SCWS HMV 14

Orkney Springs: elev. 1,485; Pop. 60. In southwest corner of county. First name was Yellow Springs; long famous for healing waters. In 1858, charter secured for development of Orkney Springs; named for Earl of Orkney, England. Wayland: HSC 18, 124; Shenandoah Co. Geog. Supplement 14

Passage Creek, near the eastern boundary of the county, flows through Powells Fort Valley. Stream leaves valley through a narrow passage with high cliffs at northern end of Massanutten Mountain. Gordon 57

Powell's Fort includes the wider area drained by Passage Creek and the ridges of the forks of Massanutten Mountain. The valley floor has been used as farm lands; an increasing area has been developed as part of the George Washington National Forest. The name came from an Englishman, Powell, early resident who made coins with greater silver content than legal money. He found precious metals, which others could not locate, and was able to elude law officers. This led to the name Powell's Fort. Area has rugged and sublime scenery. Wayland: SV 62; VaVCo Apr 1952

Quicksburg: Ry SOU; elev. 948; Pop. 150. In southeast corner of county. Earlier name Forest Station. Village built on edge Quick farm; William A. Quick had been active in promoting village and insisted that village be named in his honor. Wayland HSC 169

Rude's Hill, in southeast corner of county, received name because in 1844, Rev. A. R. Rude was living near base of hill three miles southward from Mount Jackson. Vicinity was favorite camping area of Stonewall Jackson. Elev. 946. Wayland: HSC 148, 191

Saint David's Church: elev. 914; Pop. 50. David Golladay gave land for church and parochial school. His name was used in naming the church. Painter

Seven Fountains: elev. 817; Pop. 30. In southeast corner of north half of county. Oldest postoffice in Fort Valley was Burner's Springs establish 1853; Burners were among early settlers in Fort Valley. Burners had boarders as early in 1850. Name was changed to Seven Fountains because in space of one-half acre, seven different kinds of mineral water come from separated springs. Wayland HSC 181

Shenandoah Academy: New Market. Maintained by Seventh Day Adventist denomination. College preparatory. LRI

Shenandoah Caverns, near mid-point of southern area of county, were discovered and explored in the 1880's and opened to the public in 1922. Diamond Cascade, massive formation, said to be largest calcite formation in the world. Near US Rt 11, three miles south of Mount Jackson. Wayland HSC 31; DNR 11-5-1966

Strasburg: Rys B&O, SOU; elev. 578; Pop. 2,428; increase Pop. 1950-60, 10.1%; US Rt 11; Interstate 81. Earlier names: Staufferstadt (Stovertown), Funktown, Funk's Mills, Shenandoah River. Became Strasburg legally 1761. Peter Stover purchased land 1749. Josiah Hite brought immigrants who settled in town and named for city in Alsace. In 1854, railroad through Manassas Gap; B&O extended from Winchester in 1870. Water supply, series of springs, mountain stream with impounding reservoir; supplementary, North Fork of Shenandoah River; filtered, chlorinated.   WP: Va 420; Gordon 5

Third Hill, conspicuous; used as signal station by armies in 1860's.
Wayland HSV 191

Tom's Brook: Ry SOU; elev. 745; Pop. 244; US Rt 11. Near center of north half of county. Man had cabin near creek; stream became Tom's Creek. William Border, Sr., founded Tom's Brook, using somewhat changed name.
Wayland HSC 151, 155

Woodstock: Ry SOU; Pop. 2,083; increase Pop. 1950-60, 14.7%; US Rt 11; Interstate 81. Earlier name Mullerstadt; Jacob Mueller or Miller, founder of village. Name Woodstock became legal in 1761. Jacob Miller chose name for the town but no located reason given for his choice. In January 1776, Rev. John Peter Muhlenberg preached his famous sermon. Stone courthouse built in 1791 is oldest in Northern Virginia. Water supply, Stony Creek; chlorinated.
Wayland HSC 709, 135; Painter

Zepp: Pop. 40. In northeast corner of county. In 1874, Charles M. Zepp developed tannery. Postoffice was named after him.   Painter

SMYTH COUNTY

Formed 1832; named for General Alexander Smyth, Congressman many years. Area: 435 sq.mi.; Pop. 31,066; Pop. per sq.mi., 71.4. Earliest settlement 1766 at Royal Oak, eastern edge present-day Marion. 21.9% county area in Jefferson National Forest. 65.6% county area wooded. Rank occupational groups: manufacturing, trade, agriculture. Rank agricultural income: livestock, dairy, field crops.   Roads 78

Atkins: Ry N&W; elev. 2,200; Pop. 400. Near center of eastern half of county. Atkins had water tank near railroad station. First called Atkins Switch, then Atkins Tank, then Atkins. Atkins family large land owners and very influential citizens.   Wilson 350

Blue Ridge Job Corps Center uses buildings of former Marion College, founded by Lutheran Church 1873 and continued until 1967; was two-year institution for women. Center opened in 1967 in modernized facilities for providing vocational training for women, aged 17-21, in health-related jobs. Recruits from within 150-mile radius of institution; trains enrollees to return to hospitals and health facilities of same area.   TD, B-2, 12-3-1967

Broadford: elev. 1,782; Pop. 600. Near mid-point on north side of west half of county. Community beside Laurel Creek. Earlier community at widest place on Holston River with valley road crossing, which gave name. Community moved one mile to present location, and name followed to new village. Earlier location now called Old Broadford.   Wilson 351

Chilhowie: Ry N&W; elev. 1,949; Pop. 1,169; US Rt 11. Near midpoint of west boundary of county. Early name Town House; railroad called siding Greever's Switch; village became Chilhowie. Name from Indian phrase applied to nearby valley meaning "valley of many deer". First frame house about 1748. Municipal water from two springs; chlorinated.   Wilson 288

Flattop Mountain in northwest portion. Elev. 4,000 feet. Ridges along top of ridge appear flat for several miles.   LRI

Hungry Mother State Park: 2,139.2 acres; at edge Jefferson National Park, near Marion; near center of county. Name from pioneer woman and baby captured by Shawnee raiding party; mother collapsed at foot Molly's Knob. Baby wandered to settlement, said: "Hungry — Mother — Hungry — Mother". Dead woman found; stream named Hungry Mother Creek; state park took name from creek. Has many provisions for recreation; trails entice mountain climbers.
                       Va. State Parks: Div. Conservation and Devel.

Laurel Creek in southwest portion of county. Immense stands of laurel rhododendron really, but often called laurel, covered whole section of mountain and small valley through which this creek flows. Headwaters of stream still flow through heavy beds of "laurel".   LRI

Marion: became county seat in 1832; named for General Francis Marion, "Swamp Fox" of Revolution. Ry N&W; elev. 2,125; Pop. 8,385; increase Pop. 1950-60, 20.1%; US Rt 11. Municipal water from spring, chlorinated.
                                                                        VA HSSA 48

Rye Valley, a name noted in old Fincastle records and derived from the wild rye growing abundantly along the creeks and in the glades.   Wilson 30

Saltville: Ry N&W; elev. 1,740; Pop. 2,844; increase Pop. 1950-60, 4.6%. First called Preston's Salines, after General Francis Preston living here and who made salt. In 1748, named Buffalo Lick. Town incorporated as Saltville in 1896. Olin-Mathieson Chemical Corporation uses salt brines in manufacturing products.
                                                                        Wilson 338

Seven Mile Ford: Ry N&W; elev. 2,012; Pop. 125. Mid-point in west third of county. Name from ford on river seven miles from ford at early settlement Royal Oak; claims no other place has same name.   Wilson 364

Southwestern State Hospital, founded 1887, maintained for mentally ill and criminally insane. At Marion.   Va Govt. 24, 67

Sugar Grove: Pop. 800. Near mid-point southeastern fourth of county. Fine grove sugar maples nearby, remnant of larger forest these trees, gives town its name.   Wilson 374

SOUTHAMPTON COUNTY

Formed 1749; named for third Earl of Southampton, treasurer of London Company. Or, named for a locality that was originally named for Earl of Southampton. Area: 607 sq.mi.; Pop. 27,195; Pop. per sq.mi., 44.8. In Virginia, leading county in number of hogs on farms, acres harvested and bushels of corn produced, and in both acreage and pounds peanuts produced. Rank occupational groups: agriculture, manufacturing, trade. Rank agricultural income: field crops, livestock, dairy.   Roads 64

Boykins: Ry SAL; elev. 40; Pop. 710. In southeast area of west half of county. Named for Mr. Boykins. Incorporated 1884. Water, two wells; chlorinated.   Co. Geog. Sup. 19

Branchville: Ry SAL; Pop. 158. Near North Carolina line, in southeast area of west half of county. Named for family of early settlers.   LRI

Capron: Ry NF&D; Pop. 327; US Rt 58. In northeast portion of west half of county. Early name, Princeton after Judge Princeton of Courtland. In 1889, named Cairo; was confused with Cairo, West Virginia. Capron was for general passenger agent of railroad. Water supply: well.   Co. Geog. Sup. 20

Courtland: Ry NF&D; Pop. 855; increase Pop. 1950-60, 93.0%; US Rt 58. Near mid-point of west edge of east half of county. Early name Jerusalem dated from 1750. Renamed Courtland 1788; county seat; established as town 1791. Water, well.   VaVCo 9-1959

Drewryville: Ry NF&D; Pop. 200; US Rt 58. Near mid-point of north edge of west half of county. Drewry family owned land before railroad came to vicinity, so probably named for Samuel Drewry (1800-1862), whose home still stands in village.   LRI

Flat Swamp, near Branchville. October 10, 1793, sale of 450 acres on north side of Flat Swamp.   23 V 324

Franklin (independent city): Rys ACL, NF&A, SAL; elev. 20; Pop. 7,800; increase Pop. 1950-60, 55.5%; US Rts 58, 258. Earlier name, Franklin Depot. Conflicting explanations of name: man named Franklin kept store. Another explanation: section foreman exclaimed: "This shall be Franklin"; named for Benjamin Franklin. Water: four wells.   VaVCo 12-1952

Handsom (RR Hand): Ry SAL; Pop. 90. Near center of southeast fourth of county. First section master, Mr. Hand; tradition that railroad station named for him. Postoffice has name Handsom.   LRI

Ivor: Ry N&W; Pop. 398; US Rt 460. In extreme northeast of county. Wife of Engineer Mahone chose Scott novel name. Water: two wells.

VaVCo 9-1953

Newsoms: Ry SAL; elev. 95; Pop. 423. In southeast fourth of west half of county. Named for an early store owner, Thomas Newsoms. Water: well.

Co. Geog. Sup. 20.

Poplar Swamp, about seven miles west of Capron, is mentioned in will regarding land, dated November 10, 1806.   34 V 214

Seacock Creek in northeast portion. Seacocks tribe mentioned in 1644. Seacock Swamp in will, September 21, 1708.   23 V 230; 5 V 202

Sebrell: Pop. 200. Mid-point near northeast boundary of county. Named in 1908 for James Sebrell, county's representative in legislature.   Co. Geog. Sup. 21

Sedley: Ry N&W; Pop. 500. Mid-point of south area of northeast fourth of county. President Virginian Railway gave the village its name.   LRI

Tarrara Creek in southwest portion. Local lore that stream named for small Indian tribe that lived along its banks; Tarraras were branch or sub-tribe of Meherrins.   LRI

SPOTSYLVANIA COUNTY

Formed 1720; named for Alexander Spotswood, Lieutenant-Governor 1710-22. Area: 409 sq.mi.; Pop. 13,819; Pop. per sq.mi., 33.8; increase Pop. 1950-60, 15.9%. Settlement about 1700. Battles of Fredericksburg, Chancellorsville, the Wilderness (partly), and Spotsylvania were fought in this county. Rank occupational groups: manufacturing, trade, construction. Rank agricultural income: dairy, livestock, poultry. VaVCo 4-1953; Roads 87

Belmont: Pop. 10. In extreme northwest area of county. DU

Chancellorsville: Pop. 50. In north central portion of county. Named for family in neighborhood. Battle on May 2, 3, 1863; Federals withdrew northward May 5-6, 1863. Gannett 74; SCWSHM 8

Fredericksburg (independent city): Area 6 sq.mi.; Rys RF&P, VC; elev. 70; Pop. 14,100; increase Pop. 1950-60, 12.2%; US Rts 1, 17; Interstate 95. Founded 1727; named for Frederic, Prince of Wales, father of George III. Grant May 2, 1671, for site of Fredericksburg. Fort ordered 1676; completed 1681; protected settlers from Indians, who were raiding settlements. Port of entry for many years for ocean-going vessels, at head of tidewater and navigation on the Rappahannock. Many historic shrines. First drug store in America, now museum American Pharmaceutical Association. Was county seat Spotsylvania County 1809-1838. Sylvania Industrial Corporation started April 1929; American Viccose acquired in 1946; expansion made Fredericksburg plant largest single cellophane plant in the world. Rank occupational groups: manufacturing, trade, personal services.
Roads 16; ESS county 23; VGb 29; VaVCo 4-1953; EcD county

Mary Washington College of the University of Virginia; named for the mother of George Washington, whose home and tomb are nearby. Created by Act of Assembly, March 14, 1908. Opened as State Normal School in 1911. Later became State Teachers College. In 1938, became Mary Washington College, and in 1944, the state legislature made the institution the Women's College of the University of Virginia; it is a liberal arts college. Has campus of 381 acres. Ann.Bul.

Mat River joins with Ta River to form Matta River. Name from Mattaponi.

Matta River in east central portion of county; flows east to confluence with Poni River. Name from Mattaponi.

Ni River and Po River in central Spotsylvania County unite with the Mattaponi. Names from last two syllables of Mattaponi.

Partlow: Pop. 30. In extreme southeast area of county. Named in honor of Captain Partlow.   LRI

Po River flows from central Spotsylvania to unite with Ni River in northern Caroline. The stream name is from Mattaponi as it is a tributary of that larger stream.

Post Oak: Pop. 15. Near center of county. Name derived from post and oak near the postoffice.   LRI

Snell: Pop. 100. Earlier name, Traveler's Rest, stage coach stop. Named for resident Mr. Snell. Near center of eastern half of county.   LRI

Spotsylvania: County seat. Pop. 100.

Thornburg: Pop. 50; US Rt 1. Mid-point near south boundary of county. "Mud Tavern was the old name of this place", a statement on highway marker tells regarding 1863. At that time, a place named Thornburg on Ta River farther south. At some time, the name Thornburg was moved to displace Mud Tavern. Origin of name Thornburg unknown.   SCWHM 3; LRI

Virginia Central Railway was originally chartered as Fredericksburg and Gordonsville Railroad Company; changed in 1872 to Fredericksburg, Orange and Charlottesville; in 1876 to Potomac, Fredericksburg and Piedmont Railroad and was completed to Orange as a narrow gauge line; in 1925, became Orange and Fredericksburg Railway; in 1926, it began having its present name. Then, it was converted to standard gauge. In 1938, its trackage was reduced to two and one-half miles within Fredericksburg. In 1967, it was donated to Fredericksburg in memory of the 1926 purchaser, Langbourne M. Williams, Sr.   LRI

STAFFORD COUNTY

Formed 1664; named for Staffordshire, England. Area: 271 sq.mi.; Pop. 16,876; Pop. per sq.mi., 62.3; increase Pop. 1950-60, 41.7%. First settlers 1647. Aquia sandstone quarry, one of nation's oldest, provided stone for early buildings in national capital. Early air message of April 29, 1863, using balloon. About three-fourth county area forested. Rank occupational groups: manufacturing, trade, public administration. Rank agricultural income: dairy, livestock, field crops.

Roads 60; EcD county; WP: Va 348

Brooke: Ry RF&P; Pop. 100. Near center of east half of county. Named for Colonel Brooke, a leading colonial figure living nearby. Darter

Catholic Shrine: At Aquia on US Rt 1 commemorates arrival of Spanish missionaries in September 1570 and their massacre in February 1571. First English-speaking Catholic colony in Virginia; Aquia Church erected 1757 is near crucifix and continues in use. WP: Va 347; Com Va 10-1950

Falmouth: (Branch Fredericksburg P.O.) Pop. 1,478; increase Pop. 1950-60, 25.6%; US Rt 1. At mid-point of south boundary of county. Named after Falmouth, England. Capt. Smith visited 1608. Town founded 1727 as trading center for Northern Neck; early colonial port. Darter; Roads 17

Garrisonville: Pop. 200. In north central portion of county. DU

Hartwood: Pop. 50. Two words put together give name. Large area woodland and deer there earlier. Hart is word for male deer; Hart and wood gives Hartwood. LRI

Midway Island (part of United Marine Reservation): In Sept. 1943, the General at Marine Corps School, Quantico, named the area after Midway in the Pacific. Some of the drives of area are named after deceased aviators. Midway Island, Va., postoffice was closed Dec. 30, 1965. LRI

Potomac Creek flows east across county with about one-third of county area south of the stream. Will dated Apr. 9, 1700, mentions lands owned on Potomac Creek in Stafford. In list of navigable streams, July 8, 1702, Potomac Creek listed. 1 V 363; 2 V 276

Ruby: Pop. 50. In northwest portion. DU

Stafford: Pop. 500; US Rt 1. County seat. Near center of county.

SURRY COUNTY

Formed 1652; named for Surrey County, England, having the "e" omitted. Area: 280 sq.mi.; Pop. 6,220; Pop. per sq.mi., 22.2. Early fort 1609, Smith's Fort, two miles from mouth of Grays Creek. Earliest records in county clerk's office dated April 28, 1652. Rank occupational groups: agriculture, manufacturing, trade. Rank agricultural income: field crops, livestock, dairy.

Com Va 10-1952

Chippoak Creek probably named for Chopoke, brother of Pipisco, chief of Quioughcohanocks, who lived near mouth of stream in 1610. Chippokes were a friendly Indian tribe.

Bohannon 66; Program 300th Anniversary Surry County, 19.

Claremont: Pop. 377; increase Pop. 1950-60, 0.8%. In extreme north corner of county. Named for the royal residence "Claremont" in shire Surrey, England. English colonists landed at Claremont, May 5, 1607. Water supply: three wells.

Bohannon 14; WP: Va 582

Dendron: Pop. 403. In southeast corner of county. Lumber interests established mill town near Blackwater River; later incorporated as Dendron. Town began in 1880's. Dendron, Greek word for *tree*, linked to lumbering.

Program 300th Anniversary, 25.

Elberon: Pop. 75. Earlier name Cocke's Crossroad. O. J. Cocke, an Englishman, first postmaster, links with name Elberon, considered an English name.

LRI

Gray's Creek drains the central northern portion, tributary of James. Named for Thomas Gray, who patented land upon it in 1639. Earlier names, "Smith's Fort Creek" and "Wolfe's Creek", but name Grays Creek used in 1677.

Bohannon 60.

Hog Island in northeast corner in James River. Named because colonists kept hogs there. Hog Island Waterfowl Refuge 2,100 acres. Winter home of Canadian geese and many varieties of duck. Water fowl may not be hunted on the island or within 1,000 yards of its shore. Bohannon 14; EcD county

Republican Methodists, led by James O'Kelley, formed August 4, 1794; name because linked in sympathy with French Revolution. Site of organization has stone marker beside Rt. 10, two miles east of Surry county seat. Later, the organization joined with other groups in forming the Christian Church. That denomination in 1931 united with Congregationalists in forming Congregational-Christian denomination. In 1957, the Congregational-Christian merged with Evangelical and Reformed to become United Church of Christ.

News Week 7-8-1957; VaVCo 9-1950

Spring Grove: Pop. 40. In center of northwest fourth of county. Named for a grove with a spring in it. In 1620, Richard Pace settled near present village. Chanco, Indian boy, lived here who warned of plot to massacre settlers in 1622.   Steeles 1177; V DAg 247

Surry: Pop. 288. County seat. Earliest name "the Crossroads", or "McIntosh's Cross Roads"; links to tavern keeper Robert McIntosh giving land for courthouse; deed March 23, 1796. Earlier courthouse at Troopers, two miles west. Water supply, well.   Bohannon 41; Huntley 341.

SUSSEX COUNTY

Formed 1753; named for an English county. Area: 496 sq.mi.; Pop. 12,411; Pop. per sq.mi., 25.0. Early patents on land 1701. Over three-fourths county area wooded. Rank occupational groups: agriculture, manufacturing, trade. Rank agricultural income: field crops, livestock. Roads 65

Assamoosick Swamp in southern western edge of eastern third of county. Nottoway Indians lived on Assamoosick Swamp until 1698. 7 V 351

Gray: Ry N&W; Pop. 40. In southeast part of county. Named Gray in 1897 when Gray family started sawmill operation; in mill years, population about 700. LRI

Littleton: Pop. 40. In southwest part of east half of county. Name probably contraction of Littletown, which was name of nearby plantation in 1700's. Littleton stage and postoffice too noisy so John R. Wyche built home one mile from village in 1825. LRI

Charles C. Steirly Natural Area on Blackwater River, 19-acre tract, donated by Grays to the Commonwealth. Steirly, state district forester, located in Waverly, walked along Blackwater east of Route 603; his observations and influence led to establishment of natural area. Com Va 11-1964

Stony Creek: Ry ACL; elev. 75; Pop. 437; US Rt 301. Near center of southwest fourth of county. Named by Mrs. Mahone. Incorporated 1915; chartered 1930. Water supply, two wells; treated, chlorinated. WP: Sussex Co 103

Sussex: Pop. 75. Courthouse completed 1835. Water supply, well; treated.

Wakefield: Ry N&W; elev. 95; Pop. 1,015; increase Pop. 1950-60, 6.9%; US Rt 460. In northeast corner of county. Before 1853, place known as Heath's. Wife of Engineer Mahone chose Scott novel name. Chartered 1902. Water supply, two wells. VaVCo 9-1953; WP: Sussex Co 103

Waverly: Ry N&W; elev. 115; Pop. 1,601; increase Pop. 1950-60, 6.5%; US Rt 460. Near midpoint of north boundary of county. Blackwater Depot was name in 1838. Mrs. Mahone chose Scott novel name. Chartered 1879. Water supply, two wells. VaVCo 9-1953

Yale: Pop. 150. Near mid-point of southeast fourth of county. One explanation that railroad official or member of personnel had been Yale student; railroad line abandoned later. LRI

TAZEWELL COUNTY

Formed 1799; named for Henry Tazewell, United States Senator, 1794-1799. Area: 552 sq.mi.; Pop. 44,791; Pop. per sq.mi., 85.8. First settlement 1767 on Clinch River. More than half county forested. 1.5% county area in Jefferson National Forest. 44.1% employed in mining. Rank other occupational groups: trade, manufacturing, agriculture. Rank agricultural income: livestock, dairy, field crops.
Roads 95; VaVCo 5-1953

Amonate: Ry N&W; Pop. 500. On county boundary near midpoint of west half of county. Another name for Indian princess Pocohontas. It is a coal camp. Municipal water supply, well; chlorinated.
Libr. Tz.

Bandy: Ry N&W; elev. 2,130; Pop. 500. Near center north half of west part of county. Named for a local family.
Steeles 1169

Big Ridge (4,116 ft.); mountain 3½ miles south of Bluefield. Named because of its size.
Libr. Tz.

Bishop: Ry N&W; elev. 1,779; Pop. 350. At mid-point of northern boundary of county. Named for Mr. Bishop, who was instrumental in developing a coal field in locality. Municipal water supply, spring; filtered, chlorinated.
McDonald

Bluefield: Ry N&W; elev. 2,385; Pop. 4,235; Increase Pop. 1950-60, 0.5%; US Rts 19, 21, 219, 460. On northeast boundary of county. Named for bluegrass valley in which it is situated. Higgenbotham's Farm in West Virginia later named Bluefield. Water from Bluestone River; filtered, chlorinated.
Gannett 49; VaVCo 9-1963

Bluefield College, co-educational, Baptist affiliation, established 1920.
WP: Va 533

Boisservain: Ry N&W; elev. 2,450; Pop. 600. Near northeast corner of county. Named for a local resident. Water supply from abandoned mine; chlorinated.
Steeles 1160

Burkes Garden: elev. 3,115; Pop. 100; US Rts 19, 460. In southeast corner of county. Exploring party 1748. Burke, axman or chain-carrier, planted peelings of potatoes from breakfast; covered with brush. Next year, party returned; found bed of potatoes growing; named Burke's Garden. Burke's Fort there in 1774. Broad oval valley, surrounding ridges about 1,000 feet higher than floor of area.
Pendleton 170+; WP: Va 534; Roads 57.

Cedar Bluff: Ry N&W; elev. 2,005; Pop. 995; US Rt 460. Near midpoint of west boundary of county. Named for cedar trees covering bluff. Woolen mills since 1832. Water supply, two springs; chlorinated.
Steeles 1161; WP: Va 536

Chimney Rock, 4,361 ft., 4½ miles northwest of Burke's Garden. Appearance of rock gave name.   McDonald

Cliffield: elev. 2,320; Pop. 170. In center of west half of county. Name from cliffs; level fields above.   Lib. Tz.

Dial Rock, 4,062 ft., 5 miles northeast of Burkes Garden. Legend that Indians watched the sun; when sun stood over this rock, it was twelve o'clock.   McDonald

Doran: Ry N&W; elev. 1,922; Pop. 200. Near midpoint in county boundary in northwest fourth of county. Named for Philadelphia lawyer.   Steeles 1163

East River Mountain extends through east half of county, nearly midway between north and south boundaries; 4,310 ft., 4¾ miles northwest of Burkes Garden. Named from river called East River because it flowed to the east; river flows in same direction as mountain.   Lib. Tz.

Horsepen: elev. 1,957; Pop. 400. On northern boundary east of county boundary's mid-point. A horse corral was maintained there in early days.   Steeles 1168

Hutchinson Rock (mountain), 4,503 ft., northwest rim of Burkes Garden. Named for man who had just climbed this rock on Bear Tower mountain.   McDonald

Jewell Ridge: Ry N&W; Pop. 500. Near midpoint of northwest boundary of county. Named for Jewell family who lived in community. Water supply from mountain water shed; filtered, chlorinated.   Lib. Tz.

North Tazewell (consolidated with Tazewell in 1963); was called Kelly. Elev. 2,383. Water supply, three springs; chlorinated.   WP: Va 535

Pocohontas: Ry N&W; elev. 2,320; Pop. 1,313. In extreme northeast corner of county. Indian princess name signifies "stream between two hills". Uncertain whether postoffice named for princess or coal field named for town; postoffice established June 1882. Pocohontas mine opened; first shipment from mine June 1883. Kimball's wife named Pocohontas region. 13-foot seam of coal at Pocohontas. Water supply, Big Spring Branch; filtered, chlorinated.   Gannett 249; VaVCo 9-1953; Com Va 12-1955; EcD county

Pounding Mill: an early mill pounded or crushed corn into meal. Ry N&W; elev. 2,140; Pop. 100; US Rts 19, 460. In center of west half of county.   Steeles 1174

Raven: named for local merchant. Ry N&W; elev. 1,913; Pop. 900; US Rt 460. Near midpoint of county boundary of northwest portion of county. Water supply, well.   Steeles 1174

Red Ash: Ry N&W; elev. 2,070; Pop. 500; US Rt 460. Near boundary in northwest area of county. Named for sort of coal mined there; when burned, ashes are reddish color. Steeles 1175

Richlands: Ry N&W; elev. 1,967; Pop. 4,953; increase Pop. 1950-60, 6.5%; US Rt 460. Near mid-point of west boundary. Kentucky cattle drivers found high quality pastures on bottom land along Clinch River; gave location its name. Water from two springs and Clinch River; filtered, chlorinated. WP: Va 536.

Rich Mountain, 4,041 ft., extends through east half of county, near midway between northern and southern boundaries. Name from rich soil; bluegrass grows to mountain top when ground is cleared. McDonald

Short Gap: Pop. 200. On boundary in northwest corner of county. Mountain short in length; hence gap name. Lib. Tz.

Short Mountain, 4,100+ ft., 5 miles south of Pounding Mill, in southwestern corner of county. Named for its being a short mountain. McDonald

Short Ridge, 4,198 ft., 5 miles northwest of Burkes Garden. Named from a family by name of Short. McDonald

Tannersville: Pop. 50. In southwest corner of county. A tanner operated here. Steeles 1178

Tazewell: Ry N&W; elev. 2,543; Pop. 3,713; increase Pop. 1950-60, 168.2%; US Rts 19, 460. Has had names Jeffersonville, Tazewell Court House, Tazewell. Became county seat in 1800. Named to silence a relative of Tazewell who was opposing naming for Assembly member from Russell County. Water supply, several springs and mountain watershed; chlorinated.
WP: Va 535; Gannett 297; Pendleton 396

The Peak, 4,245 ft., 1½ miles northeast of Tazewell. Was Wynne's Peak; dropped now to The Peak. McDonald

Tip Top (RR Tiptop): Ry N&W; elev. 2,755; Pop. 100. Is located on top of a hill. Steeles 1178

Tug River has name from food-needing explorers in 1756 cutting strips or thugs of hides of buffaloes and boiling them. Pendleton 221

Wilson Mountain, 4,300+ ft., 5 miles northwest of Burkes Garden. Many persons by name of Wilson in nearby section. Lib. Tz.

Wolf Pen Gap: 4,345 ft., 5 miles northwest of Burkes Garden. The rough terrain made it possible for hunters to pen or hem in the hunted wolves.
Libr. Tz.

Yards (Flat Top): Ry N&W; elev. 2,400; Pop. 400. Named from railroad yards. Steeles 1180

WARREN COUNTY

Formed 1836; named for General Joseph Warren, killed at Bunker Hill, 1775. Area: 219 sq.mi.; Pop. 14,655; Pop. per sq.mi., 66.9. Settlement developed after 1728. 16.2% county area owned by federal and state governments. About 60% county area forested. Rank occupational groups: manufacturing, trade, construction. Rank agricultural income: livestock, dairy, poultry. Roads 82

Beef Cattle Research Station: 4,222-acre tract, former U. S. Remount Station, maintained since 1949 by U. S. Department of Agriculture in cooperation with Virginia Polytechnic Institute. Investigations include in beef cattle: proportion records, total production of each sire and cow; also, investigating breeding cattle adapted to Virginia conditions. Com Va 9-1953

Bentonville: Ry N&W; elev. 737; Pop. 350; US Rt 340. In southwest corner of county. Named to honor Benton Roy, Chief of Staff, Hardie's Corps. First name used to differentiate from his brother Gibson Roy, Superintendent of Schools. LRI

Browntown: Pop. 100. In southeast corner of county. In early 1800's, Hambaugh. Presumably named for family named Brown. LRI

Carson Mountain, six miles south of Front Royal, in Shenandoah National Park, honors William E. Carson of Riverton, first chairman, 1926-1934, Virginia Conservation and Development. Active in establishing Shenandoah National Park. Com Va 10-1948

Front Royal: Pre-Revolutionary community was "Helltown" because of hilarious unapproved conduct by younger men. Was Lehewtown until 1788, when Front Royal name was adopted and incorporated. Peter Lehew purchased 200 acres at point where village grew. In colonial days, a giant oak stood in the public square — was the "royal" tree of England. During military commands and maneuvers, drill sergeant became exasperated and confused and shouted: "Front the royal oak!" Professional soldier among onlookers; he and friends kept repeating the amusing command; it became the community name. Rys N&W, SOU; elev. 490; Pop. 7,949; US Rts 340, 522. Skyline Drive starts at Front Royal. Water supply from watershed on Blue Ridge and South Fork of Shenandoah River; filtered, chlorinated. Couper II, 771; VaVCo 2-1949; VGb 37

Linden: Ry SOU; Pop. 50; elev. 905. On east boundary of north half of county. Tradition that place was named for its linden trees; one in particular was used as a landmark. LRI

Randolph-Macon Academy, military preparatory institution, established 1892. Church-related to the Methodist Church. VaVCo 2-1949

Reliance: Pop. 100. Lacking a postoffice, one night in store in 1886, proposed name Reliance because of reliable people in community; this name was approved by Postoffice Department. LRI

Riverton: Rys N&W, SOU; elev. 495; Pop. 250; US Rt 340. Near center of north half of county. Two parts of river system unite in scenic gorge; was important in river transportation before railroads in 1854. This history explains name of town. Stevens 77; WP: Va 443

Skyline Caverns are named from nearness to Skyline Drive; discovered 1937, officially opened 1946. In addition to many other kinds of formations, world's only known collection of flower-like formations, fragile andolites, which are calcite formations. Stevens 92; VaVCo 10-1949

Waterlick: Ry SOU; elev. 551; Pop. 125. In northwest corner of county. Front Royal Fish Hatchery, state-owned including 108 acres, near village. EcD county DU

WASHINGTON COUNTY

Formed 1776; named for George Washington, earliest of 31 states to name a county for him. Area: 579 sq.mi.; Pop. 38,076; Pop. per sq.mi., 65.8; increase Pop. 1950-60, 1.4%. First land grant 1752. About one-half county wooded. 4.7% county area in Jefferson National Forest. Virginia's leading producer Burley tobacco. Rank occupational groups: manufacturing, agriculture, trade. Rank agricultural income: field crops, dairy, livestock.   Tate 44

Abingdon: Ry N&W; elev. 2,055; Pop. 4,758; increase Pop. 1950-60, 1.2%; US Rts 11, 19, 58. Interstate 81. First name "Wolf Hills" because depredations by wolves in 1760. Black's Fort built in 1774. Abingdon established 1778, incorporated 1778, oldest incorporated town on waters draining into Mississippi River. Three conflicting stories regarding name: 1. Mary Washington's home town. 2. Lord Abingdon. 3. Daniel Boone's early residence, Abingdon, Pennsylvania. County seat. Water supply from encased springs administered by Washington County Sanitary District No. 1.   ESS county 19-21; Preston 93

Barter Players or Barter Theater established 1933; used buildings of Stonewall Jackson Institute, founded 1869, closed 1932. Actors exchanged products for admission to plays; depression years, products supplied food and other necessities; exchange gave name. In 1946, State of Virginia subsidized; first state-subsidized theater in America.   Com Va 8-1935

Benhams: Ry SOU; Pop. ———. In center of west fourth of county. Benham, name of fearless and determined Indian fighter, warned settlement at Castle's Woods in June 1790; this may be clue to name's derivation.   Summer's 427

Bristol (independent city): Area 4 sq.mi.; Rys N&W, SOU; elev. 1,690; Pop. 17,444; increase Pop. 1950-60, 7.6%; US Rts 11, 19, 58, 521. Name Sapling Grove in 1765; incorporated as Goodson in 1856; name from Colonel Samuel E. Goodson. General Assembly changed name to Bristol and granted new charter to city February 12, 1890. Name from Bristol, England, Interstate 81. Rank occupational groups: manufacturing, trade, educational services. Water supply from South Holston Lake; filtered, chlorinated, fluorinated.

Summers 674; EcD county

Clinchburg: Pop. 450; Ry N&W. In northeast portion of county. Was center large lumber operation in early 1930's.   DU

Damascus: Ry N&W; Pop. 1,485; elev. 1,928; US Rt 58. Early name, Mock's Mills at water gap. Railroad through gap in 1892; named Damascus because thought resembled Syrian city. Water supply from administered springs.

ESS county 22

Emory: Ry N&W; elev. 2,002; Pop. 1,000. Mid-point in east half of county. Named for Bishop John Emory. Water supply from administered springs.

Com Va 3-1956

Emory & Henry College: Founded 1836 by Holston Conference of Methodist Episcopal Church; purchased 554½ acres for $4,158.75. Named for Bishop John Emory and Patrick Henry. Martha Washington College consolidated with Emory and Henry in 1918; became co-educational in 1922. Located in town Emory. Summers 575+; Com Va 3-1956; Ann.Bul.

Glade Spring: Ry N&W; elev. 2,075; Pop. 1,407; increase Pop. 1950-60, 70.1%; Interstate 81. Railroad in 1856 called station Passawatomie, but families in village called the town Glade Spring. Pioneers in nearby early community because of a spring in a glade used the name Glade Spring; their church was Glade Spring Presbyterian Church. That gives derivation of town name. Water supply from administered springs. ESS county 21; Summers 689

Hidden Valley Wildlife Management area and lake, 6,400 acres. Name because of being so completely surrounded by mountains. Entrance is across one of the mountains. LRI

Holston: Pop. 70; US Rt 19. Mid-point of north boundary of county. Located on North Fork of Holston River.

Meadowview (RR Meadow View): Ry N&W; elev. 2,140; Pop. 750; Interstate 81. Mid-point east half of county. Name of village links to Edmondson's Meadow. Water supply from administered springs. Summers 691

Mendota: Ry SOU; elev. 1,385; Pop. 173. In northwest corner of county. Earlier name Kinderhook from owner's native Kinderhook, New York. Town merchant later named Mendota. ESS county 23

South Holston Lake on South Fork of Holston River belongs to TVA's 28-dam system.

Southwest Virginia Research Station, 21 acres, makes investigations relating to production of field crops, burley tobacco, and pasture management. At Glade Spring. Com Va 9-1953

Sullins College, established 1870, named for first president, Dr. David Sullins; was president 1870-1915. Became two-year college in 1917; confers associate degrees. 75 acre campus. Ann.Bul.

Virginia Intermont College began as Southwest Virginia Institute at Glade Spring in 1884. In 1891, moved to Bristol and name became Virginia Institute. In 1909, became Virginia Intermont College; name Intermont, "among the mountains". A junior college associated with Baptist General Association of Virginia. Ann.Bul.; Com Va 3-1956

Wallace: Ry N&W; Pop. 200. Near mid-point of southwest fourth of county. Earliest name Goforth's; Major Goforth owned nearby mill. Changed to Wallace's Switch, honoring the Rev. W. P. Wallace, community's Presbyterian minister. Became Wallace. Summers 556, 691

WESTMORELAND COUNTY

Formed 1633; named for an English county. Area: 236 sq.mi.; Pop. 11,042; Pop. per sq.mi., 46.8; increase Pop. 1950-60, 8.8%. Birthplaces of George Washington, James Monroe, and Robert E. Lee in county. Rank occupational groups: manufacturing, agriculture, trade. Rank agricultural income: field crops, livestock.
Roads 59

Acorn: Pop. 100. In southeast portion of county. When postoffice established, it was located in the shade of a huge oak tree. Hence. the name acorn.
LRI

Baynesville: Pop. 110. Between western and central parts of county, near Westmoreland State Park. Baynes family prominent 100 years ago. A Mr. Baynes was first postmaster.
LRI

Coles Point: Pop. 200; (summer Pop. 400). In northeastern corner of county. Coles Point mentioned in Carter papers in 1726. Area named Coles Point for an early settler, Mr. Cole. Postoffice Department accepted the name.
LRI; 7 V 68

Colonial Beach, on the Potomac, Pop. 1,769; popular resort. Portion of incorporated area was patented about 1650 by Samuel Bonum. Earlier name, White Beach. Developer of water front property in early 1880's named Colonial Beach. About 1909, flourishing resort. Nickname of community, Las Vegas on the Potomac. Municipal water supply from four artesian wells; exceptionally "soft", no chlorination needed.
VGb 56; LRI

Hague: Pop. 50. In eastern portion of county. Postoffice established 1824; named for Dr. Hague.
LRI

Kinsale: Pop. 250. In extreme eastern side of county. Founded 1705; named for town in Ireland. Seaport for two centuries.
Gannett 176; ESS county 18

Lerty: Pop. 10. Discontinued postoffice.
DU

Lower Machodoc River. Will dated Aug. 19, 1695, of resident of community.
36 V 297

Maple Grove: Pop. 24. Discontinued postoffice.
DU

Mattox Creek was Appomattox Creek in 1668; in list of navigable rivers 1702, Mattocks River; had become Mattox Creek in mid-eighteenth century.
14 V 295; 1 V 362; 22 V 329

Monroe Creek, bordering southwest Colonial Beach, named for family of Andrew Monroe; he was ancestor of President James Monroe.   3 W (2) 17

Montross: Pop. 394; increase Pop. 1950-60, 19%. County seat. George Robberecht Seafoods has eel traps set in rivers and territorial waters; cleaned, rinsed, frozen eels exported to mainland of Europe, where eels are considered a food delicacy. TD 8-21-1966

Mount Holly: Pop. 50. Near center of county. DU

Nomini Bay: Land transfer on Nomini Bay, Dec. 6, 1792. 4 V 452

Nomini Creek flows north in southeast portion of county into Nomini Bay of Potomac. Letter, dated Oct. 12, 1652, addressed to house upon Nominye, Potomac River. Residence on Nomini Creek, Oct. 1692. 9 V 331; 3 W (2) 32

Nomini Grove: Pop. 25. In south central part. DU

Oak Grove: Pop. 70. Near mid-point of west boundary of county. Reported there was a huge grove of oak trees at place. LRI

Oldhams: Pop. 100. In southeastern part of county. Name from family of Oldhams living in vicinity when postoffice opened. LRI

Popes Creek in northeast portion, tributary of Potomac. Thomas Pope, of Bristol, England, made will Sept. 3, 1684, probated Oct. 20, 1685, in which he mentions Popes Creek, Westmoreland County, Virginia.

3 W (2) 100; 38 V 393

Stratford: Pop. 35. In north central part of county. Thomas Lee built 1727. Richard Henry Lee, born 1732, introduced resolution in Continental Congress for Declaration of Independence. Robert E. Lee born January 19, 1807. Robert E. Lee Memorial Foundation incorporated to restore, furnish, preserve, and maintain birthplace and boyhood home at Stratford. 1,100 acres. Foundation purchased in 1932. Roads 23; Com Va 12-1958; EcD county

Templeman (Templemans Cross Roads): Pop. 50. In central eastern part of county. Advertisement in Virginia Argus, April 18, 1804, by a resident of Templeman's Crossroads. LRI

Tucker Hill: Pop. 50. In northeast corner of county. James Tucker, prominent resident in colonial days. Originally called Tucker's Hill. Mr. Tucker owned fowl and enjoyed cock fights. LRI

Washington's Birthplace (Wakefield): Pop. 5. 15 miles east of King George Courthouse. About 1774, Popes Creek plantation called "Wakefield", name from Goldsmith's "Vicar of Wakefield". George Washington Birthplace National Monument, 393.68 acres designated a unit of National Park Service, January 23, 1930. Restored story-and-a-half brick building on exact spot of home in which George Washington was born. Wakefield National Memorial Association, Federal Government, and John D. Rockefeller, Jr., made possible restoration.

June 18, 1968, this national monument was dedicated as the first "living farm" in the National Park Service. It will provide demonstrations in the use of colonial farm tools and methods in quilting, churning butter and other domestic tasks. Crops and livestock will be produced. It is expected to re-acquaint city-dwelling Americans with the role of the land in the American tradition.

George Washington Birthplace National Monument 22;
Com Va 2-1954; VaVCo 4-1949; WP: Va 549;
DNR 6-19-1968, p. 2.

Westmoreland (Sandy Point): Pop. 150. In extreme eastern part of county. Shoreline of Potomac influences currents along part of shore in northerly direction for one mile and a half. Sand accumulates when there is a storm from the east or northeast; thousands of cubic yards of sand have been hauled away, but the next storm fills the areas from which sand has been removed.   LRI

Westmoreland State Park, along the Potomac, adjoining Stratford and just east of Wakefield — a beautiful acreage developed for recreational use and over-night camping.   Va D Ag 255

Yeocomico River, in southeastern part, tributary of Potomac. Fort planned there in 1667; collector of duties appointed 1699.   19 V 252; 1 V 345

Zacata: Pop. 130. Mid-point in north edge of county. Seemingly, derived from an Indian name.   LRI

WISE COUNTY

Formed 1856; named for Henry Alexander Wise, governor of Virginia, 1856-1860. Area: 411 sq.mi.; Pop. 43,579; Pop. per sq.mi., 106.0. Coal mining employment exceeds trade. Rank occupational groups: trade, public utilities, education services. Rank agricultural income: livestock, field crops, fruit and nuts.

Roads 96

Andover: Ry INT; elev. 1,689; Pop. 250. Near northwest boundary. Named for Andover College in New England by D. B. Wentz, then president of Virginia Coal and Iron Company.

LRI

Appalachia: Rys INT, L&N, SOU; elev. 1,669; Pop. 2,456; US Rts 23, alt. 58. In center of west one-fourth of county. Appalachia takes its name from the Appalachian Mountains. Wilderness until 1891; chartered 1906. Western edge of town known locally as Intermont. Real estate dealers proposed Mineralville as town's name. Arrival of railroads, South Atlantic and Ohio used "Intermont" (now Southern Yards); Louisville & Nashville named their box-car station "Appalachia". Water from Stone Mountain; filtered, chlorinated.

Va R 6-1956; ESS county 33

Banner Rural Station: Ry N&W; elev. 2,038; Pop. 500. At mid-point of east one-fourth of county. Name from Upper Banner and Lower Banner coal seams. Formerly important coal mining vicinity.

LRI

Big Stone Gap: Rys L&N, SOU; elev. 1,488; Pop. 4,688; US Rts 23, alt. 58. Earlier name Imboden for John D. Imboden, first settler. Name Three Forks for three forks of Powell River south of the gap. Another name Mineral City. One suggested name, Wolverhampton, by Duke of Marlborough; Duke and Duchess came to see booming town. Gap in rugged stone mountain through which Powell River rushes gives town its name. Has Southwest Virginia Museum, arts and crafts of pioneers. Water from reservoir of headwaters South Fork of Powell River; chlorinated.

ESS county 16, 234; Addington 181

Bondtown, elev. 1,997, annexed to Coeburn 1956. North of Coeburn. Named for Bond family.

LRI

Clinch Valley College opened 1954. Clinch River crosses the county. In 1967, grant from Office of Economic Opportunity Upward Bound program for summer (six to eight weeks) program on college campus for high school pupils from impoverished rural and urban backgrounds. Pupils would continue to receive tutoring, academic and motivational guidance from Upward Bound staff during the regular school year. Will offer additional years so will confer bachelor's degrees in June 1970. Has 400 acre campus. At Wise.

Ann.Bul.; DNR 2-17-1967

Coeburn: Ry N&W; elev. 1,980; Pop. 2,471; increase Pop. 1950-60, 225.1%; US Rt alt 58. Is west of center of east one-fourth of county. Christopher Gist stopping place (1750) on Guest River; was Guest Station; named Coeburn after chief engineer, W. W. Coe, and Judge W. E. Burns of Lebanon, Virginia. Chartered 1892. First train 1891. First settlement near Coeburn about 1770. Water supply, three drilled wells; filtered, chlorinated.   ESS county 17, 35.

Cranes Nest Rural: Pop. 350. Cranes built nests on high cliff sides.
Steeles 1162

The Double (4,162 ft.). Six miles northwest of Big Stone Gap. Two parallel ridges extend for about two miles up the crest. The ridges suggested the name, The Doubles.   LRI

East Stone Gap (RR Elberton): Ry SOU; elev. 1,512; Pop. 475. Name from larger neighboring town.

Esserville: Ry INT; Pop. 600; US Rt 23. Near the north edge of Norton. In 1623, John A. Esser established coke company; employees named town in his honor.   Addington 220

Exeter: Pop. 350; elev. 1,972. In extreme west part of county. D. B. Wentz named for New England Academy.   Addington

High Knob (4,162 ft.). Three miles south of Norton. Highest point in Wise County; from summit five states can be viewed. High Knob Recreation Area offers wildlife refuge, swimming, picnic facilities.   LRI

Inman: Pop. 650. Near mid-point of west of center of west fourth of county. Mr. Inman, of Knoxville, Tenn., opened first mines in community in late 1890's or early 1900's.   LRI

Norton: Rys INT, L&N, N&W; elev. 2,140; Pop. 5,013; increase Pop. 1950-60, 15.8%; US Rts 23, alt. 58; Area 3 sq.mi. Became independent city 1954. First settler in Prince's Flats, Henry Frazier, probably land agent for Harry Smith; William Prince had been temporary resident. Postoffice, Eolia established 1883; later Dooly; became Norton February 7, 1890. Indications that name for Eckstein Norton, president L&N railroad, 1886-1891. Water supply, two reservoirs on Benges Branch; filtered, chlorinated.   Addington 192, 194

Pound: Ry C&O; elev. 1,557; Pop. 1,135; US Rt 23. Near mid-point of north boundary of county. Horse-power mortar and pestle in bend of river, of present cross roads. People from miles around brought grain to be pounded into meal. People said "The Pound", which explains the origin of the town's name. Water supply: three drilled wells, mountain water shed; chlorinated.
Addington 196

Roda: Ry INT; elev. 1997; Pop. 300. Shortened version of Rhodadendron; this native shrub blooms profusely in vicinity; Postoffice Department omitted the "H" from Rhoda.   LRI

Saint Paul: Rys CLIN, N&W; elev. 1,485; Pop. 1,156; Pop. increase 1950-60, 14.0%; US Rt alt 58. In southeast corner of county. Early postoffice Estonoa; about 1885, promoters sought develop St. Paul. Promoter from St. Paul, Minnesota. Incorporated Apr. 12, 1911. Water from Clinch River; filtered, chlorinated.   ESS county 32

Stonega: Ry INT; elev. 1827; Pop. 800. In center of north portion of west fourth of county. Name from Stone Gap, omitting the letter "p".

ESS county 18

Tacoma Rural Station: Rys INT, N&W; elev. 2,000; Pop. 350. Near midpoint of south half of county. Indian name meaning "high ground".   LRI

Wise: Pop. 2,164; increase Pop. 1950-60, 54.3%; US Rt 23. Originally known as Big Glades because of *gladly* (Archaic word for attractive) open view as a person looked up Gladys Creek. Became Gladeville in 1856. Confused with West Virginia town having same name. Then, known as Wise Court House; in Cleveland administration, shortened to Wise. Water supply, four wells and abandoned coal mine; filtered, chlorinated.   Addington 202, 204, 21.

WYTHE COUNTY

Formed 1789; named for George Wythe, eminent jurist, signer of Declaration of Independence. Area: 460 sq.mi.; Pop. 21,975; Pop. per sq.mi., 47.8. Settlement started in middle 1700's. 47.9% county area forested. 16.4% county area in Jefferson National Forest. Rank occupational groups: manufacturing, agriculture, trade. Rank agricultural income: livestock, dairy, poultry.   Roads 74

Austinville: Ry N&W; elev. 1,077; Pop. 750. Near mid-point of south county boundary of east half of county. Named for Moses Austin, early leader in community mining. In 1757, Colonel James Chiswell, hiding in a cave to escape Cherokees, discovered lead and zinc deposits. Fincastle County convened at Lead Mines, January 5, 1772. Water supply from New River; filtered, chlorinated.   VaVCo 7-1949; Crush 8

Barren Springs: elev. 1,908; Pop. 25. Near east county boundary in southeast part of county. James Barron (not Barren) was an important merchant; had land interests as well.   Kegley,FB

Cripple Creek: elev. 2,195; Pop. 300. Near midpoint of south boundary of west half of county. From Pennsylvania Dutch, Creeple — Swamp Creek. Village name from the creek.   Kegley, FB

Crockett: Ry N&W; elev. 2,325; Pop. 200. Near center of west half of county. Crocketts of Cripple Creek developed iron ore of region south of ridge along railroad. Crockett was their shipping point.   Kegley, FB

Fosters Falls (RR Foster Falls): Ry N&W; elev. 1,960; Pop. 200. Near mid-point of south boundary of east half of county. Name from Foster, early settler, and Falls, from falls in nearby river.   LRI

Ivanhoe: Ry N&W; Pop. 800. Near mid-point of south boundary of county. Named from Scott's novel. Ivanhoe, National Carbide corporation, manufactures calcium carbide. Water supply, well; chlorinated.   Gannett 167; VaVCo 7-1949

Max Meadows: Ry N&W; elev. 2,015; Pop. 900. Near center of east half of county. Early settler, William Mack. Another explanation, McGavocks prominent in community. Mc's Meadows probably became Max Meadows. TD 1-9-49

Reed Creek flows from northwest corner to southeast corner, tributary of New River. Derived its name from James Reed, at Dublin, Virginia.

Summers 53

Rural Retreat: Ry N&W; elev. 2,500; Pop. 413. Near mid-point of west boundary of county. Earlier name Mount Airy. In stage-coach days, old tavern of vicinity was retreat for lodging of travelers.   VaVCo 9-1953; Tate 51

Speedwell: elev. 2,303; Pop. 200. In southwest corner of county. Derived name from association of iron furnace on Cripple Creek with Speedwell Furance of North Carolina. Village name from nearby Speedwell Furnace.   Kegley, FB

Stony Creek flows from north central portion, tributary of Reed Creek. Early settlement had store; a sort of community center; became Tartar's Store, formerly a postoffice named Favonia, a story book name.   Kegley, FB

Wytheville: Ry N&W; elev. 2,230; Pop. 5,634; increase Pop. 1950-60, 2.2%; US Rts 11, 21, 52. Been county seat since organization of county. Earlier names: Abbeville, Evansham. Incorporated as Wytheville in 1839. Has animal and poultry diagnostic laboratory of Virginia Department of Agriculture. Water supply, springs and Reed Creek; filtered, chlorinated.   VGb 51; EcD county

Wytheville College: two-year community college; approved for September 1967. Opened as part of VPI in 1963.   Ann.Bul.

YORK COUNTY

Formed 1634; then Charles River County, named for King Charles I. In 1643, name changed to York County for Yorktown, England. Area: 123 sq.mi.; Pop. 21,583; Pop. per sq.mi., 27.6; increase Pop. 1950-60, 33.0%. Nearly two-fifths county federally owned. 92.1% county area forested. Rank occupational groups: manufacturing, public administration, trade. Rank agricultural income: livestock, dairy, field crops. Roads 84

Colonial Custom House, Yorktown, authorized 1680, erected 1706, oldest in America. Cradle of American tariff system, when Yorktown was port of entry for several northern cities. Restored in 1930; houses historic records and memorials. WP: Va 459; Kibler CVS 83+

Grafton: Pop. 900; US Rt 17. In southwest portion of county. Formerly Cockletown. In 1783-84, traveling Baptist preacher established congregation, naming Grafton Baptist Church after his home town in Massachusetts. About 1890, name of village changed to Grafton. LRI

Lackey: Pop. 500. Named by and for Thomas Lackey. Steeles 1169

Messick (part of Poquoson): ————. Named for William Messick, local resident. Steeles 1171

Poquoson: Pop. 4,278. In southeast portion of county. Name means land in slightly watered condition; or low wooded ground or swamp. Water supply from Newport News. GSW: CF

Poquoson River flows in southern part of county; empties into Chesapeake Bay.

Seaford: Pop. 1,100. In northeast part of south half of county. Was Crab Rock, changed to Seaford. Named by E. E. Slaight from nearness to Sand Box, thoroughfare connecting York River with Back Creek, which can be forded at low tide. GSW: CF; Steeles 1176

Tabb: Pop. 500. On southwest boundary. Named for Miss Sallie Tabb, local resident. Steeles 1178

Virginia Fisheries Laboratory at Yorktown has the responsibility of investigating the seafood industry so there will be an understanding of the habits and lives of important seafoods, an investigation of the causes of problems, and an encouraged management to form well-balanced and prosperous fishing industry.

Yorktown: Pop. 311; US Rt 17. In 1630, French engineer patented land embracing site of Yorktown. Assembly authorized port in 1680. Ship Museum has relics of British ships of Revolutionary era. Yorktown courthouse, 1697. British surrender, October 19, 1781. Water supply from Newport News. WP: Va 459, 460; EcD county

ALEXANDRIA (city)

Rys C&O, RF&P, SOU, W&OD; area: 15 sq.mi.; elev. 45; Pop. 115,000; increase Pop. 1950-60, 47.3%; US Rt 1; Interstate 495. Land first patented 1657. In 1731, warehouse built on Hunting Creek, became village of Bellhaven. In 1749, Alexandria established; named for John Alexander, who had purchased land in the vicinity in 1669. Fort built 1676 for defense against Susquehannock Indians. It was in the area of the District of Columbia 1789-1846. In the city, St. Mary's Catholic Church is the first permanent Catholic Church in Virginia. Alexandria *Gazette,* oldest daily newspaper in continuous publication in America, dating from February 5, 1784. City has lengthy list of historic places. Potomac Yards are one of the nation's most important railroad classification centers. Water supply from 550 square miles of watershed of Occoquan Creek.

Roads 19; VGb 36; Com Va 11-1963; Norris 482

Belle View, substation postoffice, named after community where located.

LRI

Episcopal High School, founded 1839, one of oldest preparatory schools for boys in the South. Used as military hospital 1861-65 by Union troops. School was a pioneer in establishing Honor Code in education. SCVSHM 10

George Washington, substation postoffice, named by postmaster. LRI

George Washington Masonic National Memorial Temple includes a memorial hall, museum and library; its pinnacle is more than 400 feet above its terraced hill. It was dedicated February 22, 1932. WPA: Alexandria 27

Hunting Creek, tributary of Potomac, along southeast boundary of city. Warehouse inspector appointed for stream, April 27, 1731. 37 V 128

Jefferson Manor. (See page 236.)

Kathmoor, substation postoffice, named by Postoffice Department. LRI

Parkfairfax, substation postoffice, was authorized July 22, 1946. Family apartments in 200-acre park development in a large garden type operation had appropriate name Park. Community name became Parkfairfax.

Amer. City 12-1946; LRI

Shirley Duke, substation postoffice, is named for community where located with names from Henry G. Shirley, State Highway Commissioner, and Duke Street on which postoffice is located. Shirley Memorial Highway crosses city.

LRI

Temple Trailer, substation postoffice, has name influenced by the Masonic Temple, after which Temple Trailer Park was named. LRI

Theological Seminary, substation postoffice, was named from the Virginia Theological Seminary, founded 1823. Seminary moved to present location in 1827; it is the Protestant Episcopal Theological Seminary in Virginia. LRI

Woodrow Wilson Memorial Bridge connects Alexandria and Prince Georges County, Maryland. It has six lanes, more than a mile in length.

Com Va, 11-1958

CHESAPEAKE (city)

Chesapeake became a city January 1, 1963. Rys N&W, ACL, NF&D, NS, SAL, SOU. Pop. 92,500. Name means "great salt water". Includes the former city of South Norfolk and all of the former Norfolk County area lying outside the cities of Norfolk and Portsmouth. South Norfolk had been incorporated as a town in 1919 and as a city in 1921. The city's port facilities are along the western side of Elizabeth River and on the southern side of James River.

Com Va 4-1963; EcD Norfolk Co

Bowers Hill (RR Bowers); substation postoffice.   DU

Camden Mills, substation postoffice.   DU

Deep Creek: Pop. ———; US Rt 17. A creek from Dismal Swamp is tributary of Elizabeth River. Indians had named it Deep Creek, which became the name of the village having the lock and spillway of the canal.   LRI

East Chesapeake, substation postoffice.

Fentress (substation postoffice): Ry NS. Fentress name in county records 1637-1710.   23 V 108

Hickory (substation postoffice): Ry NS. Formerly a railroad station Hickory Ground (now closed).   GSW-CF

Northwest: Ry NS; substation postoffice.   DU

Portlock: Ry N&W; substation postoffice. Portlock name in county records 1637-1710.   23 V 108.

Saint Brides: Ry NS; substation postoffice. Saint Brides Parish by Act of Assembly 1761. In county records 1784.   2 V 101, 215.

West Chesapeake was formerly South Norfolk postoffice. Now part of new city of Chesapeake, so area and postoffice are known as West Chesapeake.   LRI

West Norfolk, substation postoffice.   DU

HAMPTON (city)

Ry C&O; elev. 3; Pop. 110,000; increase Pop. 1950-60, 1,396.1%; US Rts 17, 60, 258; Interstate 64. Town of Hampton established by law in 1680 and named for Earl of Southampton. Indian Kecoughtan here in 1607. English village built in 1610; oldest English-speaking town in America. St. John's Episcopal Church formed in 1610 is oldest continuous parish in America and in Western World. Roads 53; McCabe 19

Kecoughtan meant "inhabitants of the great town". Hampton established as town and port in 1705; incorporated March 19, 1849; became independent city 1908. Symmes (Syms) "free school" traces to legacy in 1634 from Benjamin Syms; established 1635. Federal government installations: 12.5% area of city. First Revolutionary engagement in Virginia took place, October 25, 1775. Rank occupational groups: on duty with armed forces, public administration, trade. McCabe 11, 18; Va HSSA 54; Roads 53

Bay named for nearby Chesapeake Bay; name given this station at Fort Monroe by the Post Office. LRI

Buckroe Beach: Ry VPS. In 1620, Frenchmen sent over to plant mulberry trees and grape vines settled here. Records dating to 1617 refer to area called Buck Row (other spellings also found). Name from Buckrose in Yorkshire in England. It is identified with the ancient Wapentake of Buc-Cros. Very popular seaside resort. Roads 57; EcD city

Fort Monroe: (Old Point Comfort) Ry C&O; elev. 5; US Rts 60, 258. Fort begun in 1819 named for President James Monroe. Fort Algernourne built in 1609. In 1614, it was a stockade containing fifty people and seven cannon. Fort George in 1727 after the reigning king. Lacked being maintained 1781 until 1819. Only one in country maintained in original form, being completely surrounded by water moat. The fort was destroyed by a hurricane in 1749. Area in 1825, 80 acres; today 600 acres. Remained in possession Union forces, 1861-65. Jefferson Davis was imprisoned here, 1865-67. Roads 53; Kibler 98; VaVCo 9, 10-1948.

Hampton Institute: Authorized purchase of 125 acres on Hampton River looking out over Hampton Roads, June 1867. School for education of ex-slaves. Opened April 1868. Incorporated by Act of Virginia 1870; Hampton Normal and Industrial Institute. First permanent school for freedmen in the South. Gottman 130; Armstrong: Founding of Hampton Institute, 5+; Cartier: Amer. Univ. & Col. 1157

Hampton Institute Station: substation postoffice of Hampton.

Kecoughtan, substation postoffice. Trading post with Indians 1607.

Roads 53

Langley Air Force Base (RR Langley Field). Langley Field named for Samuel Pierpont Langley, who devoted his life to demonstrating the practicability of mechanical flight. Permanent construction of field begun 1917. Home of NACA (National Advisory Committee for Aeronautics).

Allen 12+; VaVCo 9-10 1948

Modern (substation postoffice) named for Modern Pharmacy in which station is located.   LRI

Old Point Comfort, tip of narrow peninsula at southeast corner of city, was found as a harbor and deep channel for the colonists' ships to navigate. This discovery put them in "good comfort" and they named the point "Cape Comfort". Later at this point, the first fort in the English speaking colonies of America was erected. In 1883, there was the beginning of one of the most famous resorts of the country.   Va R 6-1957; Kibler HVL 97; Wertenbaker 384.

Phoebus: Harrison Phoebus owned land, began about 1870. He developed Old Point as one of the most famous resorts of the country. Tunnel from Willoughby Spit to Phoebus connects north and south shores of Hampton Roads.

WP: Va 484; Wertenbaker 324; Va VCo 10-1952

Riverdale: Named for Riverdale Shopping Area, in which the substation postoffice is located. Riverdale housing development originated quite recently. Near Back River, which may have influenced naming.   LRI

Sherwood Park named for Sherwood Pharmacy, location of substation postoffice. Residential area gets name from farm owned by prominent family, Sherwood from the English Sherwood Forest.   **LRI**

Southampton: substation postoffice named for Southampton Shopping Area, which traces to Henry Wriothesley (pronounced Risley), Earl of Southampton, president of Virginia Company, (1620-1625).   **LRI**

Virginia State School was established in 1906 to provide academic and professional training for Negro deaf and blind youth; it is state supported.

Va. Govt., 53.

Wythe. Worshippers at spring adjoining Church Creek near present Wythe about 1614. Former magisterial district of Wythe.   VaVCo 9-10 1948, 10 1952

NEWPORT NEWS (city)

Rys C&O, PA, UAL; Area 75 sq.mi.; elev. 20; Pop. 130,000; increase Pop. 1950-60, 168.3%; US Rts 17, 60, 258; Interstate 64. Named for Sir Christopher Newport and Sir William Newce. Earliest name Point Hope, but in 1619 "Newportes Newce". In 1896, became independent city; in 1958, Newport News and Warwick merged into one city, Newport News, which includes all which was earlier Warwick County. Large coal shipments go through city. Low level dam at Walkers on Chicakahominy River in northeastern part of Charles City County is important source of municipal water supply. Rank occupational groups: manufacturing, trade, professional service.   VHSSA 39; EcD city; Com Va 8-1958

Christopher Newport College, two years; authorized 1960. Named for Captain Christopher Newport; confers Associate of Arts degrees.   Ann.Bul.

Denbigh named for Denbigh, England, in Warwickshire. First court of Warwick County held at Denbigh Plantation, owned by Samuel Mathews, who came in 1622. When court moved two miles from plantation location in 1810, retained name.   Roads 52; VaVCo 8-1947; EcD city

Fort Eustis: Named for General Abraham Eustis (1786-1853), first commandant of School of Artillery Practice, Fortress Monroe in 1824. Here, December 7, 1954, first helicopter dedicated airfield designed specifically for landing and parking helicopters.   Allen 6+; Com Va 2-1955; Roads 51

Lee Hall: named for 18th century plantation owned by the Lee family. Location factory manufacturing textile fiber ZEFRAN by Dow Chemical Company; a derivative of petroleum by-products.   Roads 52; Com Va 8-1958

Mariners' Museum, in park of 880 acres, rated as finest collection of maritime material in the world, including from most primitive raft to advent of steam production. Exhibits include water craft, navigation instruments, life saving equipment, ships' figureheads, historical pieces of china, pottery, and glass. Library contains marine prints down through the ages showing the maritime accomplishments of seagoing nations.   VaVCo 6-1951

Newport News Shipbuilding and Dry Dock Company, founded 1886 as Chesapeake Drydock and Construction Company, is the largest privately owned shipyard in the world. The plant facilities are used for manufacture of hydraulic turbines and accessories. Apprentice School of Newport News Shipbuilding and Dry Dock Company trains young men for shipbuilding industry. VaVCo 6-1951

Parkview, substation postoffice, central area of city had Parkview Elementary School and several businesses used name which led Post Office Department to choose name for postoffice.   LRI

Warwick name derived from Earl of Warwick; settlement in 1634 on Warwick River. Became courthouse of former Warwick County in 1810. Warwick County became independent city in 1952; merged with Newport News in 1958.
VaVCo 10-1952; Roads 52; EcD city

NORFOLK (city)

Area: 50 sq.mi.; Pop. 305,872; increase Pop. 1950-60, 43.3%; Rys ACL, NF&D, N&W, N&PB, NS, PA; elev. 10; US Rts 13, 58, 60, 460; Interstate 64. City name given by Col. Thorogood, one of earliest settlers, in honor of his native county in England. Norfolk, an Anglo-Saxon name as early as 1043; Nordfolc or Northfolk meaning northern people in England. City had beginning August 16, 1682, when Nicholas Wise for ten thousand pounds of tobacco purchased 50 acres for building a town on north side of Elizabeth River. Oct. 1705, Assembly established town Norfolk. Sept. 1736, Borough of Norfolk granted Royal Charter. Became a city, Febr. 11, 1845. Rank occupational groups: on duty with US armed forces, trade, public utilities.

VaVCo 4-5, 1947; VaVCo 10-1951; Burton: History Norfolk 2+

Avenue: substation postoffice, moved and kept earlier name.   LRI

Berkley: Rys N&PB, NS. Five cousins from Berkeley Castle, England, were settlers Dec. 5, 1619; named settlement Berkeley. Was county seat 1789-1801; then location name was Powder Point.

Com Va 7-1965; Norfolk Co: History & Development, 5.

Custom House, substation postoffice: 1852 appropriation by Congress for new custom house at Norfolk. Location: south side Main Street, nearly opposite Granby St., to Broad Water St., three stories high. Basement planned for postoffice; rest of building custom house. Moved to separate building on October 1951.   LRI

DeBree, substation postoffice: first location of substation on DeBree Avenue. Moved to location one block from first location; kept name DeBree.   LRI

Fleet: substation postoffice is at Norfolk Naval Base, serving Atlantic Fleet.   LRI

Hampton Roads: subdivision postoffice named for harbor area.   LRI

Milan: substation named for Norfolk's 33rd postmaster; had been Superintendent of Mails many years, then Assistant Postmaster. Was postmaster 1943-1945.   LRI

Norview: when this section was in Norfolk County, it was part way between Norfolk and Ocean View; received name from both names. Another explanation is it was "a view toward Norfolk".   LRI

Ocean View developed on a stretch of land north of Norfolk on Chesapeake Bay with invigorating breezes and almost boundless view from the beach. As the city's great seashore resort, it provided fishing, bathing, sports, entertainment, and commercialized amusements.   LRI

Old Dominion College established as Norfolk Division of College of William and Mary in 1930. Became fully accredited as four-year college in 1962; in same year, was separated from the College of William and Mary and adopted name of Old Dominion College. "Old Dominion" is a name dating to the colonial years of Virginia. In 1964, college was authorized to offer graduate degrees in four fields. Com Va 10-1964; Ann.Bul.

Sewells Point: been known by that name since 1640; Henry Sewell was among parishioners of church there. Location of eastern terminus NFBL Railroad. 1 V 327

Thomas Corner: On Virginia Beach Boulevard, intersection known as Thomas Corner. Believed that a family named Thomas lived in area and named section. Subdivision postoffice near the intersection. LRI

Virginia State College (Norfolk Division): Junior college plus four years in approved fields. Ann.Bul.

Virginia Wesleyan College is co-educational liberal arts; incorporated 1961, opened 1966; has 300-acre campus. Methodist related. Ann.Bul.

West Annex: A series of changes have been connected with this postoffice station. In World War II, old Sea Bee training center became Camp Bradford. That postoffice was in the present Naval Amphibious Base. It was called West to distinguish from other postoffices on the Base. LRI

Willoughby Spit was built of sand during a storm in 1680; this spit of 217 acres juts into Chesapeake Bay. It provides a naturally protected cove and a gentle sloping beach of white sands covering more than 15 miles. It is mostly a family vacation playground. It derives its name from the Willoughby family. TD—— Sec. H-5, May 18, 1968; 14 V 252

Wright was named for the former postmaster of Norfolk, Major Clinton L. Wright. LRI

PORTSMOUTH (city)

Rys ACL, C&O, N&FD, NPBL, NS, PA, SAL, SOU; elev. 10; Pop. 118,-000; Pop. per sq.mi., 6,376.2; increase Pop. 1950-60, 43.4%; area 18 sq.mi.; US Rts 17 58, 460; Interstate 264. Site of city patented 1659 by Captain William Carver. In 1716, total grant 1,120 acres to William Craford; laid out wide streets. Established as town 1752 and named by founder, Lt. Col. Wm. Crawford or Craford. Portsmouth was the county seat of Norfolk County. Public schools for free instruction of children opened in several localities in Norfolk County in 1799. Chartered as a city in 1858. Rank occupational groups: on duty with armed forces, manufacturing, trade. VHHMS 9; VaVCo 11-1951

Churchland, substation postoffice, originally called Sycamore Hill. Many churches in area led to popular mention of church land, which caused Churchland to displace the earlier name. LRI

Cradock, substation postoffice, named for Admiral Sir Christopher Cradock of British Navy. Development started during first World War for servicemen. Laid out in shape of an anchor with shopping center, schools and parks; early planned suburban community which has continued with encouraging permanence. LRI

Naval Hospital started 1827, country's oldest naval hospital, 17-story structure, 225 feet above grounds, has 800 beds. Com Va 3-1958, 12-1957, 5-1956

Norfolk Navy Yard, oldest naval yard in United States, established in 1767 under a British flag. Occupies considerable portion of waterfront along southern branch of the Elizabeth River; its 811 acres has 424 buildings, two ways (structures on which a vessel is built or from which launched), and seven dry docks capable of handling the world's largest ships. After American Revolution, ownership passed to the Commonwealth of Virginia; Federal Government acquired in 1801. It built the country's first battleship, the USS Texas, in 1889-1892, and the Navy's aircraft carrier, the USS Langley, in 1919-1922. Now devoted exclusively to conversions, alterations, and repairs of ships; it serves Atlantic and Mediterranean fleet vessels whose home port is Norfolk.
Bodine 30; TD 7-23-1967; Through the Years in Norfolk 160

Olive Branch: Olive Branch School and Olive Branch Cemetery in vicinity probably gave name to area and postal station. LRI

Simondale: Commandant Rear Admiral Manley H. Simons of the Norfolk Navy Yard started his tenure in 1937 and remained through World War II. He with others went into countryside and selected tract of land for development for service men in World War II. LRI

RICHMOND (city)

Rys: ACL, C&O, RF&P, SAL, SOU; Area 37 sq.mi.; elev. 160; Pop. 219,958; Pop. per sq.mi., 5,944.8; US Rts 1, 33, 60, 250, 301, 360; Interstate 95, 64. Location explored May 27, 1607; population 1634, 419; town laid out 1733; first "checkerboard" of streets 1737; established as town 1742; name because resembled Richmond on Thames in England. County seat Henrico County, 1752; capital 1779; became city 1782; construction of capitol building in 1785; first Assembly in new capitol, 19 October, 1789; capital of Confederacy 1861-1865. Inland seaport; freight vessels call regularly at Deepwater Terminal Docks. Seat of Fifth Federal Reserve District. Water supply from James. Rank occupational groups: manufacturing, trade, professional services.

VaVCo 11-1950; EcD (Henrico Co); Va Doc 25, 25-28

Ampthill: colonial name; this was name of a residence in area before Revolutionary War. Dameral

Azalea: Azalea Avenue on north side of city became name of larger shopping center and its surrounding area. Dameral

Bellevue: name of principal street in North Side and name extended to its district of city. Dameral

Belt Boulevard: earlier a broad road beyond city's residential district, so it was a belt in 1900 and its following years; now within city. Dameral

Civic Center: Civic Center Complex is being constructed in area which formerly had problematic housing. Dameral

Defense General Supply Center: principal supply center for armed services, a major installation of the Defense Department. Dameral

East End: name applies to a part of the city east of Shockoe Valley. Its area includes Church Hill, Chimborazo Hill, and hills to the northeast of these. Apparently name began to be used in first half of 20th century. Damarel

Federal Reserve: the headquarters of the Fifth Federal Reserve Bank at 9th and Franklin Streets gives the substation its name. Damarel

Forest Hill: Forest Hill Park, an amusement park laid out by Traction Company, goes back to 1836-1857; 97 acres which was acquired by the city in 1930. Became name of real estate development south of James and west of former city of Manchester. Damarel

McGuire General Hospital: Veterans Hospital. Named for Dr. Hunter Homes McGuire (1835-1900), Confederate Medical Director of Army in Shenandoah Valley. Allen 16

Medical College of Virginia began as Medical Department of Hampden-Sydney College in 1838, opened in Richmond November 5, 1838; oldest medical college in the state. Became Medical College of Virginia, February 25, 1854; was an independent institution 1854-1860. Became a state institution 1860. University College of Medicine and Memorial Hospital consolidated with Medical College in 1913. Medical College of Virginia inaugurated 1943. (See Virginia Commonwealth University). Ann.Bul.

Montrose Heights: a neighborhood name near the eastern edge of the city. DU

North Side: name describes major part of city of Richmond. Probably came into general use in first half of 20th century. Damarel

Edgar Allen Poe Shrine, 1916 East Main St., oldest house in Richmond. Inscribed on front wall letters, 'J.R.', believed to be initials of 'Jacobus Rex', James II, King of England. Believed erected 1686. WP: Va 294

Presbyterian School of Christian Education, established 1914 by General Assembly of Presbyterian Church in the United States, confers Bachelors and Masters degrees. Ann.Bul.

Richmond Professional Institute began as Richmond School of Social Economy in 1917. Became Richmond Division of William and Mary in 1925. In 1939, officially named Richmond Professional Institute of the College of William and Mary. In 1962, General Assembly separated R. P. I. from College of William and Mary; made it an independent state-supported institution. Confers associate degrees, Bachelors, and Masters. Located in downtown Richmond. (See Virginia Commonwealth University). Com Va 3-1955; Ann.Bul.

Saunders: ———. Mr. and Mrs. E. S. Saunders, Sr., built house at corner of Franklin and Shafer Streets, now property of Richmond Professional Institute. Munford 61

Shockoe Creek: Record, Oct. 12, 1740, lots and materials from Shockoe Creek vicinity for church building. Named for Peter Shaco, one of William Byrd's overseers. Previously, Indians called Chyinek. 4 V 214; Cm Va 9-1957

Southside: general name applied to all of Richmond south of James River; specifically applied to a large shopping area at the southern edge of the city. Damarel

Stewart, substation postoffice. Brook Hill house, resident of John Stewart. Munford 43.

Stuart takes its name from vicinity of J. E. B. Stuart elementary school which was named after the Confederate Cavalry General. Damarel

Union Theological Seminary began as Presbyterian Divinity School at Hampden-Sydney in 1812; moved to Richmond in 1898. Synods of Virginia and

North Carolina support institution, which gave name Union to the institution. Confers degrees: Bachelor of Divinity, Master of Theology, and Doctor of Theology. Com Va 3-1955, 8-1954; Ann.Bul.

University of Richmond began as Dunlora Academy in 1830 in Powhatan County; became Virginia Baptist Seminary in 1832. Chartered as University of Richmond in 1840. It includes with their dates of founding: Richmond College (1830); T. C. Williams School of Law (1870); Westhampton College (1914); Summer School (1920); Graduate School (1921); School of Business Administration (1949); and University College (1962). Com Va 10-1955; Ann.Bul.

Virginia Commonwealth University: On July 1, 1968, Richmond Professional Institute became part of the Virginia Commonwealth University. The nucleus of this university was created by joining Richmond Professional Institute and the Medical College of Virginia. The Richmond Professional Institute has emphasized programs related to urban needs.

Richmond News-Leader, 7-29-1968, A-2.

Virginia Treatment Center: psychiatric, short term, intensive treatment of children up to age 16 years. Va Govt 67

Virginia Union University formed in 1899 by merger of two institutions dating to 1865. Ann.Bul.

West End: Presumably was the western extremity when name generally accepted, but with growth of city, it is now within city. Damarel

Westhampton (RR Westham): developed in 19th century; now within city; is location of Westhampton College, women's division of University of Richmond. Damarel

Willow Lawn: a 20th century real estate developer's name. Originally, name of a small winding road which followed a small, winding brook. Became a major shopping area, and name is applied to whole district. Damarel

VIRGINIA BEACH (city)

Princess Anne County formed 1691, named for Queen Anne, then Princess Anne. Portions of Princess Anne County annexed to Norfolk City after 1950. Virginia Beach became independent city in 1952; Princess Anne County consolidated with Virginia Beach in 1963. Area: 255 sq.mi.; Pop. 123,000; increase Pop. 1950-60, 158.5%; Ry NS; US Rts 58, 60. First settlement in county in 1621 on Lynnhaven Bay. Present city is state's leading political unit in acreage harvest of kale. Rank occupational groups: trade, on duty with armed forces, professional services.   VaVCo 6-1950; EcD (Princess Anne County); LRI

Backbay: In southern portion of city, a large body of brackish water lying immediately behind the beach and in some places only a few hundred feet from the ocean.   LRI

Back Bay Game Refuge Area, 4,589 acres. In southeast corner of county. Name from water area Back Bay.   LRI

Bayside: Name from location on south shore of Chesapeake Bay.   LRI

Cape Henry: At extreme northeast corner of city; named for Prince of Wales, son of King James I. Site of first landing place of Virginia colonists; location of first lighthouse in 1791.
     Kibler CVS 2; VHSSA 38; EcD (Princess Anne Co.)

Creeds (substation postoffice). In south one-half of area.   DU

Dam Neck: One explanation of name is an old folks tale. As location of one of old life saving stations, the great amount of soft sand was a physical hardship on the beach horses so it was said it would break their "dam necks".   LRI

Fort Story (Military Reservation): Area 10,979.10 acres. Named for Major John Patton Story (1841-   ), teacher Coast Artillery School. Near Cape Henry.

Kempsville: Earlier name, Kemp's Landing, a port of entry in colonial days. Courthouse located 1778; was county seat until 1884. Incorporated as Kempsville, May 5, 1783.   VaVCo 6-1950; ESS (Princess Anne Co) 14.

Londonbridge (RR London Bridge): First courthouse Princess Anne County at Londonbridge. Bridge crosses small tributary of Lynnhaven River.
     VaVCo 6-1950; LRI

Lynnhaven started 1841; name from Lynnhaven River, which name traces to Captain Adam Thoroughgood, who came from King's Lynn, Norfolk, England.
     VaVCo 6-1950; EcD (Princess Anne Co.)

Lynnhaven Inlet connects Lynnhaven Bay with Chesapeake Bay.   LRI

Oceana: Ry NS. Early name Tunis; to rid of that name, changed to Oceana in 1891. Was last major stop on old Norfolk Southern Railway before reaching Virginia Beach. Mammoth jet base at United States Naval Air Station at Oceana.   ESS (Princess Anne Co.) 30; Com Va 6-1957

Pleasant Ridge: Name links to encouraging farm land in former Princess Anne County; a part of Pungo Ridge.   LRI

Princess Anne (substation postoffice): elev. 25. Was county seat of the former county Princess Anne.   Virginia (1937), 223.

Pungo: In central portion of city area. Pungo was Indian chief established trading post.   ESS (Princess Anne Co.) 32

Seapines: Pine trees grew to the edge of the ocean; this distinguished the area from nearby areas.   LRI

Seashore State Park in the northeastern corner of city. 2,770.40 acres. Marvelous dunes, lovely wooded scenery, gorgeous cypress swamps, draped with Spanish moss. Traversed by bridle paths and beautiful natural lakes. Haven for coastal birds and wildlife.   Va State Parks; EcD (Princess Anne Co)

Virginia Beach, the independent city in 1952, was on coast in northern portion of present city. That independent city had area of 2 sq.mi. Resort, three miles of white sand along ocean front. Present city has 291 miles of Atlantic Ocean shoreline. Convention center. Virginia Beach Erosion Commission and U. S. Army Engineers combat beach erosion. Repair damage by storm waves and high tides. Source of water supply from water system of Norfolk; impounded lakes on Blackwater and Nottoway Rivers.
                    EcD (Princess Anne Co); Through the Years in Norfolk 162

Virginia Truck Experiment Station. Established 1907. 107 acres at Diamond Springs. Conducts research projects including cultural methods, testing vegetable varieties in Virginia environment, control of plant diseases, control of insect pests, weed control, together with evaluation and application of fertilizers, irrigation, and crop rotation.   Va Govt 53

TITLES of REFERENCES used for DERIVATIONS

Addington—Addington: *History of Scott County.*
Agee—Agee: *Facets of Goochland County History.*
Alderman—John Alderman, Hillsville, Va.
Allen—Allen: *Origin of Names of Army and Air Corps Posts, etc.*
Ann.Bul.—Announcements or Bulletin of institution.
Arl St—Arlington Story.
Armstrong—Armstrong: *Old Homes and Buildings in Amelia.*
Arritt—Miss Gay Arritt, Covington.

Bagby—Bagby: *King and Queen County.*
Bedford—Bedford County Bicentennial.
Bedford HG—Bedford County — History and Geography Supplement.
Bell-Heartwell—Bell-Heartwell: *Brunswick Story.*
Bland—Bland County Centennial.
Bodie—Bodie: *The Face of Virginia.*
Bodine—Bodine: *The Face of Virginia.*
Bohannon—Bohannon: *Old Surry.*
Bolen—Bolen: *Lexington in Old Virginia.*
Bradshaw—Bradshaw: *History Prince Edward County.*
Bul Sps V—Bulletin: *Springs of Virginia.*
Butterworth—Ivan Butterworth, Dewitt.

C—Calendar of Virginia State Papers.
Callahan—Callahan: *Memorial to Washington.*
Carey—Information furnished by M. Patricia Carey, Fairfax County Public
    Library.
Catlett—Catlett-Fishburne: *Survey Augusta County.*
Chr-Mas—Christian-Massie: *Homes and Gardens in Old Virginia.*
Claiborne—Claiborne: *Nelson County — Historical and Industrial: Past —
    Present — Future.*
Clarke—Clarke: *Old King William Homes and Families.*
Clement—Clement: *History Pittsylvania County.*
Corp I—Information service of ownership incorporation.
Couper—Couper: *History of Shenandoah Valley.*
Crouch—Crouch: *The Names of Streams and Mountains, etc.*
Crush—Crush: *Montgomery County Story.*
CVHM—Civil War Historical Markers; Virginia.

DAI; Va—Virginia: *Dept. of Agriculture and Immigration.*
Damarel—Damarel, John E., Director Personnel, Office City Manager, Richmond.
Darter—Darter, Oscar H., Fredericksburg.

Detwiler—Detwiler: *Fairfax County Geography Supplement.*
DNR—*Daily News-Record,* Harrisonburg.
Douglas—Douglas: *Caves of Virginia.*

Early—Early: *Campbell Chronicles.*
EcD (county)—Economic Data for individual county.
ESS—Economic and Social Survey for individual county.

Fauquier—Fauquier County Bicentennial Commission: Fauquier County, 1759-
   1959.

Gannett—Gannett: *American Names.*
Gannett: PN—Gannett: *Place Names in United States.*
Garnett: TT—Garnett: *Tidewater Tales.*
G-B: GSV—Grover-Bolster: *Geol. Surv. of Va., Hydrography of Virginia.*
Glick—Glick: *Dinwiddie County Geography Supplement.*
Gordon—Gordon: *In the Picturesque Shenandoah Valley.*
Gottmann—Gottmann: *Virginia in Mid-Century.*
GSW: CF—Geological Survey (Washington, D. C.): card file.
Gwathmey—Gwathmey: *Twelve Virginia Counties.*

Hamilton—Mrs. Gladys Hamilton, Nassawadox, Virginia.
Hite—Hite: *My Rappahannock Story Book.*
Hodge—Hodge: *Handbook of American Indians.*
HR—*Highland Recorder.*
Huntley—Huntley: *Peninsular Pilgrimage.*
Hutcheson—Hutcheson, N. G., Clerk of County, Boydton.

IHS Fairfax—Industrial and Historical Sketch, Fairfax County.

Kegley—Kegley: *Virginia Frontier.*
Kegley, FB—Kegley, F. B. — Information from.
Kibler CVS—Kibler: *Colonial Virginia Shrines.*
Kibler HVL—Kibler: *Historic Virginia Landmarks.*

Lambert: Lambert: *Beautiful Shenandoah.*
Lee AC—Lee: *A History of Arlington County.*
Libr Tz—Librarian, Tazewell.
Long—Long: *Virginia County Names.*
LRI—Local Resident Information.
Lutz: Ch—Lutz: *Chesterfield; an Old Virginia County.*
Lutz: PGH—Lutz: *The Prince George-Hopewell Story.*
Lutz: RA—Lutz: *A Richmond Album.*

McCabe—McCabe: *Story of an Old Town.*
McDonald—McDonald, James L., Ext. Agt. Agr., Tazewell.
McCl—Mrs. Mary McClaugherty, Pearisburg.

Marable—Wm. Irvine Marable, Murfreesboro, No. Car.
Martin: Gaz—Martin: *Gazetteer of Virginia.*
Mathis—Mathis: *Along the Border.*
Mead—Mead: *Historic Homes of the Southwest Mountains.*
Morton—Morton: *Centennial History of Alleghany County.*
Morton: High—Morton: *History of Highland County.*
Morton: R'br—Morton: *History of Rockbridge County.*
Munford—Munford: *Richmond Homes and Memories.*

Nich—Nicholas, J. J., Rt. 3, Gloucester.
Norris—Norris: *History Lower Shenandoah Valley.*

Prid-Pr—Priddy-Price: *Charlotte County Geography Supplement.*
Page—Roswell Page, Jr., Hanover.
Painter—Fred P. Painter, Woodstock.
Parker—Parker: *History Bedford County.*
Pedigo—Pedigo: *History Patrick and Henry Counties.*
Peirce—Mrs. C. T. Peirce, Nuttsville.
Pendleton—Pendleton: *History Tazewell County and Southwest Virginia.*
Percy—Percy: *Old Place Names.*
Percy ACS—Percy: *Amherst County Story.*
PO Dept Archives—Postoffice Dept Archives; Washington, D. C.
Preston—Preston: *Historical Sketches and Reminiscences.*

Ratcliffe—R. Jackson Ratcliffe, Manassas.
Rawlings—Rawlings: *Ante-Bellum Albemarle.*
Revere—Revere: *Middlesex Geography Supplement.*
Roads—*Roads are White Pages of History in Virginia—Key to Inscriptions on Virginia Highway Historical Markers* (1929); Booklet.

St. Claire—St. Claire: *Beautiful Historic Albemarle.*
Samuels—Samuels: *Loudoun County — Past and Present.*
Schuright—Schuright: *History of German Element in Virginia.*
Scott—Scott: *History Orange County.*
SCWSHM—Selected Civil War State Historical Markers.
Snead—Snead: *Fluvanna Sketch Book.*
Sprouse—Sprouse: *Potomac Sampler.*
Stanard—Stanard: *Richmond: Its People and Its Story.*
Stevens—Stevens: *Shenandoah and Its Byways.*
Stewart—Stewart: *Names on the Land.*
Strickler MN—Strickler: *Massanutten.*
Strickler PC—Strickler: *History of Page County.*
Summers—Summers: *History Southwest Virginia.*
Sutherland—Sutherland: *Meet Virginia's Baby.*
Sweet—Sweet: *Virginia Methodism.*

Tate—Tate: *The Virginia Guide.*
TD—Richmond *Times-Dispatch.*
Turman—Turman: *Eastern Shore of Virginia.*
Turman et als (c)—Mrs. Nora Miller Turman and others, Accomac.

US Bd GN—U. S. Board of Geographic Names, etc.

V—*Virginia Magazine of History and Biography* (e.g., 11 V 217 represents
    vol. 11 of magazine, page 217).
VaCav—*Virginia Cavalier* (magazine).
Va-DAg—Virginia: *Dept of Agriculture and Immigration.*
Va Govt—Virginia Government — Va State Chamber of Commerce.
Va Guide OD—Virginia Guide to Old Dominion.
Va Highways—Virginia Highway marker system.
VA HSSA—Virginia: *Historic Shrines and Scenic Attractions.*
Va R—*Virgina Record* (magazine).
VaVCo—*Virginia and Virginia Counties* (magazine).
VGb—Virginia Guidebook.
VCG—Virginia Geological Survey: Geology Appalachian Valley.

W—W(1) = *William and Mary College Quarterly Historical Magazine,* first
        series.
        (W (1) 6 191 ===== represents the magazine, volume 6, page
        191).
    W(2) = William and Mary Quarterly, second series, etc.
Waite—Crimora Waite, Librarian, Culpeper.
Walker—Walker: *An Economic and Social Survey of Alleghany County.*
Wayland RC—Wayland: *History of Rockingham County.*
Wayland SV—Wayland: *Shenandoah Valley.*
Wertenbaker—Wertenbaker: *Norfolk Historic Southern Port.*
Whitelaw—Whitelaw: *Virginia Eastern shore.*
Willis-Walker—Willis-Walker: *Legends of the Skyline Drive and the Great
    Valley of Virginia.*
Wilson—Wilson: *Smyth County History.*
Wilstach—Wilstach: *Potomac Landings.*
Wingfield: CC—Wingfield: *History Caroline County.*
Wingfield: FC—Wingfield: *History of Franklin County.*
Witten—Witten: *Geography Supplement Brunswick County.*
Wooding—Dr. Nathaniel H. Wooding, Halifax, Va.
Woods—Woods: *History of Albemarle.*
WPA: JA—Writers Project: *Jefferson's Albemarle.*
WP: Va—Writer's Project: *Virginia.*
WWA—Who's Who in America.

Yowell—Yowell: *History of Madison County.*

ADDENDA

LARGER AREAS

Colonial National Historical Park, authorized by Congress 1930, includes Jamestown Island, parts of Williamsburg, Yorktown battlefield, Gloucester Point, and parkway connecting areas. Memorial cross on landing dune of colonists 1607 was erected by National Society of Daughters of American Colonists in 1935.

Huntley 289+; VGb 63.

FLOYD COUNTY

Burks Fork drain area in southwestern portion of county; this is name of magisterial district and a stream. Tradition that Mr. Williamson and Mr. Burke, pioneer hunters, were in area. Burke left party and went into stream drainage area; this gives stream its name. Supposed to be same person for whom Burks Garden, Tazewell County, was named.   LRI

FREDERICK COUNTY

Hogue Creek, near Gainesville, in central part of county, tributary of Back Creek.   DU

LOUISA COUNTY

Ferncliff: Pop. 50; US Rt 33.   DU

ALEXANDRIA (city)

Jefferson Manor, substation postoffice, shopping center. Name was chosen for postoffice due to location in Jefferson Manor subdivision.   LRI

INDEX

237

Russell Fork (Areas), 15
Rustburg (Campbell), 55
Ruther Glen (Caroline), 57
Ruthville (Charles City), 60
Rye Valley (Smyth), 194

Saint Brides (Chesapeake; city), 220
St. Charles (Lee), 123
Saint David's Church (Shenandoah), 191
St. Luke's Church (Isle of Wight), 111
St. Margaret's School (Essex), 75
St. Paul (Wise), 215
St. Paul College (Brunswick), 50
Saint Stephens Church (King and Queen), 116
Salem (Roanoke), 175
Salt Pond Mountain (Giles), 91
Saltville (Smyth), 194
Saluda (Middlesex), 138
Samos (Middlesex), 138
Sand Shoal Inlet (Northampton), 148
Sandston (Henrico), 106
Sandy Basin (Dickenson), 71
Sandy Creek (Halifax), 102
Sandy Hook (Goochland), 96
Sandy Level (Pittsylvania), 159
Sandy Point (Westmoreland), 212
Sandy River (Areas), 16
Sandy River (Prince Edward), 163
Sanford (Accomack), 24
Sanitarium (State Tuberculosis Hospital) (Albemarle), 27
Sapomey Church (Dinwiddie), 73
Sappony Creek (Dinwiddie), 73
Saunders (Richmond; city), 228
Saxe (Charlotte), 62
Saxis (Accomack), 24
Saxis Marsh Wildlife Refuge (Accomack), 24
Saylor's Creek Battlefield Park (Areas), 16
Schley (Gloucester), 93
Schoolfield (Pittsylvania; Danville), 159
Schuyler (Nelson), 144
Scott County, 187
Scottsburg (Halifax), 102
Scottsville (Albemarle), 27
Seaboard Coast Line Railroad (Areas), 16
Seacock Creek (Southampton), 196
Seaford (York), 218
Sealston (King George), 117
Seapines (Virginia Beach; city), 231
Seashore State Park (Virginia Beach; city), 231
Seaview (Northampton), 148
Sebrell (Southampton), 196
Sedley (Southampton), 196
Seigen Forest (Orange), 154
Selma (Alleghany), 30
Seminole Trail (Areas), 16
Seven Corners (Fairfax), 79
Seven Fountains (Shenandoah), 191
Seven Mile Ford (Smyth), 194
Severn (Gloucester), 93
Severn River (Gloucester), 93
Seward Demonstration Forest (Brunswick), 50

Sewells Point (Norfolk; city), 225
Shackelfords (King and Queen), 116
Shadow (Mathews), 133
Shanghai (King and Queen), 116
Sharps (Richmond County), 173
Shawsville (Montgomery), 140
Shenandoah (Page), 155
Shenandoah Academy (Shenandoah), 191
Shenandoah Caverns (Shenandoah), 191
Shenandoah College and Conservatory of Music (Frederick), 89
Shenandoah County, 189
Shenandoah Mountains (Areas), 16
Shenandoah National Park (Areas), 16
Shenandoah River (Areas), 16
Shenandoah Valley (Areas), 17
Shen Valley Airport (Augusta), 40
Sherwood Park (Hampton; city), 222
Shiloh (King George), 117
Shipman (Nelson), 144
Ship Shoal Island (Northampton), 148
Shirley Duke (Alexandria; city), 219
Shirley, Henry G., Memorial Highway (Fairfax), 79
Shirlington (Arlington), 36
Shockoe Creek (Richmond; city), 228
Short Gap (Tazewell), 204
Short Mountain (Tazewell), 204
Short Ridge (Tazewell), 204
Shumansville (Caroline), 57
Simonsdale (Portsmouth; city), 226
Simpsons (Floyd), 83
Singers Glen (Rockingham), 184
Sinking Creek (Areas), 17
Ski Bryce (Shenandoah), 189
Skippers (Greenville), 100
Skipwith (Mecklenburg), 135
Skyland (Page), 156
Skyline Caverns (Warren), 207
Skyline Drive (Areas), 17
Slash Christian Church (Hanover), 104
Slate (Buchanan), 52
Slate River (Buckingham), 53
Smith Creek (Areas), 17
Smithfield (Isle of Wight), 112
Smith Island (Northampton), 148
Smith Mountain Reservoir (Bedford), 45
Smith River (Areas), 17
Smyth County, 193
Snell (Spotsylvania), 198
Snow Creek (Franklin), 87
Snowden (Amherst), 33
Snowflake (Scott), 188
Snowville (Pulaski), 170
Somerset (Orange), 154
Somerton Creek (Nansemond), 142
Somerville (Fauquier), 82
Sounding Knob (Highland), 110
South (Arlington), 36
Southampton (Hampton; city), 222
Southampton County, 195
South Anna River (Areas), 17
South Boston (Halifax), 102
South Branch of the Potomac (Highland), 110
South Branch of the Shenandoah River (Areas), 17